Cabinet Office

Public Bodies 1998

THE STATIONERY OFFICE

© Crown Copyright 1998

Applications for reproduction should be made in writing to

Her Majesty's Copyright Unit, St Clements House, 2–16 Colegate, Norwich NR3 1BQ

First published 1998

ISBN 0 11 430154 9

Contents

Foreword by Mr Peter Kilfoyle MP   *v*

Introduction   *vi*

Statistical Summary   *viii*

Guide to Public Bodies 1998   *xiv*

Public Bodies 1998 Statistical Tables by Ministerial Responsibility   *1*

Annex A : Local Public Spending Bodies   *169*

Index   *172*

Foreword

by Mr Peter Kilfoyle MP
Parliamentary Secretary, Cabinet Office

The Government made a commitment in its paper *Quangos: Opening the Doors*, published in June 1998, to increase substantially the information available in future editions of *Public Bodies*. *Public Bodies 1998* now includes, for the first time, the terms of reference of each of the bodies listed, together with the names of their Chairmen and Secretaries or Chief Executives. This, together with the additional material on "local public spending bodies", provides comprehensive information about non-departmental public bodies (NDPBs) and other public sector bodies in a single document. This publication is also available on the Internet.

The Government is committed to keeping the number of NDPBs to a minimum and will ensure that a new NDPB will only be set up where it can be demonstrated that this is the most cost-effective and appropriate means of carrying out the given function. We intend to maintain the downward trend in numbers; and although some new bodies have been set up, for example to implement the Government's manifesto commitments, we have abolished a number of bodies.

The Government published in June 1998 *Quangos : Opening up Public Appointments*, which outlines how we intend to achieve our commitment to making appointments on merit in a transparent and accessible way, with equality of opportunity for all. The Government also published in December 1998 the *Executive NDPB Report 1998*, which contains information on the performance, including relevant trend data, of the largest 81 executive NDPBs, their activities and achievements. These, together with the package of reforms in *Quangos : Opening the Doors*, demonstrate that the Government is serious about putting more information than ever before in the public domain about public bodies and appointments to them, and about its commitments to open up these bodies progressively to public scrutiny and to make them more accountable.

PETER KILFOYLE MP
Parliamentary Secretary, Cabinet Office

Introduction

A guide to Public Bodies 1998

Public Bodies 1998 provides statistical and factual information about those public bodies operating at a national or regional level for which Ministers have a degree of responsibility. These bodies — commonly referred to as "quangos" — undertake a diverse range of activities, and the extent of Ministerial involvement necessarily varies from body to body. In most cases, however, Ministers are responsible for making some or all of the appointments to the boards which oversee the bodies' operations. Ministers are also responsible for ensuring that such bodies operate within a recognised and agreed management and financial control framework, and that appropriate safeguards are in place to ensure that the highest standards of propriety are maintained.

Public Appointments

Public Bodies 1998 also provides information about appointments to the boards of public bodies. Such appointments are generally made by Ministers and all appointments are governed by the overriding principle of selection based on merit. In seeking candidates for appointment, Departments use a variety of sources — including advertising — to identify a wide range of suitable individuals. Before registering an interest, however, those wishing to serve on the board of a public body should consider what skills and experience they have and what type of appointment they may most be suited to.

Individuals should approach Departments direct to register an interest in particular appointments. They may, however, also register an interest with the Cabinet Office Public Appointments Unit, which maintains a central database of individuals seeking public appointments from which Departments can draw suitable candidates. The Public Appointments Unit can be contacted at the following address:

Public Appointments Unit
Cabinet Office
Horse Guards Road
London SW1P 3AL

Tel: 0171 270 6217

Further information on those currently holding public appointments can be found on the Public Appointments website at www.open.gov.uk/pau/paupoint.htm. All Ministerial appointments (with the exception of appointments to Tribunal NDPBs and Boards of Visitors) are made in line with guidance issued by the independent Commissioner for Public Appointments.

Coverage

The following categories of public bodies are included in this publication:

- Nationalised Industries and Public Corporations;
- Non-Departmental Public Bodies (NDPBs); and
- National Health Service Bodies.

Nationalised Industries and Public Corporations

These are defined as corporate enterprises which are publicly owned and controlled, but which, at the same time, have a substantial freedom to conduct their own affairs along ordinary business lines. This includes the power, within certain limits, to hold reserves. Examples includes the British Broadcasting Corporation and the Bank of England. Nationalised industries represent a group of particularly large and important public corporations. Examples include the Post Office and the Civil Aviation Authority.

Non-Departmental Public Bodies

A non-departmental public body (NDPB) is a body which has a role in the processes of national government, but is not a government department, or part of one, and which accordingly operates to a greater or lesser extent at arm's length from Ministers. There are four types of NDPBs:

Executive NDPBs : These bodies carry out a wide variety of administrative, regulatory and commercial functions. They generally operate under statutory provisions, employ their own staff and have responsibility for their own budgets. Examples include the Environmental Agency and the Arts Councils. A number of executive NDPBs are

INTRODUCTION

classified as public corporations for public expenditure control and national accounting purposes.

Advisory NDPBs : These are generally set up administratively by Ministers to advise them and their departments on matters within their sphere of interest. Some Royal Commissions are classified as advisory NDPBs. Generally, advisory NDPBs are supported by staff from within the sponsor department, and do not incur expenditure on their own account.

Tribunal NDPBs : This category of NDPB covers bodies with jurisdiction in a specialised field of law. In general tribunals are serviced by staff from the sponsor department. There are two types of tribunal system: standing tribunals, which have a permanent membership, and tribunals that are convened from panels, so that the actual number of tribunals sitting varies.

Boards of Visitors : These comprise boards of visitors to penal establishments in England and Wales, and boards of visitors and visiting committees in Northern Ireland.

National Health Service Bodies

These include Health Authorities — or Health Boards in Scotland — NHS Trusts, Special Health Authorities, and certain other bodies operating within the NHS (and the equivalent in Northern Ireland) to which Ministers make appointments.

Other Public Bodies

The term "quango" is often used in a wider sense to describe those bodies which operate at a local level, in addition to those which have a national or regional remit. Examples include further and higher education institutions and grant-maintained schools. *Public Bodies 1998* provides a range of summary information on these and other local public spending bodies (see Annex A), together with cross-references to published source material where more detailed information about such bodies can be obtained.

Government Policy

On 29 June 1998, the Government published *Quangos: Opening the Doors*. This restated the Government's commitment to keep the number of NDPBs to a minimum and set out the action that the Government would be taking to make all NDPBs more open, accountable and effective. *Quangos: Opening the Doors* builds upon the important work which the Committee on Standards in Public Life has undertaken in recent years and which has already led to greater openness and accountability in NDPBs and to the establishment of an independent Commissioner for Public Appointments to "police" the public appointments process.

Quangos: Opening the Doors also makes it clear that new NDPBs will only be set up where it can be demonstrated that this is the most appropriate and cost effective means of carrying out a given function. Proposals for new NDPBs will be carefully scrutinised and all existing NDPBs will be subject to regular and rigorous reviews at least once every five years. Reviews of the larger executive NDPBs will be announced in advance to allow stakeholders the opportunity of submitting evidence to review teams.

Further Information

Further information about policy on non-departmental public bodies — or about any of the bodies listed in *Public Bodies 1998* — may be obtained from:

Miss Nicki Daniels
Central Secretariat
Cabinet Office
Horse Guards Road
London SW1P 3AL

Tel: 0171 270 1887
Fax: 0171 270 1874

email: NLDANIEL@cabinet-office.gov.uk

Statistical Summary

Non-departmental public bodies 1979–1998

	Number of NDPBs	Number of Staff*	Total Expenditure 1997/98	Executive NDPBs — Amount funded by government	Advisory NDPBs	Tribunal NDPBs	Boards of Visitors	Expenditure by departments in support of NDPBs	Total number of NDPBs
	No.	No.	£m†	£m†	No.	No.	No.	£m†	No.
1979	492	217,000	6,150	2,970	1,485	70	120	70	2,167
1982	450	205,500	8,330	3,910	1,173	64	123	87	1,810
1983	431	196,700	9,940	5,120	1,074	65	121	94	1,691
1984‡	402	141,200	7,280	5,160	1,087	71	121	115	1,681
1985	399	138,300	7,770	5,100	1,069	65	121	111	1,654
1986	406	146,300	8,240	5,330	1,062	64	126	116	1,658
1987	396	148,700	9,100	5,690	1,057	64	126	112	1,643
1988	390	134,600	9,450	5,930	1,066	65	127	118	1,648
1989	395	118,300	9,410	6,090	969	64	127	142	1,555
1990	374	117,500	11,870	8,630	971	66	128	114	1,539
1991	375	116,400	13,080	10,060	874	64	131	106	1,444
1992	369	114,400	13,750	10,320	846	66	131	150	1,412
1993	358	111,300	15,410	11,890	829	68	134	170	1,389
1994	325	110,200	18,330	15,080	814	71	135	170	1,345
1995	320	109,000	20,840	17,280	699	73	135	190	1,227
1996	309	107,000	21,420	17,990	674	75	136	190	1,194
1997	305	106,400	22,400	18,570	610	75	138	207	1,128
1998	304	107,800	24,130	18,420	563	69	137	196	1,073

* Figures include civil servants at the Advisory, Conciliation and Arbitration Service, and the Health and Safety Commission and Executive (see pages 147 and 43–44).
† Current prices.
‡ Staff and expenditure figures from 1984 exclude the English and Welsh Water Authorities which were reclassified as Nationalised Industries. Staff numbers in 1983 were approximately 58,000; expenditure was approximately £2,600m.

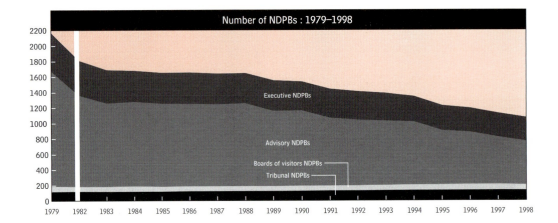

STATISTICAL SUMMARY

Non-departmental Public Bodies as at 1.4.98

	Executive NDPBs				Advisory NDPBs	Tribunal NDPBs	Boards of Visitors		
	Number of NDPBs	Number of Staff†	Total Expenditure 1997/98	Amount funded by government				Expenditure by departments in support of NDPBs	Total number of NDPBs
	No.	No.	£m	£m	No.	No.	No.	£m	No.
MAFF	37	2,200	160	44	28	4	0	3.7	69
Cabinet Office*	0	0	0	0	10	0	0	1.8	10
COI	0	0	0	0	1	0	0	0.03	1
CDL	0	0	0	0	17	0	0	0	17
DCMS	39	13,400	2,850	720	10	0	0	3.1	49
MOD	7	340	17	11	17	0	0	1.5	24
DfEE	14	14,700	9,360	9,060	6	2	0	3.1	22
OFFER	0	0	0	0	15	0	0	0.44	15
DETR	34	18,900	3,470	1,960	24	4	0	29.8	62
ECGD	0	0	0	0	1	0	0	0.01	1
FCO	7	6,700	420	220	3	2	0	0.73	12
DH	7	4,300	200	120	42	3	0	5.5	52
HO	12	2,200	360	260	10	11	133	6.0	166
IR	0	0	0	0	0	1	0	0.003	1
DFID	2	0	0.1	0.09	5	0	0	0.006	7
LCD§	2	1,400	1,670	1,240	197	1	0	13.4	200
NIO‡	35	18,500	880	790	25	16	4	9.4	80
ONS	0	0	0	0	1	0	0	0.001	1
ORR	9	31	1.6	1.6	0	0	0	0	9
Royal Mint	0	0	0	0	1	0	0	0.003	1
SCA	0	0	0	0	1	2	0	1.9	3
SO	36	8,000	1,960	1,650	61	3	0	4.4	100
DSS	2	160	8.3	7.6	33	7	0	63.6	42
OFTEL	0	0	0	0	7	0	0	0.34	7
DTI	26	14,900	1,880	1,590	24	7	0	42.6	57
HMT	1	0	27	0	0	1	0	0.46	2
OFWAT	10	48	1.9	1.9	1	0	0	0.4	11
WO	24	2,200	870	740	23	5	0	3.4	52
TOTAL	304	107,800	24,130	18,420	563	69	137	196	1,073

Note : For ease of interpretation, expenditure over £100m has been rounded to the nearest £10m; staff numbers over 1,000 have been rounded to the nearest 100. Therefore totals may not be exact.

* Includes Political Honours Scrutiny Committee.
† Figures include civil servants at the Advisory, Conciliation and Arbitration Service, and the Health and Safety Commission and Executive (see pages 147 and 43–44).
‡ Excludes those bodies which in Northern Ireland fulfil functions carried out by Local Government in Great Britain (see pages 102 and 107).
§ Figures exclude those tribunals which are part of the Court Service.

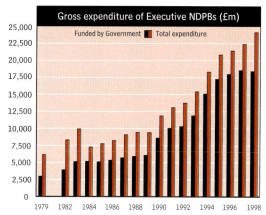

Gross expenditure of Executive NDPBs (£m)

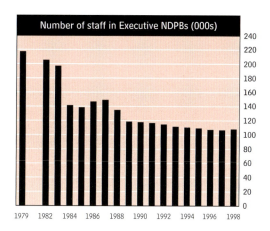

Number of staff in Executive NDPBs (000s)

STATISTICAL SUMMARY

Appointments by gender as at 1.9.98

	Executive NDPBs			Advisory NDPBs			Tribunal NDPBs[†]			Boards of Visitors[‡]		
	M	F	M:F % Ratio	M	F	M:F % Ratio	M	F	M:F % Ratio	M	F	M:F % Ratio
MAFF	365	44	89:11	397	61	87:13	363	11	97:3	0	0	
Cabinet Office*	0	0	0	68	72	49:51	0	0		0	0	
COI	0	0	0	5	3	63:37	0	0		0	0	
CDL	0	0	0	106	84	56:44	0	0		0	0	
DCMS	360	142	72:28	84	25	77:23	0	0		0	0	
MOD	50	9	85:15	238	18	93:7	0	0		0	0	
DfEE	115	41	74:26	56	31	64:36	92	78	54:46	0	0	
OFFER	0	0	0	140	78	64:36	0	0		0	0	
DETR	194	79	71:29	233	52	82:18	2,080	632	77:23	0	0	
ECGD	0	0		9	2	82:18	0	0		0	0	
FCO	63	25	72:28	18	9	67:33	4	0	100:0	0	0	
DH	64	30	68:32	436	175	71:29	151	90	63:37	0	0	
HO	139	54	72:28	134	33	80:20	161	33	83:17	934	828	53:47
IR	0	0		0	0		8	1	89:11	0	0	
DFID	13	3	81:19	46	19	71:29	0	0		0	0	
LCD#	6	3	67:33	1,162	646	64:36	2,671	563	83:17	0	0	
NIO	276	139	67:33	179	100	64:36	634	382	62:38	34	27	56:44
ONS	0	0	0	13	5	72:28	0	0		0	0	
ORR	92	26	78:22	0	0		0	0		0	0	
Royal Mint	0	0		8	2	80:20	0	0		0	0	
SCA	0	0		5	0	100:0	32	1	97:3	0	0	
SO	313	121	72:28	422	153	73:27	963	1312	42:58	0	0	
DSS	7	5	58:42	698	201	78:22	3,969	2,394	62:38	0	0	
OFTEL	0	0		40	17	70:30	0	0		0	0	
DTI	257	73	78:22	234	36	87:13	2,014	741	73:27	0	0	
HMT	3	2	60:40	0	0		23	4	85:15	0	0	
OFWAT	87	43	67:33	8	2	80:20	0	0		0	0	
WO§	234	61	79:21	153	64	71:29	293	82	78:22	0	0	
TOTAL	2,638	900	75:25	4,892	1,888	72:28	13,458	6,324	68:32	968	855	53:47

Note : Figures show total number of appointments to all Nationalised Industries, Public Corporations, Non-Departmental Public Bodies and NHS bodies listed in this publication.
In some instances, these appointments are not made by Ministers or sponsoring departments. Further information is contained, where applicable, in the detailed departmental tables.
Ministers may also make appointments to other types of bodies outside the scope of this publication.

* Includes Political Honours Scrutiny Committee.
† The Lord Chancellor makes appointments to a number of tribunal NDPBs. These are judicial appointments (see also individual tribunal entries in the departmental tables).
‡ These are Boards of Visitors to Penal Establishments in England and Wales and Boards of Visitors and Visiting Committees in Northern Ireland.
§ The Secretary of State for Wales also makes appointments to bodies outside the scope of this publication. Details of these bodies and their appointees appear in "Appointments by the Secretary of State for Wales" which is updated quarterly. Reference copies are available in the Libraries of the House of Commons and the Welsh Office, Cathays Park, Cardiff.
¶ Health and Personal Social Services Bodies in Northern Ireland.
# Figures exclude those tribunals which are part of the Court Service.

STATISTICAL SUMMARY

	Nationalised Industries			Public Corporations			NHS Bodies[¶]			Total Number of Appointments			Total Ministerial Appointments		
M	F	M:F % Ratio	M	F	M:F % Ratio	M	F	M:F % Ratio	M	F	M:F % Ratio	M	F	M:F % Ratio
0	0		3	2	60:40	0	0		1,128	118	91:9	739	109	87:13
0	0		0	0		0	0		68	72	49:51	68	24	74:26
0	0		0	0		0	0		5	3	63:37	5	3	63:37
0	0		0	0		0	0		106	84	56:44	106	84	56:44
0	0		33	15	69:31	0	0		477	182	72:28	401	165	71:29
0	0		0	0		0	0		288	27	91:9	236	18	93:7
0	0		0	0		0	0		263	150	64:36	263	150	64:36
0	0		0	0		0	0		140	78	64:36	1	0	100:0
23	3	88:12	6	3	67:33	0	0		2,536	769	77:23	741	247	75:25
0	0		0	0		0	0		9	2	82:18	9	2	82:18
0	0		0	0		0	0		85	34	71:29	38	19	67:33
0	0		0	0		1,698	1,347	56:44	2,349	1,642	59:41	2,295	1,615	59:41
0	0		0	0		0	0		1,367	948	59:41	1,314	942	58:42
0	0		0	0		0	0		8	1	89:11	8	1	89:11
0	0		8	1	89:11	0	0		67	23	74:26	67	23	74:26
0	0		0	0		0	0		3,839	1,212	76:24	3,839	1,212	63:37
0	0		7	2	78.22	152	94	62:38	1,282	744	63:37	13	5	72:28
0	0		0	0		0	0		13	5	72:28	858	491	64:36
0	0		0	0		0	0		92	26	78:22	19	4	83:17
0	0		0	0		0	0		8	2	80:20	8	2	80:20
0	0		0	0		0	0		37	1	97:3	5	0	100:0
18	1	95:5	27	5	84:16	276	160	63:37	2,019	1,752	54:46	1,920	1,727	53:47
0	0		0	0		0	0		4,674	2,600	64:36	4,674	2,600	64:36
0	0		0	0		0	0		40	17	70:30	26	11	70:30
27	2	93:7	0	0		0	0		2,532	852	75:25	2,509	849	75:25
0	0		16	2	89:11	0	0		42	8	84:16	42	8	84:16
0	0		0	0		0	0		95	45	68:32	0	0	00:00
0	0		0	0		144	63	70:30	824	270	75:25	472	176	73:27
68	6	92:8	100	30	77:23	2,270	1,664	58:42	24,394	11,667	68:32	20,676	10,487	66:34

STATISTICAL SUMMARY

Ethnic minority appointments as at 1.9.98

Ethnic Minority Appointments

Department	Total number of appointments	Total number of ethnic minority appointments	% Ratio
DCMS	659	16	2.4
DfEE	413	11	2.7
OFFER	218	16	7.3
DETR	3,305	149	4.5
FCO	119	5	4.2
DH	3,991	327	8.2
HO	2,316	141	6.1
LCD	5,051	63	1.2
NIO	2,026	11	0.5
SO	3,771	15	0.4
DSS	7,274	418	5.7
DTI	3,384	131	3.9
OFWAT	140	9	6.4
WO	1,094	9	0.8
Other Departments*	2,300	18	0.8
TOTAL	**36,061**	**1,339**	**3.7**

Note: Figures show total number of appointments to all Nationalised Industries, Public Corporations, Non-Departmental Public Bodies and NHS bodies listed in this publication.

* Includes all departments with less than 5 appointments held by members of the ethnic minorities (ie MAFF, Cabinet Office, Chancellor of the Duchy of Lancaster, COI, MOD, ECGD, Inland Revenue, DFID, ONS, Office of the Rail Regulator, Royal Mint, Scottish Courts Administration, OFTEL and HMT).

Ethnic Minority Appointments by Gender

	Male	Female	Total Appointments
Ethnic Minority Appointments	924 (69%)	415 (31%)	1,339

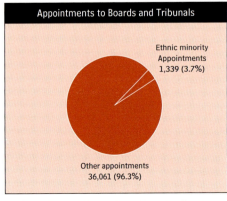

Note: Ethnic minority representation in the economically active population is 5.4%. (Source: Labour Force Survey 1998)

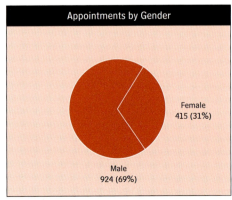

Note: Ratio of all male/female appointments is 68:32.

Public Bodies 1998
Statistical Tables & Guide

Guide to Public Bodies 1998

Explanation of row headings and abbreviations

For easy reference, explanations to the statistical tables are repeated on a lift-out flap at the rear of the book.

Row A

(All Bodies)

Shows the number of bodies where there is more than one in the same group

Row B

(Executive NDPBs and NHS Bodies)

Shows the number of employees on 1 April 1998. Part-time employees are counted as half. Among the executive NDPBs, the Advisory, Conciliation and Arbitration Service and the Health and Safety Commission and Executive are unique in that their staff, while directly employed, have civil servant status.

Row C

(All Bodies)

Shows how the body's annual report may be obtained, as follows:

Cm = published as a Command Paper (and obtainable from The Stationery Office)

HC = published as a House of Commons Paper (and obtainable from The Stationery Office)

TSO = a non-statutory Stationery Office publication

Body = obtainable only from the body or nationalised industry

NP = not published, or ad-hoc or periodic reports only.

Row D

(Executive NDPBs)

Under an Agreement between the Comptroller and Auditor General (C&AG) and Her Majesty's Treasury, the C&AG should be either the auditor of, or have inspection rights to, all executive NDPBs. Row D indicates whether the accounts are subject to full audit by the C&AG (marked 'X') or whether he has not been appointed as external auditor but nevertheless has access to the body's books and records (marked 'Y'). In the latter cases commercial auditors are usually employed as the external auditors. Where no symbol appears, access arrangements for the C&AG are in the process of being formalised. The C&AG (Northern Ireland) operates under a parallel Agreement in respect of executive NDPBs sponsored by Northern Ireland departments. However, executive NDPBs sponsored by the Northern Ireland Office are the responsibility of the GB C&AG.

Row E

(Executive NDPBs & NHS Bodies)

Shows the total gross expenditure (rounded to three decimal places) for 1997/98, before account is taken of income or revenue from any source.

Row F

(Executive NDPBs & NHS Bodies)

Shows the amount (rounded to three decimal places) of the gross expenditure met by Government grant or grant-in-aid for 1997/98. Unless otherwise noted, this does not include repayable loans, or payments for goods or services made by departments on a customer/supplier basis.

Row G

(All NDPBs)

Shows the net cost to that body's sponsoring department in carrying out its sponsorship role (rounded to the nearest £1,000) for 1997/98. The figures are made up principally of staff costs, accommodation and common services costs, fees and expenses. The figures exclude expenditure which is repaid by the body; loans to the body and payments to it for services; the direct funding of the body as shown in Row F; and expenditure on associated policy work undertaken by the department which does not depend on the existence of the body.

Row H

(Executive NDPBs, Nationalised Industries, Public Corporations & NHS Bodies)

Shows Chief Executives' remuneration details for the 1997/98 financial year. Remuneration totals are shown inclusive of basic salary, including geographical allowances such as London Weighting; performance related bonuses; any employer's contributions paid in respect of the Chief Executive under the pension scheme; any sums paid, by way of expenses allowance; the estimated money value of any other benefits receivable by the Chief Executive otherwise than in cash; and any agreed sum on taking up appointment, if applicable. Where there has been more than one Chief Executive over the period, the aggregate remuneration is shown.

Rows I–K

(All Bodies)

Shows the detail of appointments as at 1 September 1998. M=Male; F=Female.

- *Row I*

  Shows details for the Chairman or President (possibly more than one Chairman).

- *Row J*

  Shows details for the Deputy or Vice Chairman or Vice President (possibly more than one).

- *Row K*

  Shows details for members.

Ministers, civil servants or military officers who are ex-officio members of an organisation are not shown. Unless otherwise indicated, the appointments shown are made by The Queen or Her Ministers (including appointments made on their behalf or jointly, and those made by Heads of Departments in Northern Ireland), and are part-time and unpaid. However, brackets thus { } denotes an appointment by others. Bold type thus denotes a full-time appointment.

Any remuneration (rounded to the nearest pound) is shown (in some cases as a band); these are annual payments unless noted as being per day (pd), or half day (hd), or per meeting (pm), or per case (pc). Normal expenses, that is, travel and subsistence, are not included. In general, remuneration and expenses will be reflected in the expenditure figures in either row E (for executive bodies and NHS bodies) or row G (for advisory bodies, boards of visitors and tribunals).

Rows L–M

(Tribunal NDPBs)

Reflect tribunal's workload, showing the number of applications received relative to the number of cases disposed of.

Public Bodies 1998 Statistical Tables by Ministerial Responsibility

2	Ministry of Agriculture, Fisheries and Food
10	Cabinet Office
13	Cabinet Office : Ceremonial Branch
14	Central Office of Information
15	Chancellor of the Duchy of Lancaster
16	Department for Culture, Media and Sport
28	Ministry of Defence
32	Department for Education and Employment
37	Office of Electricity Regulation
41	Department of the Environment, Transport and the Regions
55	Export Credits Guarantee Department
56	Foreign and Commonwealth Office
59	Department of Health
74	Home Office
82	Inland Revenue
83	Department for International Development
85	Lord Chancellor's Department

Northern Ireland Departments

91	Northern Ireland Office
93	Department of Agriculture
95	Department of Economic Development
100	Department of Education
104	Department of the Environment
108	Department of Finance and Personnel
109	Department of Health and Social Services
116	Office for Regulation of Electricity and Gas
117	Office for National Statistics
118	Office of the Rail Regulator
121	Royal Mint
122	Scottish Courts Administration
123	Scottish Office
140	Department of Social Security
144	Office of Telecommunications
146	Department of Trade and Industry
157	HM Treasury
158	Office of Water Services
159	Welsh Office
169	Annex A : Local Public Spending Bodies
172	Index

MINISTRY OF AGRICULTURE, FISHERIES AND FOOD

Ministry of Agriculture, Fisheries & Food

Room 631, Nobel House,
17 Smith Square, London SW1P 3JR

Enquiries	Mrs Sheila Martin
Telephone	0171 238 5495
Fascimile	0171 238 6411
E-mail	s.martin@maff-sec.gov.uk
Internet	http://www.maff.gov.uk
GTN	238 5495

Public Corporations

1. Covent Garden Market Authority

Covent House
New Covent Garden Market
London
SW8 5NX
TEL : 0171 720 2211
FAX : 0171 622 5307
info@cgma.gov.uk
http://www.cgma.gov.uk
CHAIR : Mr Leif Mills ; GENERAL MANAGER : Dr Michael Liggins
TERMS OF REFERENCE : The Authority owns and manages the New Covent Garden Market. It is responsible for its operation and maintenance.

Executive NDPBs

2. Agricultural Wages Board for England and Wales

Nobel House
17 Smith Square
London
SW1P 3JR
TEL : 0171 238 6540
FAX : 0171 238 6553
CHAIR : Professor John Marsh CBE
SECRETARY : Miss Helen Baker
TERMS OF REFERENCE : The Agricultural Wages board is an independent body with a statutory obligation to fix minimum wages for agricultural workers in England and Wales. It also has discretionary powers to decide other terms and conditions eg: holiday and sick pay.

3. Agricultural Wages Committees for England

Local Committees
MAFF
Nobel House
London SW1P 3JR
TEL : 0171 238 5755
FAX : 0171 238 6553
CONTACT : Mr R G Webdale
TERMS OF REFERENCE : The Agricultural Wages Committees (AWCs) have powers to grant permits of exemption, to issue certificates regarding premium arrangements between employers and learners or apprentices, to re-value farmworkers' houses and to issue craft certificates.

	1	2	3
a. Number if a multiple body (1.4.98)	–	–	15
b. Number of staff employed by the body (1.4.98)	–	2.5*	2*
c. Annual Report	Body	TSO	TSO
d. Audit arrangements	–	X†	X†
e. Total gross expenditure of body (1997/98)	–	£0.235m†	£0.66m†
f. Amount funded by government (1997/98)	–	£0.235m	£0.66m
g. Other expenditure by sponsoring dept (1997/98)	–	–	–
h. Chief Executive's Remuneration (1997/98)	£69,500*	–	–
Appointments and Remuneration (1.9.98)			
i. Chairman/President	1M, £37,815	1M, £202pd	{14M, 1F, £86pd}‡
j. Deputy	–	–	{2M, 1F, £68pd}‡
k. Members	2M†, 2F, £7,365‡	2M, 2F, £126pd {13M, 3F}	20M, 7F, £68pd {141M, 2F}
l. Tribunal cases received	–	–	–
m. Tribunal cases disposed of	–	–	–

* General Manager's remuneration.
† Includes one member nominated by the Secretary of State for the Environment, Transport and the Regions.
‡ Three vacant posts on 1.9.98.

* Supported by staff from within the sponsoring department. Representatives of workers and employers are nominated by their respective Unions.
† Expenditure forms part of the total Ministry of Agriculture, Fisheries and Food (MAFF) expenditure. Accounts for MAFF are audited by the Comptroller and Auditor General.

* Supported by staff from within the sponsoring department. Representatives of workers and employers are nominated by their respective Unions.
† Expenditure forms part of the total Ministry of Agriculture, Fisheries and Food (MAFF) expenditure. Accounts for MAFF are audited by the Comptroller and Auditor General.
‡ Chairman and Deputies appointed by the Committees from the independent membership.

MINISTRY OF AGRICULTURE, FISHERIES AND FOOD

Executive NDPBs

4
Apple and Pear Research Council (APRC)

Bradbourne House, Stable Block, East Malling Research Station, East Malling
Kent ME19 6DZ
TEL : 01732 845115
FAX : 01732 844828
CHAIR : Professor Ian Swingland
SECRETARY : Mr Malcolm Ronald
TERMS OF REFERENCE : To promote or undertake research into the production of apples and pears; to collect and disseminate information concerning the industry and to advise on matters relating to the industry. The Council is funded by a statutory levy on growers of apples and pears.

a	–
b	1
c	Body
d	Y
e	£0.363m
f	–
g	£0.029m
h	£32,000
i	1M, £19,079
j	–
k	7M, 1F, £60pd*
l	–
m	–

* 1 post vacant at 1.9.98.

5
British Potato Council

4300 Nash Court
John Smith Drive
Oxford Business Park South
Oxford OX4 2RT
TEL : 01865 714455
FAX : 01865 782200
britishpotato@potato.org.uk
CHAIR : Mr David Walker
GENERAL MANAGER : Mr Nigel Jupe
TERMS OF REFERENCE : The Council promotes, commissions and manages a research and development programme covering potatoes. It also collects and disseminates statistical and marketing information, and is involved in market and export promotion.

a	–
b	65
c	Body
d	Y
e	£6.847m
f	–
g	£0.378m
h	£55,000pa*
i	1M, £51,000
j	–
k	14M, 1F, £100pd
l	–
m	–

* General Manager's remuneration.

6
Food from Britain

123 Buckingham Palace Road
London
SW1W 9SA
TEL : 0171 233 5111
FAX : 0171 233 9515
http://www.foodfrombritain.com
CHAIR : Mr Geoffrey John
SECRETARY : Mr Patrick Davies
TERMS OF REFERENCE : To develop and promote the marketing of British food and drink abroad, and promotion within the UK and elsewhere of the UK speciality food and drink sector. This is achieved by the promotion of a range of cost-effective business, product development and promotional services.

a	–
b	24
c	Body
d	Y
e	£11.635m
f	£5.318m
g	£0.120m
h	£81,462
i	1M, £41,841
j	–
k	11M, 3F, £1,804
l	–
m	–

7
Home-Grown Cereals Authority

Caledonian House
223 Pentonville Road
London
N1 9NG
TEL : 0171 520 3900
FAX : 0171 520 2000
admin@hgca.com
CHAIR : Mr Antony Pike ; CHIEF EXECUTIVE : Mr Tony Williams
TERMS OF REFERENCE : The Authority's remit is to improve the production and marketing of United Kingdom cereals and oilseeds.

a	–
b	44
c	Body
d	Y
e	£9.864m*
f	£0.123m
g	£0.043m
h	£80,935
i	1M, £21,324
j	1F, £7,375
k	13M, 1F, £3,671
l	–
m	–

* Forecast expenditure for the year ending 30 June.

8
Horticultural Development Council (HDC)

Bradbourne House, Stable Block, East Malling Research Station, East Malling
Kent ME19 6DZ
TEL : 01732 848383
FAX : 01732 848498
hdc@hdc.org.uk
CHAIR : Dr Margaret Charrington
CHIEF EXECUTIVE : Mr Martin Beckenham
TERMS OF REFERENCE : To promote or undertake research on behalf of the Industry (excluding apple and pear and hop growers). The Council is funded by a statutory levy on growers.

a	–
b	14
c	Body
d	Y
e	£2.790m*
f	–
g	£0.030m
h	£30,000
i	1F, 28,616
j	–
k	11M, 2F, £50pd
l	–
m	–

* Expenditure is for the period 1996/97 since the HDC financial year runs from October to September.

MINISTRY OF AGRICULTURE, FISHERIES AND FOOD

Executive NDPBs

9
Horticulture Research International

Wellesbourne
Warwick
CV35 9EF

TEL : 01789 470382
FAX : 01789 470552
chris.payne@hri.ac.uk
http://www.hri.ac.uk
CHAIR : Mr Peter Siddall
CHIEF EXECUTIVE : Professor Christopher Payne OBE
TERMS OF REFERENCE : To carry out horticultural research, whether funded by Government or by the private sector. Horticulture Research International is the principal contractor for horticultural research and development in the United Kingdom.

10
Meat and Livestock Commission (MLC)

PO Box 44, Winterhill House
Snowdon Drive
Milton Keynes
MK6 1AX

TEL : 01908 677577
FAX : 01908 609221
CHAIR : Mr Donald Curry
DIRECTOR GENERAL : Mr Colin McLean
TERMS OF REFERENCE : Promotes greater efficiency in the livestock and livestock products industry. Advises the industry on meat marketing, collecting and disseminating information and promotes meat as an important part of a balanced diet.

11
Milk Development Council (MDC)

5–7 John Princes Street
London
W1M 0AP

TEL : 0171 629 7262
FAX : 0171 629 4820
sylvia.osaji@mdc.org.uk
http://www.mdc.org.uk
CHAIR : Mr Brian Peacock
CHIEF EXECUTIVE : Mr Peter Merson
TERMS OF REFERENCE : To promote or undertake scientific research into the production, marketing, distribution and consumption of milk products.

12
Regional Flood Defence Committees*

Addresses throughout England and Wales

TERMS OF REFERENCE : Regional Flood Defence Committees of the Environment Agency carry out most of the Agency's flood defence functions in England and Wales.

13
Royal Botanic Gardens, Kew

Kew
Richmond
Surrey
TW9 3AB

TEL : 0181 332 5000
FAX : 0181 332 5197
g.prance@kew.org
CHAIRMAN OF THE TRUSTEES : Viscount Blakenham ; DIRECTOR : Professor Sir Ghillean Prance FRS
TERMS OF REFERENCE : The mission of the Royal Botanic Gardens Kew is to enable better management of the earth's environment by increasing knowledge and understanding of the plant and fungal kingdoms – the basis of life on earth.

	9	10	11	12	13
a	–	–	–	9	–
b	660*	680	5	*	512.5
c	Body	Body	Body	NP	Body
d	Y	Y	Y	*	X
e	£23.998m	£52.800m	£5.950m	*	£29.452m
f	£16.402m†	–	–	–	£20.951m
g	£0.070m	£0.274m	£0.016m	–	£0.078m
h	£69,307	£111,605	£68,195	–	£80,842
i	1M, £24,051	1M, £62,768	1M, £22,530	5M, 2F, £13,110; 2M, £10,490	1M
j	–	1M, £12,411	–	–	–
k	9M, £4,782‡	1F, £14,977*; 10M, 1F, £7,364*	8M, 2F, £100pd	43M, 4F, {101}	8M, 3F*
l	–	–	–	–	–
m	–	–	–	–	–

* 234 staff are employed direct. The rest are seconded from the Biotechnology and Biological Sciences Research Council (349 staff) and MAFF (77 staff).
† Includes £12.3m income commissioned on a customer/supplier basis.
‡ Includes 3 members appointed by the Department of Trade and Industry.

* Chairman of the MLC Consumers' Committee receives £14,977; the Commissioners receive £7,364.

* RFDCs are statutory executive committees of the Environment Agency (EA) which meets the administrative costs. They are supported by EA staff. Expenditure is accounted for by the EA to which the Comptroller and Auditor General has full inspection rights (see page 43).

* Includes one member appointed by H.M. The Queen.

4

MINISTRY OF AGRICULTURE, FISHERIES AND FOOD

Executive NDPBs

14 Sea Fish Industry Authority

8 Logie Mill
Logie Green Road
Edinburgh
EH7 4HG
TEL : 0131 558 3331
FAX : 0131 558 1442
seafish@seafish.co.uk
CHAIR : Mr Eric Davey
CHIEF EXECUTIVE : Mr Alasdair Fairbairn
TERMS OF REFERENCE : To promote the efficiency of the sea fish industry and serve the best interests of that industry and the consumers of sea fish and sea fish products.

15 United Kingdom Register of Organic Food Standards

MAFF, Room 323
Noble House
17 Smith Square
London SW1P 3JR
TEL : 0171 238 5915
FAX : 0171 238 6148
p.crofts@env.maff.gov.uk
CHAIR : Professor Sir Colin Spedding ; SECRETARY : Mr Peter Crofts
TERMS OF REFERENCE : To ensure that standards for the production of organic food are properly applied in the United Kingdom; and to maintain a register of all organic producers, processors and importers.

16 Wine Standards Board of the Vintners' Company

Five Kings House
1 Queen Street Place
London
EC4R 1QS
TEL : 0171 236 9512
FAX : 0171 236 7908
CHAIR : Mr Peter Purton ; CHIEF EXECUTIVE : Mrs Anne Kynaston
TERMS OF REFERENCE : The Board is responsible for the enforcement of European Wine Regulations at all levels except retail.

Advisory NDPBs

17 Advisory Committee on Novel Foods and Processes

Secretariat, MAFF, Ergon House, c/o Nobel House
17 Smith Square
London SW1P 3JR
TEL : 0171 238 6377
FAX : 0171 238 6382
a.acnfp@jfssq.maff.gov.uk
CHAIR : Professor Janet Bainbridge ; SECRETARY : Mr Nick Tomlinson
TERMS OF REFERENCE : To advise Ministers on any matters relating to the irradiation of food, or to the manufacture of novel foods or foods produced by novel processes, having regard, where appropriate, to the views of relevant expert bodies.

18 Advisory Committee on Pesticides

Mallard House
3 Peasholme Green
York
YO1 2PX
TEL : 01904 455701
FAX : 01904 455733
d.williams@psd.maff.gov.uk
CHAIR : Professor Sir Colin Berry
SECRETARY : Mr David Williams
TERMS OF REFERENCE : To advise Ministers in five regulatory Departments on all matters relating to the sale and effective control of pests and in particular, the measures needed to protect people and the environment from the risk of adverse effects of pesticides.

	14 Sea Fish Industry Authority	15 UK Register of Organic Food Standards	16 Wine Standards Board	17 ACNFP	18 AC on Pesticides
a	–	–	–	–	–
b	151	1.75	12.5	–	–
c	Body	NP	NP	Body	TSO
d	Y	X*	Y	–	–
e	£10.592m	£0.120m*	£0.476m	–	–
f	£0.296m	–	£0.371m	–	–
g	£0.266m	£0.089m	£0.067m	£0.155m	£0.48m*
h	£72,600	–	£43,450	–	–
i	1M, £26,300	1M, £132pm	1M, £3,500	1F, £138pm	1M, £172pm
j	1M, £16,155	–	–	1M, £109pm	1M, £136pm
k	9M, 1F, £7,370	7M, 3F, £105pm 2 vacancies	2M, 1F, £870	12M, 2F, £109pm	11M, 3F, £136pm
l	–	–	–	–	–
m	–	–	–	–	–

* Expenditure forms part of the total Ministry of Agriculture, Fisheries and Food (MAFF) expenditure. Accounts for MAFF are audited by the Comptroller and Auditor General.

* Total includes a percentage of costs which are subsequently recouped from industry. Costs are for MAFF and for the Health and Safety Executive and include staff costs incurred by the Advisory Committee's supporting panels.

MINISTRY OF AGRICULTURE, FISHERIES AND FOOD

Advisory NDPBs

19
Agricultural Dwelling House Advisory Committees (ADHAC)*

Local Committees
MAFF
Nobel House
SW1P 3JR
TEL : 0171 238 5755
FAX : 0171 238 6553
CONTACT : Mr G R Webdale
TERMS OF REFERENCE : To assist the housing authority in considering the agricultural grounds and urgency, in respect of a farmer's application to re-house workers, or former workers, living in a farm cottage needed for another agricultural worker.

20
Committee of Investigation for Great Britain

Room 323c
Whitehall Place (West Block)
London
SW1A 2HH
TEL : 0171 270 8521
FAX : 0171 270 8071
pedmunds@fdi.maff.gov.uk
CHAIRMAN : Mrs Suzan Mathews QC ; SECRETARY : Mr Philip Edmunds
TERMS OF REFERENCE : To consider, and reporting to the Minister on, any report made by a Consumers' Committee and any complaint made to the Minister as to the operation of any scheme which, in the opinion of the Minister, could not be considered by a Consumers' Committee.

21
Committee on Agricultural Valuation

Room 105, Nobel House
17 Smith Square
London
SW1P 3JR
TEL : 0171 238 5677
FAX : 0171 238 5671
TERMS OF REFERENCE : The function of the CAV is to advise the Minister and the Secretary of State for Wales on the provisions to be included in any regulations that might be made under the Agricultural Holdings Act 1986 prescribing methods of calculating compensation for improvements or tenant-right matters specified in the 1986 Act.

22
Consultative Panel on Badgers and Bovine Tuberculosis*

MAFF, Block B, Tolworth Toby Jug Site, Hook Rise,
South Tolworth,
Surrey KT56 7NF
TEL : 0181 330 8019
FAX : 0181 377 3640
j.howell@ahdc.maff.gov.uk
FORMER CHAIR : Mr Mark Thomasin-Foster ; SECRETARY : Mr James Howell
FORMER TERMS OF REFERENCE : To keep under review the evidence relating to bovine tuberculosis in badgers, including its distribution, its prevalence, and its relationship to bovine tuberculosis in cattle; to advise on operations to be undertaken to limit the transmission of tuberculosis from badgers to cattle and to recommend appropriate research.

23
Consumers' Committee for Great Britain under the Agricultural Marketing Act 1958

Room 232c
Whitehall Place (West Block)
London
SW1A 2HH
TEL : 0171 270 8521
FAX : 0171 270 8071
pedmunds@fdi.maff.gov.uk
CHAIR : Mrs Janet Laurence
SECRETARY : Mr Philip Edmunds
TERMS OF REFERENCE : Reports to the Minister on the effect of any scheme approved by the Minister, which is for the time being in force, on consumers of the regulated product.

	19	20	21	22	23
a	15	–	–	–	–
b	–	–	–	–	–
c	TSO	NP	NP	NP	NP
d	X	–	–	–	–
e	£0.185m	–	–	–	–
f	–	–	–	–	–
g	£0.185m	–	–	£0.001m	£0.011m
h	–	–	–	–	–
i	52M, 14F, £86pd	1F, £253pd	1M	–	1F
j	–	–	–	–	–
k	{219M, 1F}	3M, 3F, £130pd	12M	–	2M, 4F
l	–	–	–	–	–
m	–	–	–	–	–

* Convened on an ad hoc basis. Chairman and members for each ADHAC are selected from a panel.

* The Committee has not met since 1992 (the 11th Committee's term formally expired in February 1993). There are no plans to appoint a 13th Committee.

* Body wound up on 17.8.98.

MINISTRY OF AGRICULTURE, FISHERIES AND FOOD

Advisory NDPBs

24
Consumer Panel

Consumer Panel Secretariat, Room 306c, Ergon House, c/o Nobel House, 17 Smith Square, London SW1P 3JR
TEL : 0171 238 5779
FAX : 0171 238 6330
consumer@info.maff.gov.uk
CHAIR : Mr Jeff Rooker MP
SECRETARY : Mr Richard Sinclair
TERMS OF REFERENCE : To bring to the attention of Ministers food issues of concern to consumers and to advise on the transmission to consumers of advice and information relating to Ministers' policies on food safety, diet and nutrition.

25
Farm Animal Welfare Council

MAFF, Block D, Government Buildings, Hook Rise South, Tolworth, Surbiton, Surrey KT6 7NF
TEL : 0181 330 8077
FAX : 0181 335 4274
CHAIR : Professor Sir Colin Spedding ; SECRETARY : Mr Robert Holdsworth
TERMS OF REFERENCE : To advise Agriculture Ministers in Great Britain on all issues affecting the welfare of farm animals. The Council can also discuss issues within the European Union and correspond with the European Commission.

26
Food Advisory Committee

MAFF, Ergon House
17 Smith Square
London
SW1P 3JR
TEL : 0171 238 6267
FAX : 0171 238 6263
fac@fssg.maff.gov.uk
http://www.maff.gov.uk/food/fac/fachome.htm
CHAIR : Professor Sir Colin Campbell ; SECRETARY : Dr Sandy Lawrie
TERMS OF REFERENCE : To assess the risk to humans of chemicals which are used or occur in or on food and to advise Ministers on the exercise of powers in the Food Safety Act 1990. The Committee also advises Ministers on general matters relating to food safety.

27
Hill Farming Advisory Committee for England, Wales and Northern Ireland (HAFC)

MAFF, Nobel House,
Room 116
17 Smith Square
London SW1P 3JR
TEL : 0171 238 6307
FAX : 0171 238 6288
CHAIR : Mr Elliot Morley MP
SECRETARY : Mr David Painter
TERMS OF REFERENCE : The Committee's remit is to advise the Minister of Agriculture, Fisheries and Food and the Secretary of State for Wales on the exercise of their powers under the Hill Farming Act 1946.

28
Spongiform Encephalopathy Advisory Committee*†

MAFF, Toby Jug Site
Tolworth
Surbiton
Surrey KT6 7NF
TEL : 0181 330 8769
FAX : 0181 330 8414
m.taylor@ahbse.maff.gov.uk
CHAIR : Professor Sir John Pattison
TERMS OF REFERENCE : To provide scientifically based advice to MAFF, the Department of Health and territorial departments on matters relating to Spongiform Encephalopathies, taking account of the remits of other bodies with related responsibilities.

	24	25	26	27	28
a	–	–	–	–	–
b	–	–	–	–	–
c	Body	Body	Body	NP	TSO
d					
e	–	–	–	–	–
f	–	–	–	–	–
g	£0.092m*	£0.324m	£0.157m	£0.024m*	£0.356m
h	–	–	–	–	–
i	*	1M, £172pd	1M, £173pm	†	1M, £218–£251(max)pd‡
j	–	–	1M, £136pm	1M	1M, £186–£219(max)pd‡
k	2M, 8F £136pm†	16M, 6F, £109pd*	7M, 7F, £136pm	10M, 4F	14M, 2F, £186–£219(max)pd‡
l	–	–	–	–	–
m	–	–	–	–	–

* £0.006m of this expenditure is borne on the Department of Health's vote. The consumer panel is chaired by the Minister of State.
† An additional fee of £27 is paid to those members who provide papers for meetings.

* A member is paid £172pm when acting as Chairman of sub-group meetings.

* Excludes costs incurred by Department of Agriculture for Northern Ireland and the Welsh Office Agriculture Department.
† HFAC is chaired by the Parliamentary Secretary (Commons).

* Jointly funded by the Ministry of Agriculture, Fisheries and Food and the Department of Health.
† Department of Health, 5th Floor, Skipton House, 80 London Road, London, SE1 6LW. Tel : 0171 972 5052; Fax : 0171 972 5558.
‡ Maxima includes maximum preparatory allowance claimable and temporary exceptional circumstance allowance.

MINISTRY OF AGRICULTURE, FISHERIES AND FOOD

Advisory NDPBs

29
Sugar Beet Research and Education Committee

MAFF
Whitehall Place East
London
SW1A 2HH
TEL: 0171 270 8271
FAX: 0171 270 8188
CHAIR: Mr Hugh Dyas
SECRETARY: Mr Ray Hedley
TERMS OF REFERENCE: To advise the Minister on the drawing up of an annual programme of research and education into matters affecting the growth of home grown sugar beet.

a	–
b	–
c	NP
d	–
e	–
f	–
g	–
h	–
i	1M, £181pm
j	–
k	2M, 1 vacancy, £155pm 4M
l	–
m	–

30
Veterinary Products Committee

Veterinary Medicines Directorate, Woodham Lane, New Haw, Addlestone, Surrey KT15 3LS
TEL: 01932 336911
FAX: 01932 336618
vpc@vmd.maff.gov.uk
http://www.open.gov.uk/vmd/vmdhome.htm
CHAIR: Professor Ian Aitken
SECRETARY: Mr Chris Bean
TERMS OF REFERENCE: To give advice to the Licensing Authority with regard to the safety, quality and efficacy in relation to the veterinary use of any substance or article (not being an instrument, apparatus or appliance) to which any provision of the Medicines Act 1968 is applicable.

a	–
b	–
c	TSO
d	–
e	–
f	–
g	£0.082m
h	–
i	1M, £210pd*
j	1M*
k	18M, 4F, £165pd*
l	–
m	–

* An additional preparation fee of £60 will be paid for each additional product that a member is asked to lead upon.

Tribunal NDPBs

31
Agricultural Land Tribunals (England)

Room 105
Nobel House
London
SW1P 3JR
TEL: 0171 238 5677
FAX: 0171 238 5671
TERMS OF REFERENCE: To determine disputes between agricultural landlords and tenants (other than through the courts or arbitration) as provided for in the Agricultural Holdings Act 1986; and between agricultural neighbours as provided for in the Land Drainage Act 1991.

a	7
b	–
c	NP
d	–
e	–
f	–
g	£0.319m
h	–
i	7M, £239pd*
j	14M, 1F, £239pd*
k	232M, 3F*
l	295
m	293

* Appointments are made by the Lord Chancellor.

32
Dairy Produce Quota Tribunal

MAFF
Whitehall Place East
London
SW1A 2HH
TEL: 0171 270 8246/8259
FAX: 0171 270 8116
DEPUTY CHAIRMAN: Sir Michael Kerry; SECRETARY: Miss Kumu Adhihetty
TERMS OF REFERENCE: The tribunal was set up in 1984 following the introduction of milk quotas, to consider applications from milk producers for additional quotas. The Tribunal is currently dormant.

a	–
b	–
c	NP
d	–
e	–
f	–
g	–
h	–
i	–
j	1M
k	67M, 1F
l	–
m	–

33
Meat Hygiene Appeals Tribunals (England and Wales)

Ergon House
17 Smith Square
London
SW1P 3JR
TEL: 0171 238 6604
FAX: 0181 238 6304
CHAIR: Mr Michael Ware
SECRETARY: Mrs Margaret Tremayne
TERMS OF REFERENCE: To consider appeals against a decision to refuse or revoke a licence or to impose conditions on a licence for premises to engage in the slaughter, cutting and storage of red meat, white meat, and game meat (both farmed and wild) – in effect the wholesale industry.

a	–
b	–
c	NP
d	–
e	–
f	–
g	£0.010m
h	–
i	1M, £350pd
j	1F, £286pd
k	11M, 3F, £206pd
l	26
m	8*

* 18 appeals withdrawn.

MINISTRY OF AGRICULTURE, FISHERIES AND FOOD

Tribunal NDPBs

34
Plant Varieties and Seeds Tribunals*

MAFF, Block B
Government Buildings
Brooklands Avenue
Cambridge CB2 2DR
TEL : 01223 455925
FAX : 01223 455652
chammond@cambs.rsc.maff.gov.uk
SECRETARY : Mr C Hammond (England and Wales)
TERMS OF REFERENCE : To hear appeals against the decision of the Controller of Plant Variety Rights on Plant Breeders' Rights matters; against decisions of the Agricultural Ministers on National List and seeds matters; and against decisions of the Forestry Commissioners on matters concerning forest reproductive materials.

a	–
b	–
c	NP
d	–
e	–
f	–
g	–
h	–
i	3M, £351pd[†] £286pd[‡]
j	–
k	27M, 2F, £133pd
l	–
m	–

* One tribunal covers UK, but there are separate chairmen depending on whether it meets in England & Wales, Scotland, or Northern Ireland. Appointments of chairman are made by the Lord Chancellor (England and Wales), the Lord President of the Court of Session (Scotland) & the Lord Chief Justice (Northern Ireland). The Tribunal has not been convened since 1984.
† If a silk.
‡ If a non-silk.

Cabinet Office

Queen Anne's Chambers, 28 Broadway,
London SW1H 9JS

Enquiries	Mike Lewis
Telephone	0171 210 0340
Facsimile	0171 210 0346
Internet	http://www.open.gov.uk/co/cohome.htm
GTN	210 0340

Advisory NDPBs

	1 Advisory Committee on Business Appointments	2 Better Regulation Task Force	3 British Government Panel on Sustainable Development
	c/o Room 67/2 Cabinet Office Horse Guards Road London SW1P 3AL	Room 67a/3 Cabinet Office Horse Guards Road London SW1P 3AL	Zone 4/F5 Ashdown Hosue Victoria Street London SW1E 6DE
TEL	0171 270 5927	0171 270 6014	0171 890 4962
FAX	0171 270 5459	0171 270 6991	0171 890 4959
	CHAIR: Rt Hon Lord Carlisle of Bucklow QC; SECRETARY: Mr Jim Barron	http://www.open.gov.uk/co/bru/task.htm CHAIR: Lord Haskins SECRETARY: Mr Christian Turner	106174.2501@compuserve.com CONVENOR: Sir Crispin Tickell GCMG KCVO; SECRETARY: Dr Georgina Burney
	TERMS OF REFERENCE: To consider applications under the business appointments rules from the Permanent Secretaries and senior officials immediately below that level and to make recommendations to the Prime Minister. To provide advice, under publicised Guidelines, to former Ministers on the acceptance of appointments after leaving office.	TERMS OF REFERENCE: To advise the Government on action to improve the effectiveness and credibility of government regulation – by ensuring that it is necessary, fair, affordable, and simple to understand and administer, taking into account the needs of small businesses and ordinary people.	TERMS OF REFERENCE: To keep in view general sustainability issues at home and abroad, to identify major problems or opportunities likely to arise; to monitor progress; and to consider questions of priority.
a. Number if a multiple body/system (1.4.98)	–	–	–
b. Number of staff employed by the body (1.4.98)	–	–	–
c. Annual Report	*	Body	Body
d. Audit arrangements	–	–	–
e. Total gross expenditure of body (1997/98)	–	–	–
f. Amount funded by government (1997/98)	–	–	–
g. Other expenditure by sponsoring dept (1997/98)	£0.051m	£0.052m	£0.052m*
h. Chief Executive's Remuneration (1997/98)	–	–	
Appointments and Remuneration (1.9.98)			
i. Chairman/President	1M	1M	1M
j. Deputy	1M	1F	–
k. Members	6M	9M, 5F	2M, 1F
l. Tribunal cases received	–	–	–
m. Tribunal cases disposed of	–	–	–

* First annual report published July 1998.

* Expenditure borne on Department of the Environment, Transport and the Regions' vote.

Advisory NDPBs

4
Civil Service Appeal Board

11 Belgrave Road
London
SW1V 1RB

TEL : 0171 273 6500
FAX : 0171 273 6506
akhan@cabinet-office.gov.uk
CHAIR : Miss Patricia Downs
SECRETARY : Ms Alison Khan
TERMS OF REFERENCE : To consider appeals from civil servants against: refusal to allow participation in political activities; forfeiture of Superannuation; dismissal and compulsory early retirement; and non-payment or the amount of compensation paid on dismissal on inefficiency grounds.

5
Committee on Standards in Public Life

Horse Guards Road
London
SW1P 3AL

TEL : 0171 270 5875
FAX : 0171 270 5874
neill@gtnet.gov.uk
http://www.open.gov.uk/cspl
CHAIR : Lord Neill of Bladen QC ;
SECRETARY : Mr Richard Horsman
TERMS OF REFERENCE : To examine current concerns about standards of conduct of all holders of public office (October 1994); and to review issues in relation to the funding of political parties (November 1997); and to make recommendations as to any changes in the present arrangements in those areas.

6
Security Commission

70 Whitehall
London
SW1A 2AS

TEL : 0171 270 0182
FAX : 0171 270 1177
CHAIR : Rt Hon Lord Lloyd of Berwick ; SECRETARY : Miss E M Chivers
TERMS OF REFERENCE : To investigate and report on the circumstances in which a breach of security has occurred in the public service and to advise whether any change in security arrangements is necessary or desirable.

7
Security Vetting Appeals Panel

70 Whitehall
London
SW1A 2AS

TEL : 0171 270 0214
FAX : 0171 270 1177
CHAIR : Rt Hon Lord Justice May
SECRETARY : Mr S Reinstadtler
TERMS OF REFERENCE : To hear appeals against the withdrawal or refusal of security clearance and to make recommendations to the appropriate head of department.

8
Senior Salaries Review Board

Office of Manpower Economics
Oxford House
76 Oxford Street
London W1N 9FD

TEL : 0171 467 7244
FAX : 0171 467 7248
CHAIR : Sir Michael Perry CBE
SECRETARY : Mrs Christine Haworth
TERMS OF REFERENCE : To advise on the remuneration of holders of judicial office, senior civil servants, senior officers of the armed forces, and of certain other public appointments, in accordance with their terms of reference.

	4	5	6	7	8
a	–	–	–	–	–
b	–	–	–	–	–
c	Body	NP*	NP	NP	Cm
d	–	–	–	–	–
e	–	–	–	–	–
f	–	–	–	–	–
g	£0.295m	£0.546m	£0.008m	£0.014m	£0.500m*
h	–	–	–	–	–
i	1F, £260pd	1M, £500pd	1M	1M	1M
j	2M, £260pd	–	1F	1F	–
k	16M, 5F, £135pd	7M, 2F, £180pd†	5M, £222pd	4M, £180pd	7M, 3F
l	–	–	–	–	–
m	–	–	–	–	–

* A Legal Research study on personal liability in Public Service Organisations was published in June 1998. Fifth Report (The Funding of Political Parties in the UK) was published in October 1998 (Cm 4057).

† One member of the Committee is not entitled to an honorarium. All members are reimbursed actual expenses incurred.

* The panel was established on 1 July 1997.

* Secretariat provided by the Office of Manpower Economics (OME) part of the Department of Trade and Industry (DTI). The costs of the OME are borne on the DTI Vote.

CABINET OFFICE

Advisory NDPBs

9
Women's National Commission*

Cabinet Office
4th Floor
Horse Guards Road
London
SW1P 3AL
TEL : 0171 238 0386
FAX : 0171 238 0387
CHAIR : Mrs Valerie Evans ;
ACTING SECRETARY : Teresa Harper
TERMS OF REFERENCE : To ensure by all possible means that the informed opinion of women is given its due weight in the deliberations of Government.

a	–
b	–
c	Body
d	–

e	–
f	–
g	£0.288m

h	–

i	{1F}[†]

j	–

k	{50F}[†]

l	–
m	–

* Following the Prime Ministe's announcement on 28 July 1998, the Women's National Commission transferred to the Cabinet Office.
† Membership comprises 50 National Women's Organisations.

Cabinet Office: Ceremonial Branch

Ceremonial Branch, Cabinet Office, Ashley House, 2 Monck Street, London SW1P 2BQ

Enquiries   Anthony Merifield
Telephone   0171 276 2770
Facsimile   0171 276 2766

GTN   276 2770

Advisory NDPBs

1
Political Honours Scrutiny Committee*

Ceremonial Branch
Cabinet Office, Ashley House
2 Monck Street
London SW1P 2BQ
TEL : 0171 276 2770
FAX : 0171 276 2766
CHAIR : Lord Pym MC DL
SECRETARY : Mr Anthony Merifield CB
TERMS OF REFERENCE : To scrutinise recommendations for honours for political services put forward by the Prime Minister, and to ensure recipients are 'fit and proper persons' to receive such an honour.

a.	Number if a multiple body/system (1.4.98)	–
b.	Number of staff employed by the body (1.4.98)	–
c.	Annual Report	NP
d.	Audit arrangements	–
e.	Total gross expenditure of body (1997/98)	–
f.	Amount funded by government (1997/98)	–
g.	Other expenditure by sponsoring dept (1997/98)	–
h.	Chief Executive's Remuneration (1997/98)	–
	Appointments and Remuneration (1.9.98)	
i.	Chairman/President	–
j.	Deputy	–
k.	Members	2M, 1F
l.	Tribunal cases received	–
m.	Tribunal cases disposed of	–

*   A committee of Privy Councillors.

CENTRAL OFFICE OF INFORMATION

Central Office of Information

Hercules House, Hercules Road, London SE1 7DU

Enquiries	Ira Macmull
Telephone	0171 261 8209
Facsimile	0171 261 0942
E-mail	imacmull@coi.gov.uk
Internet	http://www.coi.gov.uk/coi
GTN	3528 8209

Advisory NDPBs

1
Advisory Committee on Advertising

Hercules House
Hercules Road
London
SE1 7DU
TEL : 0171 261 8209
FAX : 0171 261 0942
imacmull@coi.gov.uk
http://www.coi.gov.uk/coi
CHAIR : Mr Derek Dear
SECRETARY : Mr Viv Rowlands
TERMS OF REFERENCE : To advise on the nomination of suitable advertising agencies for Government Work and on the cost-effective working methods, including ways of selecting and buying.

a.	Number if a multiple body (1.4.98)	–
b.	Number of staff employed by the body (1.4.98)	–
c.	Annual Report	NP
d.	Audit arrangements	–
e.	Total gross expenditure of body (1997/98)	–
f.	Amount funded by government (1997/98)	–
g.	Other expenditure by sponsoring dept (1997/98)	£0.026m
h.	Chief Executive's Remuneration (1997/98)	–
	Appointments and Remuneration (1.9.98)	
i.	Chairman/President	1M
j.	Deputy	–
k.	Members	4M, 3F
l.	Tribunal cases received	–
m.	Tribunal cases disposed of	–

Chancellor of the Duchy of Lancaster

Duchy of Lancaster Office, Lancaster Place, Strand, London WC2E 7ED

Enquiries Colonel F N J Davies
Telephone 0171 836 8277
Facsimile 0171 836 3098

Advisory NDPBs

1
Advisory Committees on Justices of the Peace in Lancashire, Greater Manchester and Merseyside
Duchy of Lancaster Office
Lancaster Place
London
WC2E 7ED
TEL: 0171 836 8277
FAX: 0171 836 3098
SECRETARY: Col F N J Davies
TERMS OF REFERENCE: To advise the Lord Chancellor on the appointment of Justices of the Peace in Lancashire, Greater Manchester and Merseyside.

a.	Number if a multiple body (1.4.98)	17
b.	Number of staff employed by the body (1.4.98)	–
c.	Annual Report	NP
d.	Audit arrangements	–
e.	Total gross expenditure of body (1997/98)	–
f.	Amount funded by government (1997/98)	–
g.	Other expenditure by sponsoring dept (1997/98)	*
h.	Chief Executive's Remuneration (1997/98)	–
	Appointments and Remuneration (1.9.98)	
i.	Chairman/President	14M, 7F
j.	Deputy	–
k.	Members	92M, 77F
l.	Tribunal cases received	–
m.	Tribunal cases disposed of	–

* Advisory Committee expenses (of £0.012m in 1997/98) were met by the Duchy of Lancaster.

DEPARTMENT FOR CULTURE, MEDIA AND SPORT

Public Corporations

Department for Culture, Media & Sport

2–4 Cockspur Street,
London SW1Y 5DH

Enquiries	Mark Brookfield
Telephone	0171 211 6501
Facsimile	0171 211 6227
E-mail	enquiries@culture.gov.uk
Internet	http://www.culture.gov.uk
GTN	211 6501

		1 British Broadcasting Corporation	2 Channel Four Television Corporation	3 Independent Television Commission
		Broadcasting House London W1A 1AA	124 Horseferry Road London SW1P 2TX	33 Foley Street London W1P 7LB
		TEL: 0171 580 4468 FAX: 0171 580 7725 (Radio) FAX: 0181 749 6922 (TV) vlc@bbc.co.uk http://www.bbc.co.uk	TEL: 0171 396 4444 FAX: 0171 306 8369 dot4@channel4.com http://www.channel4.com	TEL: 0171 255 3000 FAX: 0171 306 7800 100731.3515@compuserve.com http://www.itc.co.uk
		CHAIR: Sir Christopher Bland DIRECTOR GENERAL: Sir John Birt	CHAIR: Vanni Treves CHIEF EXECUTIVE: Mr Michael Jackson	CHAIR: Sir Robin Biggam CHIEF EXECUTIVE: Mr Peter Rogers
		TERMS OF REFERENCE: The BBC operates two national television channels, five national radio stations, separate radio stations for Northern Ireland, Scotland and Wales, 38 local radio stations and news services such as BBC News 24 and BBC Online. It also operates World Service radio.	TERMS OF REFERENCE: Established in 1982, the Channel 4 Television Corporation produces public service broadcasting for the fourth channel, except in Wales.	TERMS OF REFERENCE: The Independent Commission (ITC) is the public body responsible for licensing and regulating commercially-funded television services provided in and from the United Kingdom.
a.	Number if a multiple body/system (1.4.98)	–	–	–
b.	Number of staff employed by the body (1.4.98)	–	–	–
c.	Annual Report	Body	Body	Body
d.	Audit arrangements	–	–	–
e.	Total gross expenditure of body (1997/98)	–	–	–
f.	Amount funded by government (1997/98)	–	–	–
g.	Other expenditure by sponsoring dept (1997/98)	–	–	–
h.	Chief Executive's Remuneration (1997/98)	£387,000	£179,000	£175,000*
	Appointments and Remuneration (1.9.98)			
i.	Chairman/President	1M, £67,420	{1M, £57,300}	1M, £67,420
j.	Deputy	1F, £17,300	{1M, £17,640}	1M, £17,300
k.	Members	3M, £17,300* 1M, £12,980† 4M, 2F, £8,660‡	{8M, 3F, £13,230}*	5M, 3F, £12,980†
l.	Tribunal cases received	–	–	–
m.	Tribunal cases disposed of	–	–	–

* National Governor.
† Chairmen of English Forum.
‡ Governors.

* Channel Four also has six Executive Members including the Chief Executive. None of the Channel Four members are Government appointees. Appointees are made by the ITC.

* The Chief Executive is paid in a range between £170,000 and £175,000.
† National Members.

DEPARTMENT FOR CULTURE, MEDIA AND SPORT

Public Corporations

Executive NDPBs

4
Radio Authority

Holbrook House
14 Great Queen Street
London
WC2 5DG
TEL : 0171 430 2724
FAX : 0171 405 7062
info@radioauthority.org.uk
http://www.radioauthority.org.uk
CHAIR : Sir Peter Gibbins
SECRETARY : Mr Tony Stoller
TERMS OF REFERENCE : The Authority licenses and regulates commercial radio (all non-BBC Services). It is funded by the commercial radio stations.

5
Sianel Pedwar Cymru (Welsh Fourth Channel Authority)

Parc Ty Glas
Llanishen
Cardiff
CF4 5DU
TEL : 01222 747444
FAX : 01222 754444
s4c@s4c.co.uk
http://www.s4c.co.uk
CHAIR : Elan Close Stephens
CHIEF EXECUTIVE : Mr Huw Jones
TERMS OF REFERENCE : To provide a high quality television service in Wales, with a substantial proportion of programmes and the majority of programmes in peak hours in the Welsh language.

6
Arts Council of England

14 Great Peter Street
London
SW1P 3NQ
TEL : 0171 333 0100
FAX : 0171 073 6590
http://www.artscouncil.org.uk
CHAIR : Mr Gerry Robinson
CHIEF EXECUTIVE : Mr Peter Hewitt
TERMS OF REFERENCE : The Arts Council of England is the national funding body for the arts in this country. It is responsible for fostering the arts through the distribution of public money from central government and revenue by the National Lottery.

7
British Film Institute

21 Stephen Street
London
W1P 2LW
TEL : 0171 255 1444
FAX : 0171 436 7950
library@bfi.org.uk
http://www.bfi.org.uk
CHAIR : Mr Alan Parker
DIRECTOR : Mr John Woodward
TERMS OF REFERENCE : To promote knowledge and understanding, and encourage the development, of the art of film in the United Kingdom.

8
British Library

96 Euston Road
London
NW1 2DB
TEL : 0171 412 7000
FAX : 0171 412 7268
press-and-pr@bl.uk
WEB : http://www.portico.bl.uk
CHAIRMAN OF THE BRITISH LIBRARY BOARD : Dr John Ashworth
TERMS OF REFERENCE : The British Library is the national library of the United Kingdom. The British Library Board is responsible for managing the library as a national centre for reference, study, bibliographical and information services.

	4 Radio Authority	5 Sianel Pedwar Cymru	6 Arts Council of England	7 British Film Institute	8 British Library
a	–	–	–	–	–
b	–	–	278	487	2,429
c	Body	Body	Body	Body	Body
d	–	–	X	Y	X
e	–	–	£481.144m*	£34.623m	£121.021
f	–	–	£185.100m	£16.000m	£87.200m
g	–	–	£0.064m	£0.066m	£0.139m
h	£140,268	£116,368	£92,231†	£55,242*	£102,000
i	1M, £50,560	1F, £39,030	1M	1M	1M, £28,363
j	1M, £17,300	–	1M, £70,000	1F	–
k	2M, 2F, £8,660	3M, 3F, £7,210	15M, 6F	15M, 2F	12M, 1F, £6,839
l	–	–	–	–	–
m	–	–	–	–	–

* This includes grant payment from the Arts Council Lottery Fund.
† The Council pays 9.4% of salary for pension purposes.

* In post for 8 months of 1997/98.

17

DEPARTMENT FOR CULTURE, MEDIA AND SPORT

Executive NPDBs

9
British Tourist Authority

Thames Tower
Black's Road
Hammersmith
London W6 9EL
TEL : 0181 846 9000
FAX : 0181 563 0302
http://www.visitbritain.com
CHAIR : Mr David Quarmby
SECRETARY : Ms Sue Garland
TERMS OF REFERENCE : To promote all of Britain as a visitor destination worldwide, generating additional tourism revenue and spreading the benefits regionally and seasonally. To provide advice to Government and others on tourism matters affecting Great Britain.

a	–
b	420
c	Body
d	X
e	£53.845m
f	£35.000m
g	£0.078m
h	£116,841
i	1M, £29,437*
j	–
k	5M, £7,340
l	–
m	–

* Chairman is joint Chairman of the British Tourist Authority and the English Tourist Board. He receives a combined salary of £58,874 per annum.

10
Broadcasting Standards Commission

7 The Sanctuary
London
SW1P 3JS
TEL : 0171 233 0544
FAX : 0171 233 0397
bsc@bsc.org.uk
http://www.bsc.org.uk
CHAIR : Lady Howe of Aberavon
DIRECTOR : Mr Stephen Whittle
TERMS OF REFERENCE : The Broadcasting Standards Commission is the statutory body for both standards and fairness in broadcasting. It is the only organisation within the regulatory framework of UK broadcasting to cover all television and radio.

a	–
b	25
c	Body
d	Y
e	£1.971m
f	£0.986m*
g	£0.040m
h	£71,666
i	1F, £45,210
j	1F, £35,990
k	4M, 6F, £14,450
l	–
m	–

* The Broadcasting Standards Commission is funded half by the Government and half by the Broadcasters.

11
Crafts Council

44A Pentonville Road
London
N1 9HF
TEL : 0171 278 7700
FAX : 0171 837 6891
http://www.craftscouncil.org.uk
CHAIR : Sir Nicholas Goodison
DIRECTOR : Mr Tony Ford
TERMS OF REFERENCE : To advance and encourage the creation of works of fine craftsmanship.

a	–
b	50
c	Body
d	Y
e	£4.933m
f	£3.250m
g	£0.050m
h	£55,156*
i	1M, £60,000
j	–
k	7M, 5F
l	–
m	–

* The Council pays 14.1% of salary for pension purposes.

12
English Sports Council

16 Upper Woburn Place
London
WC1H 0QP
TEL : 0171 273 1500
FAX : 0171 383 5740
info@english.sports.council.gov.uk
http://www.english.sports.gov.uk
ACTING CHAIR : Mr Trevor Brooking MBE
TERMS OF REFERENCE : The Council is charged with taking the lead in all aspects of sport and physical recreation in England which require administration, co-ordination or representation.

a	–
b	375
c	Body
d	X
e	£350.853m*
f	£22.343m
g	£0.185m
h	£74,657
i	1M, £22,343
j	1M, £13,463
k	10M, 3F
l	–
m	–

* This includes grant payment from the Sports Lottery Fund.

13
English Tourist Board

Thames Tower
Black's Road
Hammersmith
London W6 9EL
TEL : 0181 846 9000
FAX : 0181 563 0302
http://www.visitbritain.com
CHAIR : Mr David Quarmby
SECRETARY : Ms Sue Garland
TERMS OF REFERENCE : To assist the tourism industry to maximise tourism earnings in England. To act as a strategic body providing leadership to the industry, to develop and improve the quality of the tourism product and stimulate the domestic tourism market. To advise the Government on tourism matters affecting England.

a	–
b	63
c	Body
d	X
e	£12.784m
f	£9.866m
g	£0.078m
h	£94.009
i	1M, £29,437*
j	–
k	4M, 2F, £7,340
l	–
m	–

* Chairman is joint Chairman of the British Tourist Authority and the English Tourist Board. He receives a combined salary of £58,874 per annum.

DEPARTMENT FOR CULTURE, MEDIA AND SPORT

Executive NDPBs

	14 Football Licensing Authority	15 English Heritage (The Historic Buildings and Monuments Commission for England)	16 Great Britain Sports Council*	17 Historic Royal Palaces	18 Millennium Commission
Address	27 Harcourt House, 19 Cavendish Square, London, W1M 9AD	23 Saville Row, London, W1X 1AB	16 Upper Woburn Place, London, WC1H 0QP	Hampton Court Palace, East Molesey, Surrey, KT8 9RE	Portland House, Stag Place, London, SW1E 5EZ
TEL	0171 491 7191	0171 973 3000	0171 273 1500	0181 781 9750	0171 880 2001
FAX	0171 491 1882	0171 973 3001	0171 383 5740	0181 781 9754	0171 880 2000
Web/Email	fla@flaweb.org.uk http://www.flaweb.org.uk/fla	http://www.english-heritage.org.uk		http://www.hrp.org.uk	http://www.millennium.gov.uk
CHAIR	Mr Clive Sherling	Sir Jocelyn Stevens CVO	Sir Rodney Walker	CHAIRMAN OF THE TRUSTEES: The Rt Hon The Earl of Airlie	Rt Hon Chris Smith MP (Secretary of State)
CHIEF EXECUTIVE		Ms Pam Alexander	Mr Derek Casey		DIRECTOR: Mr Michael O'Connor
TERMS OF REFERENCE	The Football Licensing Authority is charged with ensuring the implementation of certain key recommendations of the Taylor Report concerning safety at football grounds.	The role of English Heritage is to secure the preservation of ancient monuments and historic buildings; to promote the presentation and enhancement of conservation areas; and to promote the public's enjoyment of ancient monuments and historic buildings.	Until the division of its responsibilities on 1.1.97, the Council played a strong role in fostering the knowledge and practice of sport and physical recreation among the people at large and supporting their development. The GB Sports Council will continue as a corporate body for an interim period to handle any residual issues relating to the transfer of functions.	To care for, conserve and present to the public the Unoccupied Royal Palaces; the Tower of London, Hampton Court Palace, Kensington Palace State Apartments, the Banqueting House in Whitehall, and Kew Palace with Queen Charlotte's Cottage.	The Millennium Commission distributes a fifth share of the National Lottery Distribution Fund to assist communities in marking the Millennium. It supports capital projects, bursaries to individuals, and the Millennium Festival in 2000 with the Millennium Experience at Greenwich as its centrepiece.
a	–	–	–	–	–
b	15	1,355	–	451	62
c	Body	Body	–	HC	Body
d	Y	Y	–	X	X
e	£0.896m	£127.713m	–	£44.300m	£851.650m
f	£0.896m	£105.183m	–	£7.500m	*
g	£0.011	£0.089m	–	£0.021m	£0.025m
h	£52,926	£91,000*	–	£65,000	†
i	1M, £12,662	1M, £44,625†	1M	1M	‡
j	–	–	1M	–	–
k	4M, 2F, £230pd	7M, 5F, 4 vacancies, up to £15,150	5M, 3F	6M, 2F	6M, 2F
l	–	–	–	–	–
m	–	–	–	–	–

15:
* This figure covers the salaries of an acting chief executive and a chief executive during this period.
† The Chairman is contracted to a 3 day week.

16:
* The functions and responsibility of the Council were transferred to the UK and English Sports Councils from 1.1.97.

18:
* All expenditure is funded by National Lottery.
† Eric Sorenson was Chief Executive up to 3.3.98 and received emolument amounting to £166,412 and a payment in lieu of notice of £58,025. From 4.3.98 Mike O'Connor became Director and received emolument amounting to £58,468.
‡ Chairman of the Millennium Commission is the Secretary of State.

19

DEPARTMENT FOR CULTURE, MEDIA AND SPORT

Executive NDPBs

Museums & Galleries

19 British Museum	20 Geffrye Museum	21 Horniman Museum and Gardens	22 Imperial War Museum	23 Museum of London
Bloomsbury London WC1B 3DG	Kingsland Road London E2 8AE	100 London Road Forest Hill London SE23 3PQ	Lambeth Road London SE1 6HZ	150 London Wall London EC2Y 5HN
TEL : 0171 636 1555 FAX : 0171 323 8118 pr-bm@british-museum.ac.uk http://www.british-museum.ac.uk CHAIRMAN OF THE TRUSTEES : Mr Grahame Greene SECRETARY : Ms Claire Parker TERMS OF REFERENCE : The British Museum holds in trust for the nation, and in perpetuity, those parts of the national collections in its care, to ensure their accessibility, and to promote knowledge of, and enjoyment in, the subject areas covered by their collections.	TEL : 0171 739 9893 FAX : 0171 729 5647 geffrye-museum.org.uk http://www.lattimore.co.uk/geffrye CHAIR : Baroness Brigstocke SECRETARY : Ms Nancy Loader TERMS OF REFERENCE : To collect, preserve and present, for purposes of education and enjoyment, material culture relating to English domestic furniture and interiors.	TEL : 0181 699 1872 FAX : 0181 291 5506 postmaster@horniman.demon.co.uk http://www.horniman.demon.co.uk CHAIR : Mr Donald Kirkham SECRETARY : Ms Jennifer Beever TERMS OF REFERENCE : The Horniman's aim is to use its world-wide collections and gardens to encourage a wider appreciation of the world, its people and their cultures.	TEL : 0171 416 5000 FAX : 0171 416 5216 mail@iwm.org.uk http://www.iwm.org.uk/ CHAIR : Professor Robert O'Neill AO ; SECRETARY : Mr Jonathon Chadwick TERMS OF REFERENCE : To illustrate and record all aspects of the two world wars and other military operations involving Britain and the Commonwealth since 1914.	TEL : 0171 600 3699 FAX : 0171 600 1058 info@museumoflondon.org.uk/ http://www.museum-london.org.uk CHAIR : Mr Peter Revell-Smith CBE ; SECRETARY : Ms Suika Perera TERMS OF REFERENCE : To collect and display the social history of London from prehistoric times to the present. Its collections are open to the public at the museum's buildings in the City of London.
a – b 980 c Body* d X	a – b 27 c Body d Y	a – b 82 c Body d Y	a – b 422 c Body* d X	a – b 281 c Body d Y
e £67.133m f £31.860m g £0.033m	e £1.243m f £1.122m g £0.020m	e £3.122m f £2.944m g £0.020m	e £23.622m f £10.971m g £0.033m	e £13.995m f £4.310m g £0.020m
h £96,090	h £42,824	h £41,109	h £91,148m	h £60,016
i {1M}	i 1F	i 1M	i {1M}	i {1M}
j –	j –	j {1M}	j –	j {1M}
k 12M, 2F, {5M, 3F}	k 2M, 1F, {3M, 3F}	k 3M, 1F, {4M, 2F}	k 8M, 2F, {9M, 1F}	k 3M, 4F, {3M, 1F}
l – m –	l – m –	l – m –	l – m –	l – m –

* The British Museum produces a report every three years.

* Imperial War Museum produces a report every three years.

DEPARTMENT FOR CULTURE, MEDIA AND SPORT

Executive NDPBs

Museums & Galleries

	24	25	26	27	28
	Museum of Science and Industry in Manchester	**National Gallery**	**National Maritime Museum**	**National Museums and Galleries on Merseyside**	**National Museum of Science and Industry**
Address	Station Road Castlefield Manchester M3 4FP	Trafalgar Square London WC2N 5DN	Romney Road Greenwich London SE10 9NF	127 Dale Street Liverpool L69 3LA	South Kensington London SW7 2DD
TEL	0161 832 2244	0171 839 3321	0181 858 4422	0151 207 0001	0171 938 8000
FAX	0161 833 2184	0171 930 1681	0181 312 6632	0151 478 4321	0171 938 8112
Email	all@mussci.u.net.com	information@ng-london.org.uk	http://www.nmm.ac.uk	http://www.nmgm.org.uk	h.roderick@nmsi.ac.uk
Web	http://www.edes.co.uk/mussci	http://www.nationalgallery.org.uk			http://www.nmsi.ac.uk
Chair/Secretary	CHAIRMAN OF THE TRUSTEES: Mr John Lee; SECRETARY: Mr Bob Scott	CHAIR: Mr Philip Hughes; SECRETARY: Ms Hazel Aitken	CHAIRMAN OF THE TRUSTEES: Sir David Harvey; SECRETARY: Ms Jenny Saint	CHAIRMAN OF THE TRUSTEES: Mr David McDonnell; SECRETARY: Mr Malcolm Harrison	CHAIR: Dr Peter Williams CBE; SECRETARY: Mr David Penrose
Terms of Reference	To provide permanent exhibitions on power, energy, transport, aviation, space textiles, communications, scientific instructions and social history. Changing exhibitions are also provided.	To care for, enhance and study its national collection of 13th to 19th century western European paintings; to encourage the widest possible public access to the pictures for education and enjoyment now and in the future; setting an example to other galleries.	The Museum exists to promote an understanding of the maritime history and future of Britain, the story of time and the historic sights of Greenwich.	To promote the public enjoyment and understanding of art history and science.	The Museum holds and displays the national collections of science (including medical science), engineering, transport and industry.
a	–	–	–	–	–
b	89	433	295	638.5	782
c	Body	Body	NP	HC*	HC
d	Y	X	X	X	X
e	£3.300m	£34.900m	£12.026m	£16.715m	£34.100m
f	£2.233m	£18.300m	£10.484m	£13.127m	£21.081m
g	£0.020m	£0.033m	£0.033m	£0.033m	£0.033m
h	£74,715	£103,669	£77,700	£83,650[†]	£111,813
i	1M	1M	1M	1M	1M
j	1F	–	–	–	–
k	1F, {8M, 1F}	8M, 2F	10M, 2F	9M, 6F	8M, 6F
l	–	–	–	–	–
m	–	–	–	–	–

[*] The National Museums and Galleries on Merseyside produces a report every three years.
[†] This includes a bonus payment for 1997-98 of £8,936 which was paid in 1998-99.

21

DEPARTMENT FOR CULTURE, MEDIA AND SPORT

Executive NPDBs

Museums & Galleries

29
National Portrait Gallery

St Martin's Place
London
WC2H 0HE

TEL : 0171 306 0055
FAX : 0171 306 0056
istreule@hpg.org.uk
http://www.npg.org.uk

CHAIRMAN OF THE TRUSTEES :
Mr Henry Keswick
SECRETARY : Mr John Wykeham
TERMS OF REFERENCE : The National Portrait Gallery collects and displays portraits of eminent British men and women. It houses a primary collection of over 9,000 works and a large archive.

a	–
b	137
c	Body*
d	X
e	£7.872m
f	£4.809m
g	£0.033m
h	£69,625
i	1M
j	–
k	8M, 4F, {1M, 1F}
l	–
m	–

* National Portrait Gallery produces a report every three years.

30
Natural History Museum

Cromwell Road
London
SW7 5BD

TEL : 0171 938 9123
FAX : 0171 938 8799
tac@nhm.ac.uk
http://www.nhm.ac.uk

CHAIR : Sir Robert May FRS
SECRETARY : Ms Nicola Donlon
TERMS OF REFERENCE : To maintain and develop its collections, and to use them to promote the discovery, understanding, responsible use and enjoyment of the natural world.

a	–
b	714.8
c	Body
d	X
e	£40.706m
f	£27.660m
g	£0.033m
h	£92,159
i	1M
j	–
k	5M, 3F, {3M}
l	–
m	–

31
Sir John Soane's Museum

13 Lincoln's Inn Fields
London
WC2A 3BP

TEL : 0171 405 2107
FAX : 0171 831 3957
http://www.demon.co.uk/heritage/soanes/

CHAIRMAN OF THE TRUSTEES :
Mr Richard Griffiths ; CURATOR :
Mrs Margaret Richardson
TERMS OF REFERENCE : This is the House, Museum and Collection of the architect Sir John Soane, who died in 1837. The collection comprises works of art, paintings, books, manuscripts, prints, and drawings.

a	–
b	19
c	Body
d	Y
e	£0.786m
f	£0.593m
g	£0.020m
h	£35,518
i	{1M}
j	–
k	{6M, 1F}
l	–
m	–

32
Tate Gallery

Millbank
London
SW1P 4RG

TEL : 0171 887 8734
FAX : 0171 887 8007
information@tate.org.uk
http://www.tate.org.uk

CHAIRMAN OF THE TRUSTEES :
Mr David Verey
SECRETARY : Ms Sharon Page
TERMS OF REFERENCE : The aim of the Gallery is to increase public awareness, understanding and appreciation of British art from the 16th century to the present day, and also of 20th century painting and sculpture.

a	–
b	531
c	HC*
d	X
e	£60.100m
f	£18.663m
g	£0.033m
h	£118,500
i	{1M}
j	–
k	6M, 4F, {1M}
l	–
m	–

* The Tate Gallery produces a report every two years.

33
Victoria and Albert Museum

South Kensington
London
SW7 2RL

TEL : 0171 938 8500
FAX : 0171 938 8379
postmaster@vam.ac.uk
http://www.vam.ac.uk

ACTING CHAIRMAN OF THE TRUSTEES : Mr Jonathan Scott CBE ; SECRETARY : Mr Peter Wilson
TERMS OF REFERENCE : To increase the understanding and enjoyment of art, craft and design through the Museum's collection.

a	–
b	805
c	Body*
d	X
e	£40.742m
f	£29.898m
g	£0.033m
h	£103,672
i	1M
j	–
k	7M, 4F, {1M}
l	–
m	–

* Victoria and Albert Museum produces a report every three years.

DEPARTMENT FOR CULTURE, MEDIA AND SPORT

Executive NDPBs

Museums & Galleries

	34 Wallace Collection	35 Museums and Galleries Commission	36 National Film and Television School (NFTS)	37 National Heritage Memorial Fund	38 National Lottery Charities Board
Address	Hertford House, Manchester Square, London, W1M 6BN	16 Queen Anne's Gate, London, SW1H 9AA	Beaconsfield Studios, Station Road, Beaconsfield, HP9 1LG	7 Holbein Place, London, SW1W 8NR	St Vincent House, Suffolk Street, London, SW1Y 4NL
Tel	0171 935 0687	0171 233 4200	01494 671234	0171 591 6000	0171 747 5300
Fax	0171 224 2155	0171 233 3686	01494 674042	0171 591 6001	0171 747 5214
Email	admin@wallcoll.demon.co.uk	n.poole@mgcuk.co.uk	cad@nftsfilm-tv.ac.uk	nhmf@nhmf.demon.co.uk	enquiries@nlcb.org.uk
Web	http://www.demon.co.uk/heritage/wallace		http://www.nftsfilm-tv.ac.uk	http://www.hls.org.uk	http://www.nlcb.org.uk
Chair/Chairman	Chairman of the Trustees: Mr John Lewis; Secretary: Ms Hanna Obee	Chair: Mr James Joll; Secretary: Ms Rochelle D'Andorda (Temporary)	Chair: Mr David Elstein; Director: Mr Stephen Bayly	Chairman of the Trustees: Dr Eric Anderson; Director: Ms Anthea Case	Chair: The Hon David Sieff; Chief Executive: Mr Timothy Hornsby
Terms of Reference	To maintain and display the art collection bequeathed to the nation in 1897 by Lady Wallace.	To advise the Government on matters concerning museums throughout the United Kingdom, with the central aim of promoting museum and heritage interests and raising museum standards.	The National Film and Television School (NFTS) is a leading national centre for graduate students who wish to prepare for a career in film and television.	The National Heritage Memorial Fund (NHMF) is an umbrella organisation consisting of two funds: the Heritage Lottery Fund and the Heritage Memorial Fund.	The Board distributes the proceeds of the National Lottery specifically allocated to charitable, benevolent and philanthropic organisations. It makes decisions on grants in separate committees for England, Northern Ireland, Scotland, and Wales, and for the United Kingdom as a whole.
a	–	–	–	–	–
b	68	43	94*	152	264
c	Body	HC	Body	Body	Body
d	X	X	Y	X	X
e	£2.879m	£9.514m	£8.240m†	£133.190m*	£215.700*
f	£1.870m	£9.003m	£2.100m	£5.000m	£0.800m
g	£0.033m	£0.020m	£0.047m	£0.046m	–
h	£62,306	£60,655	£62,423	£91,812	£112,662
i	1M	1M	1M	1M	1M, £56,650
j	–	–	1M	4M	1M, £38,522
k	3M, 2F	8M, 4F	11M, 7F	8M, 6F	13M, 9F
l	–	–	–	–	–
m	–	–	–	–	–

* Includes 19 staff employed by NFTS Ealing Studios Ltd, a subsidiary company.
† Includes wholly owned subsidiary companies.

* This includes grant payment from the Heritage Lottery Fund.

* This includes grant paid in year by the NLCB.

DEPARTMENT FOR CULTURE, MEDIA AND SPORT

Executive NDPBs

	39 New Millennium Experience Company Ltd*	40 Registrar of Public Lending Right (PLR)	41 Royal Armouries Museum	42 Royal Commission on Historical Manuscripts	43 Royal Commission on the Historical Monuments of England
Address	110 Buckingham Palace Road, London SW1W 9SB	Bayheath House, Prince Regent Street, Stockton-on-Tees TS18 1DF	Armouries Drive, Leeds LS10 1LT	Quality House, Quality Court, Chancery Lane, London WC2A 1HP	National Monument Record Centre, Great Western Village, Kemble Drive, Swindon SN2 2GZ
TEL	0171 808 8200	01642 604699	0113 220 1995	0171 242 1198	01793 414700
FAX	0171 808 8352	01642 615641	0113 220 1934	0171 831 3550	01793 414707
Email/Web	http://www.mx2000.co.uk	registrar@plr.octacon.co.uk; http://www.earl.org.uk/earl/members/plr	http://www.armouries.org.uk	nra@hmc.gov.uk; http://www.hmc.gov.uk	info@rchme.gov.uk; http://www.rchme.gov.uk
CHAIR	Mr Robert Ayling	Dr James Parker	The Rt Hon Viscount Younger of Leckie	—	The Rt Hon Lord Faringdon
CHIEF EXECUTIVE / SECRETARY / etc.	CHIEF EXECUTIVE: Ms Jennifer Page		SECRETARY: Mr Dick Mundell	CHAIRMAN OF COMMISSIONERS: Rt Hon Lord Bingham of Cornhill (Lord Chief Justice); SECRETARY: Dr Christopher Kitching	SECRETARY: Mr Tom Hassall FSA
TERMS OF REFERENCE	To develop, build and operate a national Millennium Experience at Greenwich and an associated programme of events and activities across the UK, to provide the focus for the country's millennium celebrations.	The Registrar and his staff administer the Public Lending Right Scheme.	To promote the public's enjoyment and understanding of arms and armour, by ensuring that the collection is exhibited to the public, and that the objects are available for study and research.	To locate, report on and disseminate information about historical papers outside the Public Records; and act as the central advisory body in the UK with regard to this part of the nation's written heritage.	To compile and make available the national record of England's ancient monuments and historic buildings for use by individuals and bodies concerned with understanding, interpreting and managing the historic environment.
a	–	–	–	–	–
b	94	15	108	34.5	236
c	Body†	HC	Body*	TSO	Body
d	Y	X	X	X*	X
e	‡	£4.924m	£6.364m	£1.033m†	£11.450m
f	‡	£4.921m	£5.223m	£1.089m	£11.050m
g	£0.025m	£0.043m	£0.021m	£0.037m	£0.057m
h	£150,000§	£40,782	£65,935	£51,757	£60,094*
i	1M	–	1M	1M	1M
j	1M	–	–	–	1F
k	6M, 2F#	–	5M, 1F, {1M}	11M, 4F	9M, 4F; 1 vacancy
l	–	–	–	–	–
m	–	–	–	–	–

* Peter Mandelson MP holds the company shares, on behalf of the Government and is accountable to Parliament.
† Annual report and accounts cover the period 12.2.97–31.3.98.
‡ Expenditure figures are included in the expenditure totals for the Millennium Commission.
§ Excludes pension contributions and future performance bonus award.
\# Non-executive directors only. Chief Executive, Managing Director and Finance Director also sit on the Board as executive directors.

* The Royal Armouries Museum produces a triennial report.

* Accounts for DCMS are audited by the Comptroller and Audit General.
† Expenditure forms part of the total Department for Culture, Media and Sport (DCMS) expenditure.

* Chief Executive is a member of the Principal Civil Service Pension Scheme. The Commission pays the ordinary 'employers' contributions.

DEPARTMENT FOR CULTURE, MEDIA AND SPORT

Executive NDPBs

44
United Kingdom Sports Council

Walkden House
10 Melton Street
London
NW1 2EB
TEL : 0171 380 8000
FAX : 0171 380 8005
info@uksport.gov.uk
CHAIR : Sir Rodney Walker
TERMS OF REFERENCE : To foster, support and encourage the development of sport and physical recreation and the achievement of excellence in the UK.

Advisory NDPBs

45
Advisory Committee for the Public Lending Right

Bayheath House
Prince Regent Street
Stckton-on-Tees
Cleveland TS18 1DF
TEL : 01642 604699
FAX : 01642 615641
registrar@pir.octacon.co.uk
CHAIR : Mr Michael Holroyd
TERMS OF REFERENCE : To provide expert advice to the Secretary of State for Culture, Media and Sport and to the Registrar of the Public Lending Right on the operation of the Public Lending Right Scheme.

46
Advisory Committee on Historic Wreck Sites

2–4 Cockspur Street
London
SW1Y 5DH

TEL : 0171 211 2099
FAX : 0171 211 2040
enquiries@culture.gov.uk
http://www.culture.gov.uk
CHAIR : Lady Merrison
SECRETARY : Mr Gwyn Owens
TERMS OF REFERENCE : To advise the Government on the suitability of wreck sites to be designated for protection under the grounds of historical, archaeological or artistic interest.

47
Advisory Committee on the Government Art Collection*

c/o Department for Culture, Media and Sport, Public Enquiry Unit, 2–4 Cockspur Street, London SW1Y 5DH
TEL : 0171 211 6200
CHAIR : Mr John Tusa
TERMS OF REFERENCE : To guide the purchasing and commissioning activities of the Governnment Art Collection and to advise other governments on the acquisition and care of works of art.

48
Advisory Council on Libraries

Secretariat
Libraries Division
2–4 Cockspur Street
London SW1Y 5DH
TEL : 0171 211 6124
FAX : 0171 211 6130
CHAIR : Mr Michael Messenger
SECRETARY : Mr Andrew Robson
TERMS OF REFERENCE : To advise the Secretary of State upon matters connected with the provision or use of library facilities under the Public Libraries and Museums Act 1964.

	44	45	46	47	48
a	–	–	–	–	–
b	33	–	–	–	–
c	Body	NP	Body	Body	HC
d	X	–	–	–	–
e	£12.040m	–	–	–	–
f	£11.824m	–	–	–	–
g	£0.140m	£0.006m	£0.022m	–	£0.015m
h	£84,278	–	–	–	–
i	1M, £22,343	1M	1F	1M	1M
j	1M	–	–	–	–
k	4M, 3F	3M, 4F	8M, 3F 1 vacancy	4M, 2F	6M, 3F
l	–	–	–	–	–
m	–	–	–	–	–

* This body was formed in June 1935 but became inactive during and immediately after the Second World War. It was reconstituted in 1946, and again in 1956, since when it has been in continuous existence.

DEPARTMENT FOR CULTURE, MEDIA AND SPORT

Advisory NDPBs

49
Football Task Force

c/o The Football Trust
Walkden House
10 Melton Street
London NW1 2EB
TEL : 0171 388 4504
FAX : 0171 388 6688
CHAIR : David Mellor PC QC
ADMINISTRATOR : Mr Andy Burnham
TERMS OF REFERENCE : To consider, and make recommendations to the Minister for Sport on, appropriate measures to deal with public concern on issues such as racism, access for the disabled, ticket prices and the increasing commercialisation of football.

50
Library and Information Commission

2 Sheraton Street
London
W1V 4BH
TEL : 0171 411 0078
FAX : 0171 411 0057
libcom@lic.bl.uk
http://www.ukoln/services/lic
CHAIR : Mr Matthew Evans
SECRETARY : Mrs Margaret Haines
TERMS OF REFERENCE : To be a national focus of expertise in the field of library and information services.

51
Reviewing Committee on the Export of Works of Art

2–4 Cockspur Street
London
SW1Y 5DH
TEL : 0171 211 6160
FAX : 0171 211 6170
cultural.property@culture.gov.uk
CHAIR : Mr John Guinness CB
SECRETARY : Ms Elizabeth Foxell
TERMS OF REFERENCE : To make recommendations to the Secretary of State for Culture, Media and Sport about the granting or deferral of export licenses for works of art.

52
Royal Fine Art Commission

7 St James's Square
London
SW1Y 4JU
TEL : 0171 839 6537
FAX : 0171 839 8475
http://www.royal-fine-art.gov.uk
CHAIR : Rt Hon The Lord St John of Fawsley ; SECRETARY : Mr Francis Golding
TERMS OF REFERENCE : To advise public bodies on questions of public amenity or of artistic importance. Its principal purpose is to promote good contemporary architecture, although it takes an interest in all aspects of the visual environment.

53
Theatres Trust

Doric House
22 Charing Cross Road
London
WC2 0HR
TEL : 0171 836 8591
FAX : 0171 836 3302
CHAIR : Mr Laurence Harbottle
DIRECTOR : Mr Peter Longman
TERMS OF REFERENCE : The Trust was set up to promote the protection of theatres for the benefit of the nation. Its remit covers the whole of the United Kingdom.

	49	50	51	52	53
a	–	–	–	–	–
b	1	–	–	–	–
c	–	Body	Cm	Cm	Body
d	–	–	–	–	–
e	£0.043m	–	–	–	–
f	–	–	–	–	–
g	£0.022m	£0.460m*	£0.016m	£0.770m	£0.055m
h	–	–	–	–	–
i	1M	1M	1M	1M	1M
j	{1M}*	–	–	–	1M
k	{13M, 1F}	7M, 3F	5M, 2F	12M, 4F, 1 vacancy	10M, 2F
l	–	–	–	–	–
m	–	–	–	–	–

* Appointed by Task Force chairmen.
* Includes £0.430m grant-in-aid.

Advisory NDPBs

54
Treasure Valuation Committee

Secretariat, Department of Culture, Media and Sport,
2–4 Cockspur Street
London SW1Y 5DH
TEL : 0171 211 2105
FAX : 0171 211 2006
CHAIR : The Rt Hon The Lord Stewartby FBA ; SECRETARY : Ms Lisa Ray
TERMS OF REFERENCE : To recommend to the Secretary of State a fair market value for the items of treasure brought before it. The Committee's remit covers finds from England, Wales and Northern Ireland.

a	–
b	–
c	Cm
d	–

e	–
f	–
g	£0.001m

h	–

i	1M

j	–

k	5M

l	–
m	–

DEPARTMENT FOR CULTURE, MEDIA AND SPORT

MINISTRY OF DEFENCE

Ministry of Defence

Northumberland House, Northumberland Avenue, London WC2N 5BP

Enquiries   Richard Berthon
Telephone   0171 218 4814
Facsimile   0171 218 0223
E-mail   domd@gtnet.gov.uk
Internet   http://www.mod.uk

GTN   2188 4814

Executive NDPBs

1 Fleet Air Arm Museum

Box D6, RNAS
Yeovilton
Ilchester
Somerset BA22 8HT
TEL : 01935 840565
FAX : 01935 840181
CHAIR : Rear Admiral Terrence Loughran CB
TERMS OF REFERENCE : To provide an effective and accessible repository, both now and in the future, for the heritage of the Navy and to raise public awareness of naval aviation.

2 National Army Museum

Royal Hospital Road
London
SW3 4HT
TEL : 0171 730 0717
FAX : 0171 823 6573
nam@enterprise.net
http://www.failte.com/am/
DEPUTY CHAIR : General Sir John Waters GCB CBE
TERMS OF REFERENCE : The Museum collects, conserves and displays objects relating to the story of Britain's land forces from the 15th century to the present, including the Indian Army up to independence in 1947.

3 Oil and Pipelines Agency

35–38 Portman Square
London
W1H 0EU
TEL : 0171 935 2585
FAX : 0171 935 3510
CHAIR : Mr Geoffrey Richards
TERMS OF REFERENCE : To manage the Government Pipeline and Storage System on behalf of the Ministry of Defence.

		1	2	3
a.	Number if a multiple body (1.4.98)	–	–	–
b.	Number of staff employed by the body (1.4.98)	48*	82	17
c.	Annual Report	Body	Body	Body
d.	Audit arrangements	X	X	Y
e.	Total gross expenditure of body (1997/98)	£1.500m†	£3.39m	£1.719m
f.	Amount funded by government (1997/98)	£0.423m	£3.39m	£1.510m
g.	Other expenditure by sponsoring dept (1997/98)	£0.009m	–	£0.047m
h.	Chief Executive's Remuneration (1997/98)	£43,253	£57,357*	£86,666
	Appointments and Remuneration (1.9.98)			
i.	Chairman/President	‡	†	1M, £9,800
j.	Deputy	‡	{1M}†	–
k.	Members	{6M, 1F}§	{6M, 1F}†	1M, £4,300
l.	Tribunal cases received	–	–	–
m.	Tribunal cases disposed of	–	–	–

* An additional 15 temporary staff are employed in the summer months.
† Figures unaudited at time of going to press.
‡ The Chairman and Deputy are ex-officio.
§ Appointed by the respective museum boards.

* Not including the Performance. Related Bonus (which has not been calculated for 1997/98).
† Chairman is ex-officio. Deputy and Members appointed by the Army Board.

MINISTRY OF DEFENCE

Executive NDPBs

Advisory NDPBs

4
Royal Air Force Museum

Hendon
London
NW9 5LL

TEL : 0181 205 2266
FAX : 0181 200 1751
rafmus@dircon.co.uk
http://www.rafmuseum.org.uk
CHAIR : Marshall of the RAF, Sir Michael Beetham GCB CBE DFC AFC
TERMS OF REFERENCE : To preserve, conserve and exhibit the history of aviation, focusing primarily on the Royal Air Force and associated air forces. It does this through the integrated use of exhibitions, collection, its restoration and conservation work, research facility and education service.

a	–
b	122*
c	Body
d	X
e	£6.661m†
f	£4.058m
g	£0.044m
h	£71,205
i	1M
j	–
k	12M, 2F
l	–
m	–

* Including 9 temporary 'Explainers' for the new interactive suite.
† Includes £1.87m provided through grants from Heritage Lottery and European Regional Development Funds for development at RAF Museum, Cosford.

5
Royal Marines Museum

Eastney
Southsea
Hampshire
PO4 9PX

TEL : 01705 819385
FAX : 01705 838420
CHAIR : Lieutenant General Sir Henry Beverley KCB OBE
TERMS OF REFERENCE : The preservation and presentation of all aspects of the Royal Marines' history through the acquisition, conservation, recording of and research into documents, pictures, books, medals, uniforms, weapons, and other artefacts.

a	–
b	21
c	Body
d	X
e	£1.024*
f	£0.590m
g	£0.009m
h	£42,397
i	{1M}†
j	–
k	{5M, 2F}†
l	–
m	–

* Figures unaudited at time of going to press.
† Appointed by the respective museum boards.

6
Royal Naval Museum

HM Naval Base
Portsmouth
PO1 3LR

TEL : 01705 727562
FAX : 01705 727575
genenq@RN-museum.compulink.co.uk
CHAIR : Vice-Admiral Sir Barry Wilson KCB
TERMS OF REFERENCE : To provide an effective and accesible repository, both now and in the future, for the heritage of the Navy and to raise public awareness of the Royal Navy and to encourage scholarship and research into the history of the Royal Navy.

a	–
b	34
c	Body
d	X
e	£2.189m*
f	£0.824m
g	£0.009m
h	£53,763
i	{1M}†
j	–
k	{8M, 2F}†
l	–
m	–

* Figures unaudited at time of going to press.
† Appointed by the respective museum boards.

7
Royal Navy Submarine Museum

Haslar Jetty Road
Gosport
Hampshire
PO12 2AS

TEL : 01705 510354/529217
FAX : 01705 511349
rnsubs@submarine-museum.demon.co.uk
http://www.submarine-museum.demon.co.uk/index
CHAIR : Rear Admiral Sir Anthony Whetstone CB
TERMS OF REFERENCE : To promote an understanding of the role that the Royal Navy, and in particular the Royal Navy Submarine branch, has played in the nation's history through the centuries.

a	–
b	20
c	–
d	X
e	£0.517m*
f	£0.319m
g	£0.009m
h	£37,312
i	{1M}†
j	–
k	{6M, 1F}†
l	–
m	–

* Figures unaudited at time of going to press.
† Appointed by the respective museum boards.

8
Advisory Committee on Conscientious Objectors*

C&L(F&S), Legal 1, Room 3/17
Metropole Building
Northumberland Avenue
London WC2N 5BP

TEL : 0171 218 0509
FAX : 0171 218 0844
CHAIR : Judge John Willis Rogers QC ; SECRETARY : Mr Richard Chandler
TERMS OF REFERENCE : To provide advice on appeals by officers and men of the armed forces whose applications for permission to retire or to resign their commissions or for discharge on grounds of conscience have been refused by the Service authorities.

a	–
b	–
c	Body
d	–
e	–
f	–
g	£0.001m
h	–
i	1M, £178pm†
j	1M, £178pm†
k	1M, 2F, £153pm†
l	–
m	–

* The Advisory Committee on Conscientious Objectors did not meet during the 1997/98 period.
† Appointed by the Lord Chancellor.

MINISTRY OF DEFENCE

Advisory NDPBs

9
Animal Welfare Advisory Committee

Defence Evaluation & Research Agency, Room 2019,
Farnborough, Hants
GU14 0LX
TEL : 01252 414573
FAX : 01252 414571
CHAIR : Dr Jeremy Lucke
SECRETARY : Mrs Christine Peet
TERMS OF REFERENCE : The Animal Welfare Advisory Committee consults, inspects and makes all necessary enquiries into all aspects of animal care and their use in research in DERA establishments, advises Sectoral Directors and reports directly to the Chief Scientific Adviser at the Ministry of Defence.

10
Armed Forces Pay Review Body

Office of Manpower Economics
Oxford House
76 Oxford Street
London W1N 9FD
TEL : 0171 467 7244
FAX : 0171 467 7248
CHAIR : Sir Gordon Hourston
SECRETARY : Mr Gregor McGregor
TERMS OF REFERENCE : To advise on the remuneration and charges for members of the Naval, Military and Air Forces of the Crown, in accordance with their terms of references.

11
Dartmoor Steering Group and Working Party*

HQ Devcor
Ministry of Defence
Mount Wise
Plymouth PL1 4JH
TEL : 01752 501488
CHAIR : Sir Anthony Barrowclough ; SECRETARIES : Lieutenant-Colonel Tony Clark OBE, Dr Nick Atkinson
TERMS OF REFERENCE : The Dartmoor Steering Group and Working Party reviews progress in reconciling the interests of military training, conservation, and public access.

12
Defence Scientific Advisory Council

Room 2276
MoD Main Building
Whitehall
London SW1A 2HW
TEL : 0171 218 0333
FAX : 0171 218 4066
CHAIR : Professor Peter Clarricoats ; SECRETARY : Dr Chris Morgan
TERMS OF REFERENCE : To advise the Secretary of State on matters of concern to the Ministry of Defence in the fields of science, engineering and technology.

13
Independent Board of Visitors for Military Corrective Training Centres (MCTC)

c/o Adjutant, Royal Military Corrective Training Centre,
BERE Church Hall Road,
Colchester, Essex, CO2 9NU
TEL : 01206 783473
CHAIR : Mr Philip Holmes
TERMS OF REFERENCE : The Board inspects relevant military premises in order to ensure that the state of the premises, their administration and the treatment of detainees is satisfactory.

	9	10	11	12	13
a	–	–	2	6	–
b	–	–	–	–	–
c	Body	Cm	HC	Body	Body
d	–	–	–	–	–
e	–	–	–	–	–
f	–	–	–	–	–
g	£0.005m	£0.500m*	–	£0.503m	–
h	–	–	–	–	–
i	1M, £250pd	1M	1M	5M, 1F, £265–£315pd	1M
j	–	–	–	–	1M
k	1M, 1F, £200pd	5M, 2F	†	169M, 9F, £210pd*	3M, 1F
l	–	–	–	–	–
m	–	–	–	–	–

* Secretariat provided by the Office of Manpower Economics (OME) part of the Department of Trade and Industry (DTI). The costs of the OME are borne on the DTI Vote.

* Joint MOD/Department for the Environment, Transport and the Regions sponsored committee.
† 12 members are ex-officio.

* Council members appointed by Ministers; board and register members appointed by MOD officials.

MINISTRY OF DEFENCE

Advisory NDPBs

	14 National Employers' Liaison Committee	15 Nuclear Powered Warships Safety Committee	16 Nuclear Weapons Safety Committee	17 Review Board for Government Contracts	18 Royal Military College of Science Advisory Council (RMCS)
Address	Duke of Yorks' Headquarters, Chelsea, London SW3 4SS	ACSA(N) Secretariat, Room 2270, MoD Main Building, Whitehall, London SW1A 2HW	ACSA(N) Secretariat, Room 2270, MoD Main Building, Whitehall, London SW1A 2HW	Secretaries to the Review Board for Government Contracts, Binder Hamlyn, 20 Old Bailey, London EC4M 7BH	Shrivenham, Swindon, Wiltshire SN6 8LA
TEL	0171 218 5625	0171 218 9433/9435	0171 218 9433/9435	0171 489 9000	01793 785438
FAX	0171 218 4888	0171 218 0758	0171 218 0758	0171 489 6060	01793 785677
Email					p.a.j.sheridan@rmcs.cranfield.ac.uk
CHAIR	Mr John S Bridgeman	Professor Sir John Cadogan CBE FRSE	Professor Sir John Cadogan CBE FRSE	Sir Peter Webster	Lord John Gregson TD
SECRETARY	Lieutenant Colonel John Bolton-Clark			Mr James Scott	Col P A J Sheridan
TERMS OF REFERENCE	To advise Ministers on ways to win and maintain the support of employers for those who wish to serve in the Volunteer Reserve Forces (VRF); and to improve retention of volunteers by countering work-related difficulties.	To advise the Secretary of State for Defence and other Ministers concerned on all safety matters associated with the construction, operation and maintenance of nuclear powered warships.	To advise the Secretary of State for Defence, the Services and other Ministry of Defence authorities on all safety matters pertaining to nuclear weapons systems, including issues of design, manufacture, transport, storage, handling and operational training.	To review periodically (normally at three-yearly intervals) the operation of the profit formula used in pricing non-competitive Government contracts.	To advise on matters of policy concerning the RMCS, which acts as the centre for higher education in Science, Technology and Management; and to act as a focus for scientific thought and development applied to Defence.
a	–	–	–	–	–
b	–	–	–	–	–
c	Body	NP	NP	Body	NP
d	–	–	–	–	–
e	–	–	–	–	–
f	–	–	–	–	–
g	£0.005m	£0.050m	£0.050m	£0.227m	£0.002m
h	–	–	–	–	–
i	1M*	1M, £225pd*	1M, £225pd*	1M, £10,990	{1M}*
j					
k	{11M, 2F}†	11M, £200pd	11M, £200pd	4M, £7,320	{5M}*
l	–	–	–	–	–
m	–	–	–	–	–

* The Chairman is unpaid but claims minimal expenses. He is appointed by the Secretary of State for Defence.
† Members are appointed by the Chairman.

* Present Chairman does not claim fees.

* Present Chairman does not claim fees.

* Appointed by the Army Board.

DEPARTMENT FOR EDUCATION AND EMPLOYMENT

Department for Education and Employment

Caxton House, 6–12 Tothill Street,
London SW1H 9NF

Telephone   0171 273 6194
Facsimile   0171 273 6067
Enquiries   Mr Guy Longhorn
E-mail   guy.longhorn@dfee.gov.uk

GTN   273 6194

Executive NDPBs

	1 British Educational Communications and Technology Agency (BECTA)*	2 Centre for Information on Language Teaching and Research (CILT)	3 Education Assets Board (EAB)
	Milburn Hill Road Science Park Coventry CV4 7JJ	20 Bedfordbury London WC2N 4LB	Capitol House Bond Court Leeds LS1 5SS
	TEL : 01203 416994 FAX : 01203 411418 enquiry-desk@becta.org.uk http://www.becta.org.uk CHAIR : Mrs Heather Du Quesnay : CHIEF EXECUTIVE : Mr Owen Lynch TERMS OF REFERENCE : To identify the relevance of new technologies to education and to evaluate the potential of new technologies to enhance learning and to raise standards.	TEL : 0171 379 5101 FAX : 0171 379 5082 CHAIR : Mr Stephen Jones TERMS OF REFERENCE : To promote greater national capability in languages and, in particular, to provide professional support for teachers of languages.	TEL : 0113 234 8888 FAX : 0113 246 0569 CHAIR : Mr Keith Bridge TERMS OF REFERENCE : The Board is responsible, under the 1988 Act, for the transfer of certain property, rights and liabilities from local authorities to higher education institutions and to governing bodies of grant-maintained schools.
a. Number if a multiple body/system (1.4.98)	–	–	–
b. Number of staff employed by the body (1.4.98)	121	30	7
c. Annual Report	Body	Body	Body
d. Audit arrangements	Y	Y	X
e. Total gross expenditure of body (1997/98)	£29.576m	£1.813m	£0.635m
f. Amount funded by government (1997/98)	£4.493m	£1.000m	£0.635m
g. Other expenditure by sponsoring dept (1997/98)	£0.099m	£0.015m	£0.020m
h. Chief Executive's Remuneration (1997/98)	£66,112†	£48,072	£74,000
Appointments and Remuneration (1.9.98)			
i. Chairman/President	1F	1M	1M, £27,252
j. Deputy	–	–	–
k. Members	2M, 5F, 6 vacancies	–	4M, 4F, £173pm
l. Tribunal cases received	–	–	–
m. Tribunal cases disposed of	–	–	–

* Formerly the National Council for Educational Technology.
† This is an aggregate figure for two post holders in the 1997/98 financial year.

DEPARTMENT FOR EDUCATION AND EMPLOYMENT

Executive NDPBs

	4 Equal Opportunities Commission (EOC)	5 Funding Agency for Schools	6 Further Education Funding Council for England (FEFC)	7 Higher Education Funding Council for England (HEFCE)	*Industrial Training Boards* 8 Construction Industry Training Board*
	Overseas House Quay Street Manchester M3 3HN TEL: 0161 833 9244 FAX: 0161 835 1657 info@eoc.org.uk CHAIRWOMAN: Ms Kamlesh Bahl TERMS OF REFERENCE: To work towards the elimination of sex and marriage discrimination and to promote equality of opportunity between men and women.	Albion Wharf 25 Skeldergate York YO1 2XL TEL: 01904 661661 FAX: 01904 661684 CHAIR: Sir Anthony Tippet TERMS OF REFERENCE: The Agency currently provides financial support for grant-maintained schools in England; and it has specific responsibilities for planning the supply of school places in certain Local Education authority areas.	Cheylesmore House Quinton Road Coventry CV1 2WT TEL: 01203 863000 FAX: 01203 863100 http://www.fefc.ac.uk CHAIR: Lord Bryan Davies of Oldham; CHIEF EXECUTIVE: Professor David Melville TERMS OF REFERENCE: The Council was set up in July 1992 under the Further and Higher Education Act 1992. The purpose of the Council is to secure further education provision which meets the needs and demands of individuals, employers and the requirements of government in respect of the location, nature and quality of provision.	Northavon House Coldharbour Lane Bristol BS16 1QD TEL: 0117 931 7317 FAX: 0117 931 7203 hefce@hefce.gov.uk http://www.hefce.ac.uk CHAIR: Sir Michael Checkland TERMS OF REFERENCE: To advise the Secretary of State for Education and Employment on the funding needs of higher education; and to distribute available funds.	Bircham Newton Near Kings Lynn Norfolk PE31 6RH TEL: 01485 577577 resource@citb.org.uk http://www.citb.org.uk CHAIR: Mr Hugh Try TERMS OF REFERENCE: The Board was established to help employers by ensuring that there are, and will be in the future, enough trained people to meet the needs of construction industry employers.
a	–	–	–	–	–
b	165.5	348	385	166	936
c	Body	Body	Body	Body	Body
d	X	X	X	X	Y
e	£6.036m	£2,008.200m	£3,138.780m	£3,537.387m	£98.749m
f	£5.792m	£2,008.200m	£3,138.780m	£3,537.387m	–
g	£0.021m	£0.261m	£0.053m	£0.100m	£0.482m
h	£69,128	£110,000	£118,855	£126,000	£86,478
i	1F, £58,471	1M, £30,600	1M, £37,754	1M, £38,862	1M, £27,293
j	2F, £237pd	–	–	–	1M, £16,678
k	4M, 5F, £123pd, 3 vacancies	5F, £155pd	13M, 1F, £4,000	8M, 5F, £4,000	17M, 2 vacancies
l	–	–	–	–	–
m	–	–	–	–	–

* Both Industrial Training Boards operate a December financial year end.

33

DEPARTMENT FOR EDUCATION AND EMPLOYMENT

Executive NDPBs

Industrial Training Boards

9	10	11	12	13
Engineering Construction Industry Training Board (ECITB)*	**Investors in People UK (IiP UK)**	**Qualifications Curriculum Authority (QCA)***	**Remploy Limited**	**Student Loans Company Ltd (SLC)**
Blue Court Kings Langley Hertfordshire WD4 8JP	4th Floor 7–10 Chandos Street London W1M 9DE	29 Bolton Street London W1Y 7PD	415 Edgware Road Cricklewood London NW2 6LR	100 Bothwell Street Glasgow G2 7JD
TEL : 01923 260000 FAX : 01923 270969 ecitb@ecitb.org.uk http://www.ecitb.org.uk	TEL : 0171 467 1900 FAX : 0171 636 2386 investors-in-people-uk@dial.pipex.co.uk http://www.iip-uk.co.uk	TEL : 0171 509 5555 FAX : 0171 509 6975 http://www.open.gov.uk/qca	TEL : 0181 235 0500 FAX : 0181 235 0501 http://www.remploy.co.uk	TEL : 0141 306 2000 FAX : 0141 306 2005 http://www.sic.co.uk
CHAIR : Mr Norman Dunlop CHIEF EXECUTIVE : Mr Peter Griffiths	CHAIR : Sir Michael Checkland	CHAIR : Sir William Stubbs	CHAIR : Mr David Heywood	CHAIR : Sir Ron Norman ODE DL
TERMS OF REFERENCE : The Board was established to help employers by ensuring that there are, and will be in the future, enough trained people to meet the needs of engineering construction industry employers.	TERMS OF REFERENCE : To provide business leadership and development for the Investors in People Standard and to lead and undertake national promotion of the Standard.	TERMS OF REFERENCE : To work with and assist the Secretary of State for Education and Employment to ensure that the curriculum and qualifications available to young people and adults are high quality, coherent and flexible.	TERMS OF REFERENCE : Remploy Ltd aims to provide jobs for 7,000 severely disabled people in over 90 factories and seeks to assist another 2,800 people through its Interwork programme.	TERMS OF REFERENCE : To administer the student loans scheme within the policy context set by the Government and the legislative framework of the Education (Student Loans) Act 1990 and the Education (Student Loans)(Northern Ireland) Order 1990 and associated regulations.
a –	a –	a –	a –	a –
b 37	b 25	b 459	b 11,478*	b 432
c Body	c Body	c –	c Body	c Body
d Y	d Y	d Y	d Y	d Y
e £13.653m	e £4.754m	e £38.096m	e £252.367m	e £18.930m
f –	f £2.272m	f £33.072m	f £94.200m	f £18.930m
g £0.228m	g £0.050m	g £0.300m	g £0.398m†	g £0.074m
h £72,199	h £87,815	h £43,563	h £117,000	h £92,463
i 1M, £9,097	i 1M	i 1M, £40,800	i 1M, £14,250	i 1M, £20,000
j –	j –	j 1M	j –	j –
k 16M, 1F	k 12M, 2F, 2 vacancies	k 7M, 4F, 1M Chief Executive	k 1M, Chief Executive 3M, Executive Directors 4M, 1F Non-Executive posts	k 1M, Non-Executive Director, £9,000 1M, Executive Director 3 vacancies
l –	l –	l –	l –	l –
m –	m –	m –	m –	m –

* Both Industrial Training Boards operate a December financial year end.

* QCA was created by the merger of the National Council for Vocational Qualifications (NCVQ) and the School Curriculum and Assessment Authority (SCAA) and commenced business on 1.10.97.

* This is an average figure, which includes 10,021 people with severe disabilities.

† This includes £167,200 of Employment Service costs.

DEPARTMENT FOR EDUCATION AND EMPLOYMENT

Executive NDPBs

14
Teacher Training Agency (TTA)

Portland House
Stag Place
London
SW1E 5TT
TEL : 0171 925 3700
FAX : 0171 925 3792
tta@gtnet.gov.uk
http://www.teach-tta.gov.uk
CHAIR : Mr Clive Booth
TERMS OF REFERENCE : To fund the provision of teacher training in England, to accredit providers of initial training for teachers, to provide information and advice on teaching as a career.

Advisory NDPBs

15
Disability Rights Task Force

Level 4, Caxton House
6–12 Tothill Street
London
SW1H 9NA
TEL : 0171 273 5631
CHAIR : Margaret Hodge
CONTACT : Nella Mitchell
TERMS OF REFERENCE : To consider how best to secure comprehensive, enforceable civil rights for disabled people within the context of our wider society and to make recommendations on the role and functions of a Disability Rights Commission.

16
National Disability Council

Level 4, Caxton House
6–12 Tothill Street
London
SW1H 9NA
TEL : 0171 273 5636
FAX : 0171 273 5929
chairman.ndc@ofee.gov.uk
http://www.open.gov.uk/ndc/ndchome.htm
CHAIR : Mr David Grayson
SECRETARY : Ms Richard Timm
TERMS OF REFERENCE : To advise the Government on the reduction and elimination of discrimination against disabled people; and on the operation of the Disability Discrimination Act.

17
New Deal Task Force

Level 3, Caxton House
6–12 Tothill Street
London
SW1H 9NA
TEL : 0171 273 5556
CHAIR : Sir Peter Davis
CONTACT : Ms Sinead O'Sullivan
TERMS OF REFERENCE : To ensure that the design of the New Deal meets the needs of the client groups; to harness the commitment of all partners, and particularly the business community; to the success of New Deal; and to monitor the New Deal on the ground and advise the government on its future development.

18
School Teachers' Review Body

Office of Manpower Economics
Oxford House
76 Oxford Street
London W1N 9FD
TEL : 0171 467 7244
FAX : 0171 467 7248
CHAIR : Tony Vineall
SECRETARY : Mr Gregor McGregor
TERMS OF REFERENCE : To examine and report matters relating to the statutory conditions and employment of school teachers in England and Wales as may from time to time be referred to them by the Secretary of State for Education and Employment.

	14	15	16	17	18
a	–	–	–	–	–
b	93	–	–	–	–
c	Body	NP	HC	NP	Cm
d	X	–	–	–	–
e	£212.262m	–	–	–	–
f	£212.262m	–	–	–	–
g	£0.085m	£0.036m	£0.181m	£0.168m	£0.500m*
h	£99,150	–	–	–	–
i	1M, £16,074	1F	1M, £260pd	1M	1M
j	–	–	1M, £125pd	–	–
k	7M, 3F 1F, Chief Executive	15M, 9F	10M, 8F, £125pd	11M, 4F	4M, 3F
l	–	–	–	–	–
m	–	–	–	–	–

* Secretariat provided by the Office of Manpower Economics (OME) part of the Department of Trade and Industry (DTI). The costs of the OME are borne on the DTI Vote.

35

DEPARTMENT FOR EDUCATION AND EMPLOYMENT

Advisory NDPBs

19
Skills Task Force

Room W901
Moorfoot
Sheffield
S1 4PQ
TEL : 0114 259 3281
CHAIR : Chris Humphries
CONTACT : Ms Alison Webster
TERMS OF REFERENCE : To assist the Secretary of State in developing a national skills agenda which will ensure that Britain has the skills needed to sustain high levels of employment, compete in the global market and provide opportunities for all.

20
Supported Employment Consultative Group*

DSB, Level 3
Rockingham House
123 West Street
Sheffield S1 4ER
TEL : 0114 259 5737
FAX : 0114 259 6990
CHAIR : Mr Paul Keen
SECRETARY : Mrs Ann Jepson
FORMER TERMS OF REFERENCE : To consider common ways of implementing general policies relating to supported employment, and to contribute to consideration of general policies relating to supported employment and to the views of people concerned with its provision.

Tribunal NDPBs

21
Registered Inspectors (RgI) Appeals Tribunal

Department for Education and Employment, Sanctuary Buildings, Great Smith Street
London SW1P 3BT
TEL : 0171 925 6458/5814
FAX : 0171 925 6001
SECRETARIAT : Ms Sue Davey
TERMS OF REFERENCE : To hear appeals from individuals, who have been removed from the Register of Inspectors by the Office for Standards in Education (OFSTED).

22
Special Educational Needs Tribunal (SENT)

71 Victoria Street
London
SW1H 0HW
TEL : 0171 925 6925
FAX : 0171 925 6926
sen.tribunal@gtnet.gov.uk
CHAIR : Mr Trevor Aldridge QC
SECRETARY : Mr Peter Craggs
TERMS OF REFERENCE : To hear and adjudicate on appeals made by parents against Local Education Authority decisions about their children's special educational needs.

	19	20	21	22
a	–	–	–	–
b	–	–	–	–
c	NP	NP	NP	Body
d	–	–	–	–
e	–	–	–	–
f	–	–	–	–
g	–	£0.003m†	–	£0.030m
h	–	–	–	–
i	1M	*	*	President 1M, £382pd Chairs 24M, 24F, 268pd
j	–	–	–	–
k	11M, 6F	*	4M, 8F, £203pd	63M, 46F, £149pd
l	–	–	–	2,051*
m	–	–	–	981*

* The SECG ceased to exist as an Advisory NDPB on 16.6.98. Membership at that date was 1M, Chairman, 10M, 1F Members.
† Represents Employment Service staff costs, refreshments, travel and subsistence.

* Appointments are made only when required, and on an ad hoc basis, by the Lord Chancellor's Department. A Chairman would receive £282pd.

* Based on the 1996/97 academic year.

Office of Electricity Regulation

*Committees' Unit, Hagley House,
Hagley Road, Edgbaston,
Birmingham B16 8QG*

Enquiries Jane Morris
Telephone 0121 456 6359
Facsimile 0121 455 6277
E-mail JaneMorris@offer-caff.demon.co.uk
Internet http://www.open.gov.uk/offer/offerhm.htm

Advisory NDPBs

Electricity Consumers' Committees

	1 National Consumers' Consultative Committee (NCCC)	2 Eastern Region	3 East Midlands Region
	OFFER, Consumer Affairs 16th Floor, Hagley House Hagley Road, Edgbaston Birmingham B16 8QG TEL: 0121 456 6359 FAX: 0121 455 6277	4th Floor, Waveney House Handford Road Ipswich Suffolk IP9 2BJ TEL: 01473 216101 FAX: 01473 215838	Suite 3c, Langford House 40 Friar Lane Nottingham NG1 6DQ TEL: 0115 950 8738 FAX: 0115 941 3472
	CHAIR: Professor Stephen Littlechild; SECRETARY: Mrs Jane Morris	CHAIR: Mr Malcolm Roberts SECRETARY: Mrs Lorna Marriott	CHAIR: Mrs Irene Bloor SECRETARY: Mr Anton Draper
	TERMS OF REFERENCE: The NCCC meet four times a year to discuss matters of concern to all electricity customers and to exchange information.	TERMS OF REFERENCE: To represent the interests of all electricity customers – commercial, industrial and domestic.	TERMS OF REFERENCE: To represent the interests of all electricity customers – commercial, industrial and domestic.
a. Number if a multiple body (1.4.98)	–	–	–
b. Number of staff employed by the body (1.4.98)	–	–	–
c. Annual Report	Body	Body	Body
d. Audit arrangements	–	–	–
e. Total gross expenditure of body (1997/98)	–	–	–
f. Amount funded by government (1997/98)	–	–	–
g. Other expenditure by sponsoring dept (1997/98)	£0.010m	£0.042m*	£0.034m*
h. Chief Executive's Remuneration (1997/98)	–	–	–
Appointments and Remuneration (1.9.98)			
i. Chairman/President	1M*	{1M, £15,400}†‡	{1F, 15,400}†‡
j. Deputy	–	–	–
k. Members	{8M, 6F}†	{9M, 4F}§	{11M, 3F}§
l. Tribunal cases received	–	–	–
m. Tribunal cases disposed of	–	–	–

* The NCCC is chaired by the Director General of Electricity.
† Members are also Chairmen of the Electricity Consumers' Committees.

* Figures in Row 'g' include the Chairmen's remuneration and expenditure by the Committees on running costs. They do not include costs for shared facilities, OFFER's staff costs or the full extent of OFFER's support for the Committee's national activities. The total cost of supporting the Consumers' Committees and their work in the financial year 97/98 has been estimated at approximately £969,585.
† Pay award pending for all chairmen.
‡ Committee Chairmen are appointed by the Director General after consultation with the Secretary of State.
§ Committee Members are appointed by the Director General after consultation with individual Chairmen.

OFFICE OF ELECTRICITY REGULATION

Advisory NDPBs

Electricity Consumers' Committees

4	5	6	7	8
London Region	**Merseyside and North Wales Region**	**Midlands Region**	**North Eastern Region**	**North Western Region**
11 Belgrave Road London SW1V 1RB	4th Floor, Hamilton House Hamilton Place Chester CH1 2BH	11th Floor, Hagley House Hagley Road Edgbaston Birmingham B16 8QG	7th Floor, Pearl Assurance House, 7 New Bridge Street Newcastle upon Tyne NE1 8AQ	5th Floor, Boulton House 17–21 Chorlton Street Manchester M1 3HY
TEL: 0171 233 6366 FAX: 0171 233 6449	TEL: 01244 320849 FAX: 01244 320857	TEL: 0121 456 4424 FAX: 0121 456 6181	TEL: 0191 221 2071 FAX: 0191 233 0300	TEL: 0161 236 3484 FAX: 0161 236 3740
CHAIR: Mrs Yvonne Constance SECRETARY: Mrs Selvi Jegatheswara	CHAIR: Mr David Owen SECRETARY: Mrs Jacky Bradshaw	CHAIR: Mr Raymond O'Brien SECRETARY: Mr Keith Windsor	CHAIR: Mrs Elizabeth Derrington; SECRETARY: Mrs Carole Pitkeathley	CHAIR: Professor Lorraine Baric SECRETARY: Mr Brian Sykes
TERMS OF REFERENCE: To represent the interests of all electricity customers – commercial, industrial and domestic.	TERMS OF REFERENCE: To represent the interests of all electricity customers – commercial, industrial and domestic.	TERMS OF REFERENCE: To represent the interests of all electricity customers – commercial, industrial and domestic.	TERMS OF REFERENCE: To represent the interests of all electricity customers – commercial, industrial and domestic.	TERMS OF REFERENCE: To represent the interests of all electricity customers – commercial, industrial and domestic.

	4	5	6	7	8
a	–	–	–	–	–
b	–	–	–	–	–
c	Body	Body	Body	Body	Body
d	–	–	–	–	–
e	–	–	–	–	–
f	–	–	–	–	–
g	£0.029m*	£0.026m*	£0.026m*	£0.031m*	£0.022m*
h	–	–	–	–	–
i	{1F, £23,099}[†‡]	{1M, £15,400}[†‡]	{1M, £15,400}[†‡]	{1F, £15,400}[†‡]	{1F, £15,400}[†‡]
j	–	–	–	–	–
k	{5M, 6F}[§]	{9M, 5F}[§]	{9M, 5F}[§]	{10M, 6F}[§]	{7M, 6F}[§]
l	–	–	–	–	–
m	–	–	–	–	–

* Figures in Row 'g' include the Chairmen's remuneration and expenditure by the Committees on running costs. They do not include costs for shared facilities, OFFER's staff costs or the full extent of OFFER's support for the Committee's national activities. The total cost of supporting the Consumers' Committees and their work in the financial year 97/98 has been estimated at approximately £969,585.

† Pay award pending for all chairmen.

‡ Committee Chairmen are appointed by the Director General after consultation with the Secretary of State.

§ Committee Members are appointed by the Director General after consultation with individual Chairmen.

OFFICE OF ELECTRICITY REGULATION

Advisory NDPBs

Electricity Consumers' Committees

	9 North of Scotland Region	10 South Eastern Region	11 South of Scotland Region	12 South Wales Region	13 South Western Region
	Regent Court 70 West Regent Street Glasgow G2 2QZ TEL : 0141 331 2552 FAX : 0141 331 2777 CHAIR : Mr Hugh Duncan SECRETARY : Mrs Eileen Findlay TERMS OF REFERENCE : To represent the interests of all electricity customers – commercial, industrial and domestic.	1–4 Lambert's Yard Tonbridge Kent TN9 1ER TEL : 01732 351356 FAX : 01732 355388 CHAIR : Mrs Pauline Ashley SECRETARY : Mrs Marcelle Lingham TERMS OF REFERENCE : To represent the interests of all electricity customers – commercial, industrial and domestic.	Regent Court 70 West Regent Street Glasgow G2 2QZ TEL : 0141 331 2552 FAX : 0141 331 2777 CHAIR : Mr Graeme Millar SECRETARY : Mrs Eileen Findlay TERMS OF REFERENCE : To represent the interests of all electricity customers – commercial, industrial and domestic.	5th Floor, St David's House West Wing Wood Street Cardiff CF1 1ES TEL : 01222 228388 FAX : 01222 229388 CHAIR : Mrs Janet Candler SECRETARY : Miss Wendy Davies TERMS OF REFERENCE : To represent the interests of all electricity customers – commercial, industrial and domestic.	Unit 1, Hide Market West Street Bristol Avon BS2 0BH TEL : 0117 954 0934 FAX : 0117 955 7145 CHAIR : Mr Peter Weston SECRETARY : Ms Katherine Holland TERMS OF REFERENCE : To represent the interests of all electricity customers – commercial, industrial and domestic.
a	–	–	–	–	–
b	–	–	–	–	–
c	Body	Body	Body	Body	Body
d	–	–	–	–	–
e	–	–	–	–	–
f	–	–	–	–	–
g	£0.044m*	£0.030m*	£0.028m*	£0.030m*	£0.036m*
h	–	–	–	–	–
i	{1M, £15,400}†‡	{1F, £15,400}†‡	{1M, £15,400}†‡	{1F, £15,400}†‡	{1M, £15,400}†‡
j	–	–	–	–	–
k	{9M, 2F}§	{12M, 4F}§	{7M, 4F}§	{9M, 6F}§	{9M, 5F}§
l	–	–	–	–	–
m	–	–	–	–	–

* Figures in Row 'g' include the Chairmen's remuneration and expenditure by the Committees on running costs. They do not include costs for shared facilities, OFFER's staff costs or the full extent of OFFER's support for the Committee's national activities. The total cost of supporting the Consumers' Committees and their work in the financial year 97/98 has been estimated at approximately £969,585.
† Pay award pending for all chairmen.
‡ Committee Chairmen are appointed by the Director General after consultation with the Secretary of State.
§ Committee Members are appointed by the Director General after consultation with individual Chairmen.

OFFICE OF ELECTRICITY REGULATION

Advisory NDPBs

Electricity Consumers' Committees

14	15
Southern Region	**Yorkshire Region**
30–31 Friar Street Reading Berkshire RG1 1DX	Symons House Belgrave Street Leeds LS2 8DD
TEL : 0118 956 0211	TEL : 0113 234 1866
FAX : 0118 956 7662	FAX : 0113 234 2018
CHAIR : Mr Ken Prior	CHAIR : Mr Rodney Brooke
SECRETARY : Mr Marcus Clements	SECRETARY : Ms Morag Lockhart
TERMS OF REFERENCE : To represent the interests of all electricity customers – commercial, industrial and domestic.	TERMS OF REFERENCE : To represent the interests of all electricity customers – commercial, industrial and domestic.

a	–		a	–
b	–		b	–
c	Body		c	Body
d	–		d	–
e	–		e	–
f	–		f	–
g	£0.024m*		g	£0.032m*
h	–		h	–
i	{1M, £15,400}[†‡]		i	{1M, £15,400}[†‡]
j	–		j	–
k	{8M, 5F}[§]		k	{9M, 5F}[§]
l	–		l	–
m	–		m	–

* Figures in Row 'g' include the Chairmen's remuneration and expenditure by the Committees on running costs. They do not include costs for shared facilities, OFFER's staff costs or the full extent of OFFER's support for the Committee's national activities. The total cost of supporting the Consumers' Committees and their work in the financial year 97/98 has been estimated at approximately £969,585.

† Pay award pending for all chairmen.

‡ Committee Chairmen are appointed by the Director General after consultation with the Secretary of State.

§ Committee Members are appointed by the Director General after consultation with individual Chairmen.

DEPARTMENT OF THE ENVIRONMENT, TRANSPORT AND THE REGIONS

Department of the Environment, Transport & the Regions

Ashdown House, 123 Victoria Street, London SW1E 6DE

Enquiries Clive Rowlinson
Telephone 0171 890 6796
Facsimile 0171 890 6769
Internet http://www.detr.gov.uk

GTN 3533 6796

Nationalised Industries

	1 British Railways Board	2 Civil Aviation Authority	3 London Regional Transport*
	Whittle's House 14 Pentonville Road London N1 9HF	45–49 Kingsway London WC2B 6TE	55 Broadway London SW1H 0DB
	TEL : 0171 904 5008 FAX : 0171 904 5018	TEL : 0171 379 7311 FAX : 0171 240 1153	TEL : 0171 222 5600 FAX : 0171 222 5719
	CHAIR : Mr John Welsby SECRETARY : Mr Peter Trewin	CHAIR : Sir Malcolm Field CHIEF EXECUTIVE OF NATIONAL AIR TRAFFIC SERVICES LTD : Mr William Kerr Semple	CHAIR : Mr Brian Appleton CHIEF EXECUTIVE : Mr Dennis Tunnicliffe
	TERMS OF REFERENCE : Many of the services provided by the Board have now been privatised under the provisions of the Railway Act 1993. The board retains responsibilities for non-operational railway land, the British Transport Police Force and residual liabilities.	TERMS OF REFERENCE : Responsible for the regulation of civil aviation in the United Kingdom and specific responsibility for aviation safety, and economic regulation of civil aviation. It also provides air traffic control services through National Air Traffic Services Ltd.	TERMS OF REFERENCE : To provide or secure the provision of public passenger transport services for Greater London.
a. Number if a multiple body/system (1.4.98)	–	–	–
b. Number of staff employed by the body (1.4.98)	–	–	–
c. Annual Report	Body	Body	Body
d. Audit arrangements	–	–	–
e. Total gross expenditure of body (1997/98)	–	–	–
f. Amount funded by government (1997/98)	–	–	–
g. Other expenditure by sponsoring dept (1997/98)	–	–	–
h. Chief Executive's Remuneration (1997/98)	£282,000*	–	–
Appointments and Remuneration (1.9.98)			
i. Chairman/President	1M, £282,000*†	1M, £71,780*	1M, £77,500†‡
j. Deputy	1M, £164,000*†	1M, £46,804	–
k. Members	1M, £223,000*† 4M, 1F, £8,232*	1M, £103,000* 1M, £88,000* 1M, 85,490* 1M, £47,792 1M, £60,000 1M, 1F, £24,375 1M, £12,185 1M, £8,122	1M, £169,318†‡ 1M, £109,590†‡ 1M, £21,478 3M, 1F £17,899† 3 vacancies
l. Tribunal cases received	–	–	–
m. Tribunal cases disposed of	–	–	–

* All salaries are at 1997/98 prices.
† Salaries of the Chairman and the executive members include bonus and compensation awards. The Chief Executive and Chairman are the same person.

* A performance related bonus of up to 35% of salary is payable to the Chairman and three full-time executive members.

* Trading name from 1.5.90 is London Transport.
† All salaries are at 1998/99 prices.
‡ A performance related bonus scheme for executive board members provides for a bonus of up to 40% of basic salary.

41

DEPARTMENT OF THE ENVIRONMENT, TRANSPORT AND THE REGIONS

Public Corporation

4
British Waterways Board*

Willow Grange
Church Road
Watford
Hertfordshire WD1 3QA
TEL : 01923 226422
FAX : 01923 201400
CHAIR : Mr Bernard Henderson
CHIEF EXECUTIVE : Dr David Fletcher
TERMS OF REFERENCE : To manage and operate Britain's inland waterways system efficiently for the increasing benefit of the economy, particularly from leisure and tourism.

Executive NDPBs

5
Audit Commission for Local Authorities and the National Health Service in England and Wales*

1 Vincent Square
London
SW1P 2PB
TEL : 0171 828 1212
FAX : 0171 976 6187
http://www.audit-commission.gov.uk
CHAIR : Mr Roger Brooke
CONTROLLER OF AUDIT : Mr Andrew Foster
TERMS OF REFERENCE : The Audit Commission appoints the external auditor for local authorities and the NHS in England and Wales, carries out national value for money studies and defines and publishes performance indicators.

6
British Board of Agrément

PO Box 195, Bucknall's Lane
Garston
Watford
Hertfordshire WD2 7NG
TEL : 01923 665300
FAX : 01923 665301
bba@btinternet.com
http://www.bbacerts.co.uk
CHAIR : Mr Tony Jackson CBE
SECRETARY : Dr Peter Hewlett
TERMS OF REFERENCE : To award Agrément Certificates to products and systems for the construction industry which, in the BBA's opinion are fit for their intended purpose.

7
Commission for New Towns

Central Business Exchange,
414–428 Midsummer Boulevard, Milton Keynes
MK9 2EA
TEL : 01908 692692
FAX : 01908 691333
http://www.cnt.org.uk/
CHAIR : Sir Alan Cockshaw
CHIEF EXECUTIVE : Mr John Walker
TERMS OF REFERENCE : To dispose of assets and liabilities inherited from 21 English New Town Corporations, having due regard to persons residing, working or carrying on business in them. To act as a residuary body for assets and liabilities of urban development corporations and Housing Action Trusts.

8
Countryside Commission

John Dower House
Crescent Place
Cheltenham
Gloucestershire GL50 3RA
TEL : 01242 521381
FAX : 01242 584270
info/hq/cci@countryside.gov.uk
http://www.countryside.gov.uk
CHAIR : Mr Richard Simmonds CBE ; CHIEF EXECUTIVE : Mr Richard Wakeford
TERMS OF REFERENCE : The Commission aims to make sure that the English countryside is protected, and that it can be used and enjoyed now and in the future.

	4 British Waterways Board	5 Audit Commission	6 British Board of Agrément	7 Commission for New Towns	8 Countryside Commission
a	–	–	–	–	–
b	–	1,307	90	266	240.6
c	Body	TSO	Body	Body	Body
d	–	X	Y	Y	X
e	–	£98.500m	£4.293m	£94.624m	£25.308m
f	–	–	£0.633m	–	£24.903m
g	–	£0.056m	£0.049m	£0.012m	£0.016m
h	£110–120,000	£122,808†	£85,872	£145,884	£64,770*
i	1M, £45,414†	1M, £21,030	1M, £14,081	1M, £38,154	1M, £41,015
j	1M, £11,980†	1M, £7,210	–	1M, £11,419	–
k	4M, 3F, £9,082†	7M, 8F, £3,260–£6,520	8M, 2F, £2,326, 1M*	2M, 2F, £7,370	6M, 2F, £5,890
l	–	–	–	–	–
m	–	–	–	–	–

* The British Waterways Board, formerly a Public Corporation, was reclassified as a Nationalised Industry on 1.4.98.
† 1 July 1997 rates.

* In 1997 the Commission moved annual accounting arrangements to end on 31 October each year. The figures in Row 'e', 'g', and 'h' relate to the full year ending 31.10.98 and include an estimated element as final figures were not available at time of publication. Actual costs from 1.4.97 to 31.10.97 for these entries were £58.650m, £0.0047m, and £94.346m respectively.
† Excludes any bonus award.

* Paid as Executive Director.

* Excludes any bonus award.

DEPARTMENT OF THE ENVIRONMENT, TRANSPORT AND THE REGIONS

Executive NDPBs

General Lighthouse Authorities

	9 English Partnerships	10 Environment Agency	11 Northern Lighthouse Board	12 Trinity House Lighthouse Service	13 Health and Safety Commission
Address	16–18 Old Queen Street London SW1H 9HP	Rio House, Waterside Drive Aztec West Almondsbury Bristol BS32 4UD	84 George Street Edinburgh EH2 3DA	Trinity Square Tower Hill London EC3N 4DH	Rose Court 2 Southwark Bridge London SE1 9HS
TEL	0171 976 7070	01454 624400	0131 473 3100	0171 480 6601	0171 717 6000
FAX	0171 976 7740	01454 624409	0131 220 2093	0171 480 7662	0171 717 6717
	CHAIR: Rt Hon Lord Walker of Worcester; CHIEF EXECUTIVE: Mr Anthony Dunnett	enquiries@environment-agency.gov.uk http://www.environment-agency.gov.uk CHAIR: Lord De Ramsey; CHIEF EXECUTIVE: Mr Ed Gallagher	CHAIR: Sir Michael Livesay KCB CHIEF EXECUTIVE: Captain James Taylor	CHAIRMAN AND CHIEF EXECUTIVE: Rear Admiral Patrick Rowe	http://www.open.gov.uk/hse/hsehome.htm CHAIRMAN OF THE COMMISSION: Mr Frank Davies CBE
TERMS OF REFERENCE	To regenerate derelict, vacant and under used land and buildings throughout England, working in partnership in every region to transform areas of need into quality places for people to live and work.	To protect and improve the environment in England and Wales through regulation of pollution, management of water resources and flood defence duties in relation to conservation, fisheries, navigation and recreation.	Responsible for the provision and maintenance of marine aids to navigation for Scotland and the Isle of Man.	Responsible for the provision and maintenance of marine aids to navigation for England, Wales and the Channel islands.	The Health and Safety Commission's function is to ensure that risks to people's health and safety from work activities are properly controlled. The Health and Safety Executive is the means whereby this is carried out.
a	–	–	–	–	–
b	462.5	9,668	220	433.5	5*
c	Body	Body	HC	HC	Body
d	Y	Y	X	X	X
e	£397.365m	£603.755m	£26.459m	£29.342m	£0.378m
f	£268.779m	£163.915m*	–	–	£0.378m
g	£0.125m	£0.245m	–	–	£0.414m†
h	£140,000	£141,384	£54,628	£57,682	–
i	1M*	1M, £53,975	{1M}*	{1M, £57,682}	1M, £63,103
j	1M, £29,518	–	{1M}*	–	–
k	4M, £7,175 2M, 1F†	8M, 2F, £12,585–£22,025 1M†	2M, £7,236 {3M, £7,236}* {11M, 1F}	{6M}* 3M, £7,045†	6M, 3F, £1,273+£137pd
l	–	–	–	–	–
m	–	–	–	–	–

* Remuneration declined.
† Paid as an executive director

* Includes MAFF/Welsh Office flood defence capital grant and MAFF grant-in-aid for fisheries.
† Paid as Chief Executive.

* The NLB board membership comprises 11 ex-officio and 6 co-opted members elected by the Commissioners of Northern Lights. 1 is nominated by the Manx Government and appointed by the Secretary of State for the Environment, Transport and the Regions and 1 is nominated by the Secretary of State and appointed by the Commissioners.

* These comprise 3 Elder Brethren and 3 non-voting officers. (The 3 Elder Brethren and the 3 non-voting officers are on the board by virtue of the posts they hold.)
† These are nominated by the Secretary of State for Environment, Transport and the Regions. Appointments are made by the Court of Trinity House.

* Although directly employed, staff are civil servants.
† Total amount spent on sponsorship of both HSE and HSC.

43

DEPARTMENT OF THE ENVIRONMENT, TRANSPORT AND THE REGIONS

Executive NDPBs

Housing Action Trusts

	14 Health and Safety Executive	15 Castle Vale Housing Action Trust	16 Liverpool Housing Action Trust	17 North Hull Housing Action Trust	18 Stonebridge Housing Action Trust
Address	Rose Court, 2 Southwark Bridge, London SE1 9HS	Castle Vale School, Farnborough Road, Birmingham B35 7NL	2nd Floor, Cunard Building, Water Street, Liverpool L3 1EG	Pavilion Offices, 536 Hall Road, Hull HU6 9BS	Kassinga House, 37–41 Winchelsea Road, Brent, London NW10 8UN
TEL	0171 717 6000	0121 776 6784	0151 227 1099	01482 856160	0181 961 0278
FAX	0171 717 6717	0121 776 6786	0151 236 3360	01482 856162	0181 961 0291
Web/Email	http://www.open.gov.uk/hse/hsehome.htm	cvhat@cvhat.org.uk http://www.cvhat.org.uk	http://www.liverpoolhat.org.uk		
CHAIR		Mr Richard Temple Cox	Paula Ridley OBE	Lord Bellwin of Leeds	Mr Ivan Weekes
CHIEF EXECUTIVE / DIRECTOR GENERAL	DIRECTOR GENERAL OF THE EXECUTIVE: Miss Jenny Bacon CB	Mr Angus Kennedy	David Green	Mr Stephen Brindley	Ms Sorrel Brookes
TERMS OF REFERENCE	The Health and Safety Commission's function is to ensure that risks to people's health and safety from work activities are properly controlled. The Health and Safety Executive is the means whereby this is carried out.	Castle Vale Housing Action Trust, established in March 1993 took over a single 195 hectare estate of mixed houses and flats on the outskirts of Birmingham. Houses, parks and new streets are being developed on the sites of the old high-rise blocks.	The Trust took over 5,337 properties in 1993 from Liverpool City Council. There were 67 tower blocks on 35 sites, scattered throughout the City. Some of the blocks are being refurbished and others demolished to be replaced with traditional housing.	Since 1991 the Trust has modernised over 2,000 houses and 310 new homes have also been built. Tenants have been offered a choice of future landlord and access to training, education and employment opportunities will continue. The Trust closes on 31 December 1998.	Stonebridge Housing Action Trust manages a single estate in the London Borough of Brent. Properties are a mixture of high and medium-rise flats and town houses which the Trust plans to replace or refurbish. The Trust also has a programme of community initiatives.
a	–	–	–	–	–
b	3,873*	129	137	53	75
c	Body	Body	Body	Body	Body
d	X	Y	Y	Y	Y
e	£215.675m	£28.354m	£19.454m	£7.897m	£12.589m
f	£178.222m	£20.990m	£18.200m	£2.200m	£9.000m
g	£0.414m†	£0.119m	£0.57m	£0.120m	£0.130m
h	–	£64,783*	£61,642*	£66,261	£69,883
i	‡	1M, £29,556	1F, £29,556	1M, £29,556	1M, £29,556
j	‡	1M, £10,032	1M, £10,032	1M, £10,032	1F, £10,032
k	‡	6M, 4F, £5,868	4M, 4F, £5,868 1M†	8M, 1F, £5,868	5M, 5F, £5,868
l	–	–	–	–	–
m	–	–	–	–	–

Column 14 notes:
* Although directly employed, staff are civil servants.
† Total amount spent on sponsorship of both HSE and HSC.
‡ Board membership comprises 3 civil servants only.

Column 15 notes:
* Excludes any bonus award.

Column 16 notes:
* Excludes employers' pension contribution.
† Remuneration declined.

44

DEPARTMENT OF THE ENVIRONMENT, TRANSPORT AND THE REGIONS

Executive NDPBs

Housing Action Trusts

	19	20	21	22	23
	Tower Hamlets Housing Action Trust	**Waltham Forest Housing Action Trust**	**Housing Corporation**	**Joint Nature Conservation Committee (JNCC)**	**Local Government Residuary Body**
	73 Usher Road Bow London E3 2HS TEL: 0181 983 4698 FAX: 0181 204 1556 jackie.odunoye@thhat.demon.co.uk CHAIR: Dr Michael Barraclough ACTING CHIEF EXECUTIVE: Mrs Jackie Odunoye TERMS OF REFERENCE: THHAT took over three estates of 1,667 flats in Bow in 1993 and is replacing them with new homes (mostly houses). Also provides training and employment schemes. Recently gone into partnership with Circle 33 for it to take on responsibility for the homes.	4th Floor, Kirkdale House Kirkdale Road Leytonstone London E11 1HP TEL: 0181 539 5533 FAX: 0181 539 8074 davidfoster.101317.1175@compuserve.com CHAIR: Mr John Chumrow CHIEF EXECUTIVE: Mr Mike Wilson TERMS OF REFERENCE: Waltham Forest Housing Action Trust manages four estates in East London. These are being demolished in staged phases and replaced with a traditional street pattern, with a mix of houses, flats and sheltered accomodation.	149 Tottenham Court Road London W1P 0BN TEL: 0171 393 2000 FAX: 0171 393 2111 http://www.open.gov.uk/hcorp CHAIR: The Rt Hon The Baroness Dean of Thornton-le-Fylde; DEPUTY CHAIR: Mr Anthony Mayer TERMS OF REFERENCE: The Corporation regulates funds and promotes the proper performance of registered social landlords. These are non-profit making bodies run by voluntary committees.	Monkstone House City Road Peterborough PE1 1JY TEL: 01733 62626 FAX: 01733 562626 http://www.jncc.gov.uk CHAIR: Sir Angus Stirling ACTING CHIEF OFFICER: Deryck Steer TERMS OF REFERENCE: JNCC is a committee of three conservation bodies – English Nature, Scottish Natural Heritage and the Countryside Council for Wales, through which their functions relating to nature conservation in Great Britain and beyond are jointly exercised.	Zone 3/H30 Ashdown House 123 Victoria Street London SW1E 6DE TEL: 0171 890 6150 FAX: 0171 890 6152 CHAIR: Mr Roy Swanston SECRETARY: Mr Harry Fawcett TERMS OF REFERENCE: To make arrangements for the transfer or disposal of any property, rights or liabilities which have been vested in the Residuary Body as a result of local government re-organisation; or to advise the Secretary of State on effecting such orders.
a	–	–	–	–	–
b	80	61	545	85	2
c	Body	Body	Body	Body	Body
d	Y	Y	Y	X	Y
e	£14.125m	£29.328m	£981.498m	£4.317m	£0.319m
f	£10.000m	£23.998m	£964.428m*	£3.884m*	£0.030m
g	£0.120m	£0.097m	£0.130m	£0.035m	£0.008m
h	£51,745*	£70,992	£113,788[†]	–	–
i	1M, £29,556	1M, £29,556	1F, £39,002	1M, £27,340	1M, £347pd
j	1F, £10,032	1M, £10,032	1M, £22,306	–	–
k	7M, 3F, £5,868 1M, £2,934	4M, 5F, £5,868	7M, 4F, £10,171 1M[‡] 1M, £12,337	2M, 1F, £7,370	2M, 1F, £210pd
l	–	–	–	–	–
m	–	–	–	–	–

* Excludes any bonus award.

* Grant-in-aid including Capital, revenue, and administrative expenditure.
† Excludes £20k one off bonus for the successful implementation of the recommendations of the Finance, Management and Policy Review withhin agreed timetable.
‡ Paid as Executive Director.

* JNCC is funded from the grant-in-aid of English Nature, the Countryside Council for Wales and Scottish Natural Heritage.

45

DEPARTMENT OF THE ENVIRONMENT, TRANSPORT AND THE REGIONS

Executive NDPBs

24 London Pensions Fund Authority

Dexter House
2 Royal Mint Court
London
EC3N 4LP
TEL : 0171 369 6000
FAX : 0171 369 6111
lpfa@msn.com
CHAIR : Mr Maurice Stonefrost
CHIEF EXECUTIVE : Mr Peter Scales
TERMS OF REFERENCE : The London Pensions Fund Authority is the administering authority within the Local Government Pension Scheme Regulations for the former Greater London Council Pension Fund.

25 London Regional Passengers' Committee

Clements' House
14–18 Gresham Street
London
EC2V 7PR
TEL : 0171 505 9000
FAX : 0171 505 9003
CHAIR : Sir Alan Greengross
DIRECTOR : Mr Rufus Barnes
TERMS OF REFERENCE : To represent, protect and promote the interests of users of public transport in London, and – as part of the Rail Users Consultative Committee – users of the national rail network in London and the surrounding area.

26 National Forest Company

Enterprise Glade, Bath Lane
Moira
Swadlincote
Debyshire DE12 6BD
TEL : 01283 551211
FAX : 01283 552844
CHAIR : Mr Rodney Swarbrick CBE ; CHIEF EXECUTIVE : Ms Susan Bell
TERMS OF REFERENCE : The creation of the National Forest over an area of approximately 200 square miles of the English Midlands.

27 English Nature

Nortminster House
Peterborough
PE1 1UA
TEL : 01733 455500
FAX : 01733 568834
http://www.english-nature.org.uk
CHAIR : Baroness Young of Old Scone ; CHIEF EXECUTIVE : Dr Derek Langslow
TERMS OF REFERENCE : English Nature is the Government's adviser on nature conservation in England and promotes the conservation of England's wildlife. Amongst its activities are the notification of Sites of Special Scientific Interest and the declaration of National Nature Reserves.

28 Rural Development Commission

Dacre House
19 Dacre Street
London
SW1H 0DH
TEL : 0171 340 2900
FAX : 0171 340 2910
http://www.argonet.co.uk/rdc
CHAIR : Mr Miles Middleton
CHIEF EXECUTIVE : Mr John Edwards.
TERMS OF REFERENCE : To keep under review and advise the Government on all matters relating to the economic and social development of English rural areas; to promote and assist others to carry out measures to further regeneration and community action in the countryside.

	24	25	26	27	28
a	–	–	–	–	–
b	65	12	14	689	274
c	Body	Body	–	Body	Body
d	Y*	Y	Y	X	X
e	£263.000m†	£0.524m	£2.544m	£41.165m	£43.625m
f	–	£0.524m	£2.493m	£39.195m*	£38.291m
g	£0.030m	–	£0.037m	£0.095m*	£0.110m
h	£84,500	–	£63,354	£69,720	£78,363
i	1M, £21,073	1M, £12,095	1M, £12,954	1F, £41,010	1M, £42,725
j	–	1F	–	–	Vacant
k	6M, 3F, £4,379	14M, 10F	5M, 2F, £2,375, 1F*	6M, 2F, £7,370; 1M, £10,315, 1M†; 1 vacancy	3M, 2F, £5,731; 5 vacancies
l	–	–	–	–	–
m	–	–	–	–	–

* Audited by the District Auditor.
† Includes payments from the Superannuation Fund.

* Paid as an Executive Director

* Pre-audit figures; actual amounts not available at time of printing.
† Paid as Executive Director.

DEPARTMENT OF THE ENVIRONMENT, TRANSPORT AND THE REGIONS

Executive NDPBs

Urban Development Corporations

	29 Traffic Director for London	30 United Kingdom Eco-labelling Board (UKEB)	31 Birmingham Heartlands*	32 Black Country*	33 London Docklands (LDDC)‡
Address	College House, Great Peter Street, London SW1P 3LN	30–34 Albert Embankment, London SE1 7TL	Zone 4/G10, Eland House, Bressenden Place, London SW1E 5DU	Zone 4/G10, Eland House, Bressenden Place, London SW1E 5DU	Zone 4/G10, Eland House, Bressenden Place, London SW1E 5DU
TEL	0171 222 4545	0171 820 1199	0171 890 3748	0171 890 3748	0171 890 3748
FAX	0171 976 8640	0171 820 1104	0171 890 3759	0171 890 3759	0171 890 3759
	messages@tdfl.gov.uk http://www.tdfl.gov.uk	ACTING CHAIR: Mr Kenneth Miles CHIEF EXECUTIVE: Mr Jerry Rendell	CONTACT: Ian Lennard	CONTACT: Ian Lennard	CONTACT: Ian Lennard
	DIRECTOR: Mr Derek Turner				
TERMS OF REFERENCE	To manage the introduction of the Priority (Red) Route Network which covers 315 miles of London's strategic roads. Work includes co-ordinating the design, implementation and maintenance of a comprehensive package of traffic management measures on these roads.	To administer the European Community Eco-Labelling scheme within the United Kingdom; to promote the scheme to industry, retailers and consumers; and to contribute to the development of Eco-Labelling product criteria.	FORMER TERMS OF REFERENCE: To secure the regeneration of its designated urban area.	FORMER TERMS OF REFERENCE: To secure the regeneration of its designated urban area.	FORMER TERMS OF REFERENCE: To secure the regeneration of its designated urban area.
a	–	–	–	–	–
b	25	5.5	6	5	14
c	Body	Body	Body	Body	Body
d	Y	Y	Y	Y	Y
e	£21.349m	£0.717m	£15.478m	£43.554m	£255.677m
f	£20.912m	£0.667m*	–	£20.000m	£59.600m
g	–	£0.050m	£0.017m	£0.034m	£0.105m
h	–	£70,290	£44,000†	£91,305	£228,334†
i	1M, £78,604*	1M, 12,970	–	–	–
j	–	–	–	–	–
k	–	8M, 3F, £2,710 1F, unpaid	–	–	–
l	–	–	–	–	–
m	–	–	–	–	–

* Appointee is the Traffic Director.

* UKEB budget is funded from grant-in-aid by DETR.

* Formally dissolved on 1.7.98.
† Excludes employers' pension contribution.

* Formally dissolved on 1.7.98.

* On 1.4.92, the Docklands Light Railway (DLR) became wholly owned by the LDDC. In 1997/98 DLR received grant-in-aid of £32.5m from the LDDC.
† LDDC had two joint Chief Executives in 1997/98, with remuneration of £116,251 and £112,083 respectively.
‡ Formally dissolved on 1.7.98.

DEPARTMENT OF THE ENVIRONMENT, TRANSPORT AND THE REGIONS

Executive NDPBs

Urban Development Corporations

	34 Merseyside*	35 Plymouth*	36 Teesside*	37 Trafford Park*	38 Tyne and Wear*
Address	Zone 4/G10 Eland House Bressenden Place London SW1E 5DU	Zone 4/G10 Eland House Bressenden Place London SW1E 5DU	Zone 4/G10 Eland House Bressenden Place London SW1E 5DU	Zone 4/G10 Eland House Bressenden Place London SW1E 5DU	Zone 4/G10 Eland House Bressenden Place London SW1E 5DU
TEL	0171 890 3748	0171 890 3748	0171 890 3748	0171 890 3748	0171 890 3748
FAX	0171 890 3759	0171 890 3759	0171 890 3759	0171 890 3759	0171 890 3759
CONTACT	Ian Lennard	Ian Lennard	Ian Lennard	Ian Lennard	Ian Lennard
FORMER TERMS OF REFERENCE	To secure the regeneration of its designated urban area.	To secure the regeneration of its designated urban area.	To secure the regeneration of its designated urban area.	To secure the regeneration of its designated urban area.	To secure the regeneration of its designated urban area.
a	–	–	–	–	–
b	12	7	8.5	7	11
c	Body	Body	Body	Body	Body
d	Y	Y	Y	Y	Y
e	£52.341m	£10.666m	£38.238m	£21.773m	£61.193m
f	£18.300m	£14.326m	£28.884m	–	£27.600m
g	£0.072m	£0.042m	£0.091m	£0.039m	£0.059m
h	£76,500	£70,752	£92,900	£72,000*	£88,336
i	–	–	–	–	–
j	–	–	–	–	–
k	–	–	–	–	–
l	–	–	–	–	–
m	–	–	–	–	–

* Formally dissolved on 1.7.98.   *Formally dissolved on 1.7.98.   * Formally dissolved on 1.7.98.   † Excludes employers' pension contribution.   * Formally dissolved on 1.7.98.

DEPARTMENT OF THE ENVIRONMENT, TRANSPORT AND THE REGIONS

Advisory NDPBs

	39 Advisory Committee on Business and the Environment*	40 Advisory Committee on Hazardous Substances	41 Advisory Committee on Packaging	42 Advisory Committee on Plant and Machinery*	43 Advisory Committee on Releases to the Environment
	Room 6/F8 Ashdown House 123 Victoria Street London SW1E 6DE	Room 3/E7 Ashdown House 123 Victoria Street London SW1E 6DE	Packaging Unit, DETR Room 6/F8, Ashdown House 123 Victoria Street London SW1E 6DE	LGT Division Zone 5/J1, Eland House Bressenden Place London SW1E 5DU	Biotechnology Unit, Zone 3/G9 Ashdown House 123 Victoria Street London SW1E 6DE
TEL	0171 890 6568	0171 890 5265	0171 890 6622	0171 890 4222	0171 890 5275
FAX	0171 890 6559	0171 890 5229	0171 890 6559	0171 890 4209	0171 890 5259
					paulburrows@detrbiotech.demon.co.uk
CHAIR	Mr David Davies	Professor Peter Callow	Sir Peter Parker		Professor John Beringer
SECRETARY	Ms Emily Hay	Mr Brian Collins			Dr Paul Burrows
TERMS OF REFERENCE	The Committee provides a forum for a strategic dialogue between business and government on environmental issues.	To advise generally on hazardous substances, and in particular to advise the Secretary of State on the exercise of his powers under Sections 140 and 142 of the Environmental Protection Act.	To advise the Secretary of State on implementation of the Producer Responsibility Obligations (Packaging Waste) Regulations, which came into force in March 1997.	FORMER TERMS OF REFERENCE: To consider the extent to which the plant and machinery of industries currently subject to prescribed rating assessments would be rateable under existing legislation.	To advise the Secretaries of State on the exercise of their powers under Part VI of the Environmental Protection Act 1990 and in particular on the risks to the environment and human health from releases of genetically modified organisms into the environment.

	39	40	41	42	43
a	–	–	–	–	–
b	–	–	–	–	–
c	Body	TSO	NP*	NP	Body
d					
e	–	–	–	–	–
f	–	–	–	–	–
g	£0.114m	£0.025m	£0.013m	£0.021m	£0.029m
h	–	–	–	–	–
i	1M	1M, £178pd	1M	–	1M, £172pd
j	–	–	–	–	1M, £132pd
k	14M	6M	8M	–	8M, 3F, £132pd
l	–	–	–	–	–
m	–	–	–	–	–

* Jointly sponsored by DETR and DTI.

* Ad hoc reports of recommendations to the Secretary of State available from the Packaging Unit.

* Body formally wound up on 14.5.98.

49

DEPARTMENT OF THE ENVIRONMENT, TRANSPORT AND THE REGIONS

Advisory NDPBs

44
Advisory Panel on Standards for the Planning Inspectorate

c/o DETR, Floor 4/J1
Eland House
Bressenden Place
London SW1E 5DU
TEL : 0171 890 3936
FAX : 0171 890 3949
CHAIR : Michael Fitzgerald QC
TERMS OF REFERENCE : To advise the Secretaries of State for the Environment, Transport and the Regions and Wales on the maintenance and enhancement of professional standards in the Planning Inspectorate.

a	–
b	–
c	Body
d	–
e	–
f	–
g	£0.017m
h	–
i	1M
j	–
k	2M, 1 vacancy
l	–
m	–

45
Building Regulations Advisory Committee

Room 3/D1
Eland House
Bressenden Place
London SW1E 5DU
TEL : 0171 890 5738
FAX : 0171 890 5739
CHAIR : Professor Jack Anderson
SECRETARY : Mr Alec Custerson
TERMS OF REFERENCE : To advise the Secretary of State on the exercise of his powers to make building regulations and on other subjects connected with building regulations.

a	–
b	–
c	NP
d	–
e	–
f	–
g	£0.038
h	–
i	1M
j	–
k	16M, 4F
l	–
m	–

46
Committee on Chemicals & Materials of Construction For Use In Public Water Supply & Swimming Pools

Drinking Water Inspectorate
Floor 2/E5, Ashdown House
123 Victoria Street
London SW1E 6DE
TEL : 0171 890 5996
FAX : 0171 890 5979
dwi@dial.pipex.com
http://www.dwi.detr.gov.uk/list/index.htm
CHAIR : Dr Norman King
TECHNICAL SECRETARY : Dr Toks Ogunbiyi
TERMS OF REFERENCE : The Committee advises the Secretaries of State on approvals issues under the Water Supply (Water Quality) Regulations 1989. The Committee also operates a non-statutory approval system for chemicals used in the treatment of swimming pool water.

a	–
b	–
c	*
d	–
e	–
f	–
g	–
h	–
i	1M, £201pd
j	–
k	4M, £172pd / 1F, £172pd
l	–
m	–

* Various documents are published throughout the year.

47
Darwin Initiative Advisory Committee

Room 4/A2, Ashdown House
123 Victoria Street
London
SW1E 6DE
TEL : 0171 890 6204
FAX : 0171 890 6239
vrichardson@epint.demon.co.uk
CHAIR : Sir Crispin Tickell
SECRETARY : Mr Jonathan Tillson
TERMS OF REFERENCE : To use UK scientific and educational strengths in collaborative biodiversity projects to help developing countries meet their obligations.

a	–
b	–
c	NP
d	–
e	–
f	–
g	£0.003m
h	–
i	1M
j	–
k	5M, 2F
l	–
m	–

48
Disabled Persons Transport Advisory Committee

Great Minster House
76 Marsham Street
London
SW1P 4DR
TEL : 0171 890 4916
FAX : 0171 890 6102
mu.detr@gtnet.gov.uk
http://www.mobility-unit.detr.gov.uk
CHAIR : Mr Robert Taylor
SECRETARY : Mr Neil Priest
TERMS OF REFERENCE : To advise the Secretary of State for Transport on transport issues affecting disabled and elderly people. It also offers advice and guidance to transport manufacturers and operations and to local authorities.

a	–
b	–
c	Body
d	–
e	–
f	–
g	£0.055m*
h	–
i	1M†
j	1M
k	6M, 10F, 2 vacancies
l	–
m	–

* Comprises expenditure on travel and subsistence, working lunches, attendance at conferences and costs of DPTAC publications.
† Current appointments made in January 1996 and will run until December 1998.

Advisory NDPBs

DEPARTMENT OF THE ENVIRONMENT, TRANSPORT AND THE REGIONS

49
Expert Group on Airborne Particles

National Environmental Technology Centre, AEA Technology, Culham, Abingdon, Oxon OX14 3DB
TEL : 01235 463554
FAX : 01235 463005
CHAIR : Professor Ray Harrison
SECRETARY : Dr Beth Conlan
TERMS OF REFERENCE : To review current knowledge and advise Ministers on levels and sources of particles in the UK, physical and chemical characteristics of particles and long range transport capabilities of particles.

50
Expert Panel on Air Quality Standards

Air and Environmental Quality Division, Room 4/H16, Ashdown House, 123 Victoria Street, London SW1E 6DE
TEL : 0171 890 6315
FAX : 0171 890 6290
CHAIR : Professor Anthony Seaton ; SECRETARY : Dr Stephanie Coster
TERMS OF REFERENCE : To advise on the establishment and application of air quality standards in the United Kingdom, for the purposes of developing policy on air pollution control and increasing public knowledge and understanding of air quality.

51
Expert Group on Cryptosporidium In Water Supplies

Drinking Water Inspectorate Floor 2/E1, Ashdown House 123 Victoria Street London SW1E 6DE
TEL : 0171 890 5976
FAX : 0171 890 5969
dwi@dial.pipex.com
CHAIR : Professor Ian Bouchier
SECRETARY : Mr David Drury
TERMS OF REFERENCE : To assess the lessons learned from suspected water borne outbreaks of cryptosporidiosis, and to advise the Government as to whether or not further safeguards are necessary for the protection of drinking water.

52
Expert Panel on Sustainable Development Education

Zone 7/F8
Ashdown House
123 Victoria Street
London SW1E 6DE
TEL : 0171 890 6693
FAX : 0171 890 6659
CHAIR : Sir Geoffrey Holland
SECRETARIES : Mrs Gill Beauchamp (DfEE) and Ms Helen Morris (DETR)
TERMS OF REFERENCE : To identify gaps, opportunities, priorities and partnerships for action in providing sustainable development education. To advise the Deputy Prime Minister and the Secretary of State for Education and Employment and other stakeholders.

53
Expert Action Group for Building Materials

DETR/CEPMS, Zone 3/H4
Eland House
Bressenden Place
London SW1E 5DU
TEL : 0171 890 5697
FAX : 0171 890 5669
CHAIR : Michael Rose CD
SECRETARY : Mr Steve Brandl
TERMS OF REFERENCE : To provide advice on methods and priorities for pursuing business opportunities overseas for UK suppliers of building materials and construction products. To advise on measures to improve co-ordination and presentation of export opportunities within the industry and between government and industry.

	49	50	51	52	53
a	–	–	–	–	–
b	–	–	–	–	–
c	NP	NP*	*	Body	NP
d	–	–	–	–	–
e	–	–	£3,084.26m	–	–
f	–	–	£3,084.26m	–	–
g	£0.010m	£0.024m	–	–	£0.007m
h	–	–	–	–	–
i	1M, £172pd	1M, £500pd	1M, £26.80 per hour	1M	1M, £250pd
j	–	–	–	–	–
k	10M, 2F	11M, 1F	10M, 2F	15M, 8F	9M, 2F
l	–	–	–	–	–
m	–	–	–	–	–

* Ad hoc reports of recommendations available from The Stationery Office.

* A report of the group's recommendations is to be published shortly.

DEPARTMENT OF THE ENVIRONMENT, TRANSPORT AND THE REGIONS

Advisory NDPBs

54 Inland Waterways Amenity Advisory Council

City Road Lock
38 Graham Street
Islington
London N1 8JX
TEL : 0171 253 1745
FAX : 0171 490 7656
CHAIR : Viscountess Knollys
SECRETARY : Mr Anthony McCann
TERMS OF REFERENCE : To advise the British Waterways and the Government on the recreational and amenity development of the inland waterways.

55 Local Government Commission for England*

Dolphyn Court
10–11 Great Turnstile
London
WC1V 7JU
TEL : 0171 430 8400
FAX : 0171 404 6142
CHAIR : Professor Malcolm Grant ; CHIEF EXECUTIVE : Ms Barbara Stephens
TERMS OF REFERENCE : To review and make recommendations to the Government on whether there should be changes to the structure of local government, to the boundaries of individual local authority areas and to their electoral arrangements (such as the number of councillors for each area).

56 Local Government Staff Commission (England)*

Zone 5/A1
Eland House
Bressenden Place
London SW1E 5DU
TEL : 0171 890 4252
FAX : 0171 890 4109
CHAIR : Mr Alan Atherton
FORMER TERMS OF REFERENCE : To assist DETR on the transfer of local authority staff as a result of local government reorganisation.

57 Property Advisory Group

Zone 3/G10
Eland House
Bressenden Place
London SW1E 5DU
TEL : 0171 890 5567
FAX : 0171 890 5539
detr.pag@gtnet.gov.uk
CHAIR : Mr Robin Broadhurst FRICS ; SECRETARY : Mr Patrick Martin
TERMS OF REFERENCE : To keep under review changes in the land and property market, advise on matters concerning the development process, and advise the Department generally on property issues.

58 Radioactive Waste Management Advisory Committee

Room 4/D9
Ashdown House
123 Victoria Street
London SW1E 6DE
TEL : 0171 890 6260
FAX : 0171 890 6319
CHAIR : Sir Gordon Beveridge
SECRETARY : Dr Robert Jackson
TERMS OF REFERENCE : To advise DETR, Scottish Office and Welsh Office Ministers on the technical and environmental implications of major issues concerning the development and implementation of an overall policy for all aspects of the management of civil radioactive waste, including research and development.

	54	55	56	57	58
a	–	–	–	–	–
b	–	–	–	–	–
c	NP	Body	NP	Body	Body*
d	–	–	–	–	–
e	–	–	–	–	–
f	–	–	–	–	–
g	£0.024m	£0.032	£0.004m	£0.043m	£0.117m
h	–	–	–	–	–
i	1F, £178pd	1M, £29,025	–	1M	1M, £201pd
j	–	–	–	–	–
k	13M, 3F	4M, 2F, £5,405	–	11M, 3F	14M, 2F, £172pd†
l	–	–	–	–	–
m	–	–	–	–	–

* The Commission also carries out some executive functions in addition to its advisory role.

* Body formally wound up on 12.5.98.

* The Committee's advice is published in the form of ad hoc reports.
† New appointments exercise ongoing as at 1.9.98. On this date the Committee (excluding the Chairman) consisted of 16 members — either appointed or co-opted.

DEPARTMENT OF THE ENVIRONMENT, TRANSPORT AND THE REGIONS

Advisory NDPBs

Tribunals

59
Royal Commission on Environmental Pollution

1st Floor
Steele House
11 Tothill Street
London SW1H 9NS
TEL : 0171 273 6635
FAX : 0171 273 6640
rcep@dial.pipex.com
http://www.rcep.org.uk
CHAIR : Sir Tom Blundell
TERMS OF REFERENCE : To advise the Crown, Government, Parliament and the public on matters, both national and international, concerning the pollution of the environment; on the adequacy of research in this field, and on the future possibilities of danger to the environment.

60
Standing Advisory Committee on Trunk Road Assessment

HETA, 3rd Floor
Great Minster House
Marsham Street
London SW1P 4DR
TEL : 0171 890 6177
FAX : 0171 890 2198
CHAIR : Ms Eileen McKay CB
TECHNICAL SECRETARY : Mrs Rachel Chandler
TERMS OF REFERENCE : To advise on issues related to the appraisal of trunk roads.

61
UK Round Table on Sustainable Development

Room 4/F4
Ashdown House
123 Victoria Street
London SW1E 6DE
TEL : 0171 890 4963
FAX : 0171 890 4959
CHAIR : Sir Richard Southwood
TERMS OF REFERENCE : To advise Government and to build concensus between people with different perspectives and responsibilities to identify ways of making development more sustainable.

62
Water Regulations Advisory Committee

Room 3/G18
Ashdown House
123 Victoria Street
London SW1E 6DE
TEL : 0171 890 5372
FAX : 0171 890 5398
CHAIR : Professor John Swaffield ; SECRETARY : Mr Mike Williamson
TERMS OF REFERENCE : To advise the Government on the requirements for plumbing installations and fittings to be included in the Water Regulations and on other related technical matters. To report to the Government on enforcement of the Regulations.

63
Commons Commissioners

4th Floor
35 Old Queen Street
London
SW1H 9JA
TEL : 0171 222 0038
FAX : 0171 222 0133
CHIEF COMMISSIONER : Mr David Burton
TERMS OF REFERENCE : To adjudicate on any disputes arising from the provisional registration of common land.

	59	60	61	62	63
a	–	–	–	–	–
b	–	–	–	–	–
c	NP*	NP	NP	NP*	NP
d	–	–	–	–	–
e	–	–	–	–	–
f	–	–	–	–	–
g	£0.774m	£0.036m*	–	£0.006m	£0.178m*
h	–	–	–	–	–
i	1M, £208pd†	1F, £175pd	1M	1M	1M, £34,720m†
j	–	–	–	–	–
k	9M, 1F, £178pd†	7M, £150pd	18M, 3F	11M, 1F	1M, £13,958†
l	–	–	–	–	456
m	–	–	–	–	11

* Periodic reports published as Command Papers.
† Established by Royal Warrant. Chairman and Members are appointed by the Crown on the advice of the Prime Minister.

* Comprises expenditure on fees, travel and subsistence, working lunches and attendance of conferences.

* The Committee undertook a public consultation on its draft recommendations to the Government during the Summer of 1997.

* Includes £0.030m contribution from Welsh Office.
† Appointments are made by the Lord Chancellor.

DEPARTMENT OF THE ENVIRONMENT, TRANSPORT AND THE REGIONS

Tribunals

64
Rent Assessment Panels (RAPS)*

Room 2/J6
Eland House
Bressenden Place
London SW1E 5DU
TEL: 0171 890 3562
FAX: 0171 890 3519
TERMS OF REFERENCE: To provide members to sit on Rent Assessment Committees and Leasehold Valuation Tribunals.

65
Traffic Commissioners

Traffic Area Network Unit,
Zone 2/05, Great Minster House, 76 Marsham Street,
London SW1P 4DR
TEL: 0171 676 2120
FAX: 0171 676 2109
SENIOR TRAFFIC COMMISSIONER: Mr Michael Betts; DEPUTY CHAIR: Brigadier M H Turner
TERMS OF REFERENCE: Traffic Commissioners are responsible for the licensing of operators and drivers of heavy goods and passenger service vehicles in the eight traffic areas covering England, Scotland and Wales.

66
Valuation Tribunals

DETR
Room 5/J3
Eland House
London SW1E 5DU
TEL: 0171 890 4195
FAX: 0171 890 4209
CONTACT: Stephen Londesborough
TERMS OF REFERENCE: To list, hear and determine appeals concerning valuations for non-domestic rating purposes and for Council Tax, and also concerning liability for Council Tax.

	64		65		66
a	9	a	6	a	56
b	–	b	–	b	–
c	–	c	Body	c	NP
d	–	d	–	d	–
e	–	e	–	e	–
f	–	f	–	f	–
g	£5.26m	g	£9.089m*	g	£10.899m
h	–	h	–	h	–
i	8M, 1F, £12,545–39,165	i	6M, £51,382–56,520	i	{51M, 5F}*
j	9M, 3F, £11,865–37,125	j	16M, 3F, £206pd	j	{327M, 78F}*
k	267M, 104F, £132–262pd†	k	–	k	{1,394M, 438F}*
l	15,888	l	27,133	l	257,718
m	12,925	m	27,743†	m	412,219

* Rent Assessment Committees, Rent Tribunals and Leasehold Valuation Tribunals are drawn from the RAPs.
† The daily fee rates shown were effective from 1 April 1998.

* Recouped through fees. This figure includes the cost of 6 Traffic Area Offices directly funded by Department.
† Comprises 25,784 applications for Road Freight Licensing and 1,959 for Road Passenger Licensing.

* Appointments are made by local authorities.

Export Credits Guarantee Department

2 Exchange Tower, Harbour Exchange Square, London E14 9GS

Enquiries   Mr Dave Hannah
Telephone   0171 512 7208
Facsimile   0171 512 7021
E-mail   dhannah@ecgd.gtnet.gov.uk
Internet   http://www.open.gov.uk/ecgd/

Advisory NDPBs

1
Export Guarantees Advisory Council

PO Box 2200
2 Exchange Tower
Harbour Exchange Square
London E14 9GS
TEL : 0171 512 7000
FAX : 0171 512 7649
dhannah@ecgd.gtnet.gov.uk
http://www.open.gov.uk/ecgd/
CHAIR : Mr David Harrison
SECRETARY : Mr David Hannah
TERMS OF REFERENCE : To advise ECGD on sovereign risk underwriting – in particular on market ceilings and other controls that ECGD imposes on its exposure. The Council also gives guidance on many other areas of ECGD's activities – such as portfolio and debt management and Overseas Investment Insurance.

a.	Number if a multiple body (1.4.98)	–
b.	Number of staff employed by the body (1.4.98)	–
c.	Annual Report	HC*
d.	Audit arrangements	–
e.	Total gross expenditure of body (1997/98)	–
f.	Amount funded by government (1997/98)	–
g.	Other expenditure by sponsoring dept (1997/98)	£0.010m
h.	Chief Executive's Remuneration (1997/98)	–
	Appointments and Remuneration (1.9.98)	
i.	Chairman/President	1M
j.	Deputy	–
k.	Members	8M, 2F, 1 vacancy
l.	Tribunal cases received	–
m.	Tribunal cases disposed of	–

* From 1997–98 a report on the work of the 'Export Guarantees Advisory Council' will be included within ECGD's annual report.

Foreign & Commonwealth Office

1 Palace Street, London SW1

Enquiries   Steve Townson
Telephone   0171 238 4019
Facsimile   0171 238 4004
E-mail   rfd.fpd.fco@gtnet.gov.uk
Internet   http://www.fco.gov.uk

GTN   238 4019

Executive NDPBs

	1 Britain-Russia Centre	2 British Association for Central and Eastern Europe	3 British Council
	14 Grosvenor Place London SW1X 7HW	4th Floor 50 Hans Crescent London SW1X 0NA	10 Spring Gardens London SW1A 2BN
	TEL : 0171 235 2116 FAX : 0171 259 6254 CHAIR : Sir Rodric Braithwaite DIRECTOR : Dr Iain Elliot TERMS OF REFERENCE : The Britain-Russia Centre incorporating the British East-West Centre promotes high level contacts with Russia and the other republics of the former Soviet Union and furthers the development of democratic institutions through visits, seminars and training workshops.	TEL : 0171 584 0766 FAX : 0171 584 8831 bacee@compuserv.com CHAIR : Giles Radice MP CHIEF EXECUTIVE : Sir John Birch TERMS OF REFERENCE : The Association promotes better understanding between Britain and the countries of Central and Eastern Europe through a programme of exchanges, conferences, seminars and grants in the field of civil society and democratic institutions.	TEL : 0171 930 8466 FAX : 0171 839 6347 WEB : http://www.britcoun.org CHAIR : Helena Kennedy QC ACTING DIRECTOR GENERAL : Tom Buchanan TERMS OF REFERENCE : The British Council promotes a wider knowledge of the UK and the English language and encourages cultural, scientific, technological and educational co-operation between Britain and other countries.
a. Number if a multiple body/system (1.4.98)	–	–	–
b. Number of staff employed by the body (1.4.98)	5.5	4	6,659*
c. Annual Report	Body	Body	Body
d. Audit arrangements	Y	Y	X
e. Total gross expenditure of body (1997/98)	£0.417m	£0.422m	£413.9m†
f. Amount funded by government (1997/98)	£0.225m	£0.221m	£212.0m‡
g. Other expenditure by sponsoring dept (1997/98)	£0.048m	–	£0.288m
h. Chief Executive's Remuneration (1997/98)	£45,983*	£47,954	£165,436§
Appointments and Remuneration (1.9.98)			
i. Chairman/President	{1M, 1F}	{1M}*	{1F, £35,000}¶
j. Deputy	{6M}	{2M}	{1M, 1F, 1 vacancy}¶
k. Members	–	{8M, 3F}	{13M, 5F}
l. Tribunal cases received	–	–	–
m. Tribunal cases disposed of	–	–	–

* Plus £1,287 language allowance.

* The Chairman is appointed by British Association for Central and Eastern Europe with the approval of the Secretary of State for Foreign and Commonwealth Affairs.

* Full time equivalents as at 1.4.98.
† Includes £125.7m reimbursable agency expenditure.
‡ Includes £78.2m reimbursable agency expenditure.
§ Takes account of aggregate remuneration during changeover of Director General.
¶ Chairman, Deputy Chairmen, two vice chairmen elected by the Board having previously been approved by the SoS for Foreign and Commonwealth Affairs.

FOREIGN AND COMMONWEALTH OFFICE

Executive NDPBs

Advisory NDPBs

4 Commonwealth Institute

Kensington High Street
London
W8 6NQ

TEL : 0171 603 4535
FAX : 0171 602 7374
http://www.commonwealth.org.uk
CHAIR : Mr David Thompson
DIRECTOR-GENERAL : Mr David French
TERMS OF REFERENCE : Representing the Commonwealth to the British public; mounting exhibitions and maintaining collections; and providing educational programmes, library and information services, and operating a major conference and events centre.

5 The Great Britain-China Centre

15 Belgrave Square
London
SW1X 8PS

TEL : 0171 235 6696
FAX : 0171 245 6885
gbcc@gn.apc.org
http://www.gbcc.org.uk
CHAIR : Mr David Brewer
DIRECTOR : Ms Katie Lee
TERMS OF REFERENCE : To promote closer economic, professional, cultural and academic relations between Britain and China; and to encourage mutual knowledge and understanding.

6 Marshall Aid Commemoration Commission

Association of Commonwealth Universities,
36 Gordon Square,
London WC1H 0PF
TEL : 0171 387 8572
FAX : 0171 387 2655
macc@acu.ac.uk
http://www.castor.acu.ac.uk/marshall/index.html
CHAIR : Dr Robert Stevens
EXECUTIVE SECRETARY : Professor Michael Gibbons
TERMS OF REFERENCE : The Marshall Aid Commission has responsibility for the British Marshall Scholarships.

7 Westminster Foundation for Democracy

Clutha House
10 Storey's Gate
Westminster
London SW1P 3AY
TEL : 0171 976 7565
FAX : 0171 976 7464
wfd@wfd.org
CHAIR : Mr Ernie Ross MP
CHIEF EXECUTIVE : Ms Alexandra Jones
TERMS OF REFERENCE : To assist the development of pluralist democratic institutions overseas. Priority regions are Central/Eastern Europe, the former Soviet Union and anglophone Africa.

8 Diplomatic Service Appeal Board

Room 3.2.1
1 Palace Street
Westminster
London SW1E 5HE
TEL : 0171 238 4404
FAX : 0171 238 4420
CHAIR : Sir Keith Morris
SECRETARY : Mr Paul Chatt
TERMS OF REFERENCE : The Board's aim is to advise the Secretary of State whether premature retirement, or termination of an appointment on grounds of failed probation, or on dismissal grounds is fair.

	4 Commonwealth Institute	5 The Great Britain-China Centre	6 Marshall Aid Commemoration Commission	7 Westminster Foundation for Democracy	8 Diplomatic Service Appeal Board
a	–	–	–	–	–
b	32	4.5	–	6	–
c	Body	Body	Cm	Body	NP
d	X	Y	X	Y	–
e	£2.779m	£0.503m	£1.486m	£2.853m	–
f	£0.800m	£0.245m	£1.486m	£2.713m	–
g	£0.316m	£0.001m	£0.010m	£0.010m	£0.001m
h	£60,000	–	–	£67,862	–
i	1M, £15,000	{1M}*	1M	1M	1M, £255pd*
j	–	{1F}	–	3M	1M, £255pd*
k	1M, 1F, 10 vacancies*	{14M, 3F}†	4M, 5F	5M, 4F, 1 vacancy	1M, 4F, 1 vacancy, £182pd*
l	–	–	–	–	–
m	–	–	–	–	–

* The term of office for 10 members expired in November 1997. Confirmation of the new appointees to be announced.

* The Chairman is elected by the executive committee, with the approval of the Secretary of State for Foreign and Commonwealth Affairs.
† All new members to the executive committee are elected by the executive committee.

* Remuneration is only paid when the Board meets. It did not meet in 1997/98.

FOREIGN AND COMMONWEALTH OFFICE

Advisory NDPBs

Tribunal NDPBs

9
Government Hospitality Fund Advisory Committee for the Purchase of Wine

8 Cleveland Row
London
SW1A 1DH

TEL : 0171 210 4290/4292
FAX : 0171 930 1148
CHAIR : Sir Ewen Fergusson GCMG GCVO
TERMS OF REFERENCE : To advise on the purchasing of wine for Government hospitality.

10
Wilton Park Academic Council

c/o Wilton Park
Wiston House
Steyning
West Sussex BN44 3DZ

TEL : 01903 815020
FAX : 01903 879647
CHAIR : Mrs Liliana Archibald
CHIEF EXECUTIVE : Mr C B Jennings
TERMS OF REFERENCE : The council aims to ensure that Wilton Park retains full academic independence; it oversees Wilton Park's programme with this objective.

11
Foreign Compensation Commission

4 Central Buildings
Matthew Parker Street
London SW1H 9NL

CHAIR : Mr Arthur Wheeler
SECRETARY : Mr Alexander Grant
TERMS OF REFERENCE : The Commission primarily distributes funds received from other Governments in accordance with agreements to pay compensation for expropriated British property and other losses sustained by British Nationals.

12
Intelligence Services Tribunal

PO Box 4823
London
SW1A 9XD

TEL : 0171 273 4383
PRESIDENT : Rt Hon Lord Justice Brown ; SECRETARY : Mr E Wilson
TERMS OF REFERENCE : The Tribunal investigates complaints from any person who believes that the Secret Intelligence Service or Government Communications Headquarters have done something to them or their property.

	9	10	11	12
a	–	–	–	–
b	–	–	–	1
c	NP	NP	Cm	NP
d	–	–	–	–
e	–	–	–	–
f	–	–	–	–
g	£0.001m	£0.004m	£0.025m	£0.030m
h	–	–	–	–
i	1M	1F	1M*†	1M
j	–	–	–	1M
k	4M	10M, 4F	–	1M, £316pd
l	–	–	–	3*
m	–	–	–	6*

* Paid by Department of Social Security
† Appointment made by the Lord Chancellor.

* 1997 Calendar Year.

Department of Health

DEPARTMENT OF HEALTH

Executive NDPBs

Richmond House, 79 Whitehall,
London SW1A 2NS

Enquiries Lee McGill
Telephone 0171 210 5978
Facsimile 0171 210 4904
E-mail   lmcgill@doh.gov.uk
Internet   http://www.open.gov.uk/doh

GTN   210 5978

1 Central Council for Education and Training in Social Work (UK)

Derbyshire House
St Chad's Street
London
WC1H 8AD
TEL : 0171 278 2455
FAX : 0171 278 2934
zuima.wickenden@ccetsw.org.uk
http://www.ccetsw.org.uk
CHAIR : Ms Ziggy Alexander
CHIEF EXECUTIVE : Jennifer Bernard
TERMS OF REFERENCE : The promotion and development of training; the regulation of professional training; the awarding of qualifications; and the funding of students undertaking training.

2 English National Board for Nursing, Midwifery and Health Visiting

Victory House
170 Tottenham Court Road
London
W1P 0HA
TEL : 0171 388 3131
FAX : 0171 388 4031
enb.link@easynet.co.uk
http://www.enb.org.uk
CHAIR : Professor Ron de Witt MA BA(HONS) SRN
TERMS OF REFERENCE : The ENB was set up under the Nurses, Midwives and Health Visitors Act 1979. The Board's core aim is to ensure that the institution and education programmes it approves and the advice given to Local Supervising Authorities concerning the supervision of midwifery practice meet the standards of the UKCC.

3 Human Fertilisation and Embryology Authority

Paxton House
30 Artillery Lane
London
E1 7LS
TEL : 0171 377 5077
FAX : 0171 377 1871
WEB : http://www.hfea.gov.uk
CHAIR : Mrs Ruth Deech
TERMS OF REFERENCE : To control and monitor licensed centres providing infertility treatment involving IVF, AID, egg, sperm and embryo donation; and related research.

		1	2	3
a.	Number if a multiple body/system (1.4.98)	–	–	–
b.	Number of staff employed by the body (1.4.98)	205	128	28
c.	Annual Report	Body	Body	Body
d.	Audit arrangements	X	X	X
e.	Total gross expenditure of body (1997/98)	£38.501m	£7.427m	£1.410m
f.	Amount funded by government (1997/98)	£36.834m*	£5.864m	£1.484m*
g.	Other expenditure by sponsoring dept (1997/98)	£0.169m	£0.022m	£0.065m
h.	Chief Executive's Remuneration (1997/98)	£75,000	£85,573	£54,710
	Appointments and Remuneration (1.9.98)			
i.	Chairman/President	1F, £20,000	1M, 22,135	1F, £8,210
j.	Deputy	1 vacancy†, £5,000	1F	1F, £143pd
k.	Members	5M, 3F, 8 vacancies 2M‡, 2 vacancies‡	2M, 3F	12M, 7F, £131pd
l.	Tribunal cases received	–	–	–
m.	Tribunal cases disposed of	–	–	–

* This is Grant Aid, not grant-in-aid.
† As Chair of CCETSW Finance Committee receives remuneration of £5,000.
‡ As Chairs of CCETSW National Committee each receives remuneration of £5,000.

* Revenue only.

59

DEPARTMENT OF HEALTH

Executive NDPBs

Advisory Bodies

	4 Medical Practices Committee	5 National Biological Standards Board (UK)	6 National Radiological Protection Board	7 Public Health Laboratory Service Board	8 Administration of Radioactive Substances Advisory Committee
	Room 116 Eileen House 80–94 Newington House London SE1 6EF TEL : 0171 972 2930 FAX : 0171 972 2985 WEB : http://www.open.gov.uk/doh/mpc/mpch.htm CHAIR : Miss Mary Leigh TERMS OF REFERENCE : To ensure the number of general practitioners (GPs) in all areas of England and Wales is adequate and to ensure GPs are distributed equitably, in accordance with the health care needs of the populations of different areas.	Blanche Lane South Mimms Potter's Bar Hertfordshire EN6 3QG TEL : 01707 654753 FAX : 01707 646730 nibsc@nibsc.ac.uk http://www.nibsc.ac.uk CHAIR : Dr N J B Evans SECRETARY : Dr Richard Stewart TERMS OF REFERENCE : The aim of the National Biological Standards Board is to safeguard and enhance public health through the standardisation and control of biologicals used in medicine.	Chilton OXON OX11 0RQ TEL : 01235 831600 FAX : 01235 833891 nrpb@nrpb.org.uk http://www.nrpb.org.uk CHAIR : Professor Sir Keith Peters ; ACTING SECRETARY : Mr David Talbot TERMS OF REFERENCE : To provide scientific advice to the Government, as well as to a range of public and private sector organisations and professional bodies, on matters relating to radiation hazards.	61 Colindale Avenue London NW9 5DF TEL : 0181 200 1295 FAX : 0181 200 8130 webmaster@phls.co.uk http://www.phls.co.uk CHAIR : Sir Leslie Turnberg SECRETARY : Mr Keith Saunders TERMS OF REFERENCE : The Public Health Laboratory Service Board aims to protect the population from infection through detection, diagnosis, surveillance, prevention and control of infections and communicable diseases in the UK and world-wide on the sources and control of infection.	ARSAC Secretariat Room 525, Wellington House 133–155 Waterloo Road London SE1 8UG TEL : 0171 972 4802 FAX : 0171 972 4800 CHAIR : Professor James McKillop ; SECRETARY : Ms Patricia Brown TERMS OF REFERENCE : To advise Health Ministers with respect to the grant, renewal, suspension, revocation and variations of certificates to administer radioactive substances to humans.
a	–	–	–	–	–
b	13	275	306	3,301	–
c	Body	Body	Body	Body	NP
d	X*	X	X	X	–
e	£0.480m*	£16.100m	£14.600m	£124.973m	–
f	£0.480m	£11.253m	£6.613m	£59.553m	–
g	£0.210m	£0.039m	£0.036m	£0.050m	£0.016m
h	–	£71,715	£74,860	£128,129	–
i	1F, £34,294	1M	1M, £10,920	1M, £15,125	1M
j	–	1F	–	1M, £3,060	–
k	7M, 2F, £155.80pn	10M, 1F	7M, 5F, £131pd	14M, 3F, £131pd 1 vacancy	13M, 7F
l	–	–	–	–	–
m	–	–	–	–	–

* Expenditure forms part of the total Department of Health (DH) expenditure. Accounts for DH are audited by the Comptroller and Auditor General.

DEPARTMENT OF HEALTH

Advisory NDPBs

	9	10	11	12	13
	Advisory Board on the Registration of Homeopathic Products	**Advisory Committee on Borderline Substances**	**Advisory Committee on Dangerous Pathogens***	**Advisory Committee on Design Quality in the NHS***	**Advisory Committee on Distinction Awards**
	c/o Market Towers 1 Nine Elms Lane London SW8 5NQ	P&P Branch, Room 153 Department of Health Richmond House, 79 Whitehall London SW1A 2BS	Dept of Health, HSE, 6th Floor North Wing, Rose Court 2 Southwark Bridge London SE1 9HS	NHS Estates Agency Room 1 South Trevelyan Square Leeds LS1 6AE	Room 2N35D Quarry House Quarry Hill Leeds LS2 7UE
TEL	0171 273 0451	0171 210 5737	0171 717 6266	0113 254 7148	0113 254 5921
FAX	0171 273 0453	0171 210 5585	0171 717 6199	0113 254 7299	0113 254 5798
			acdp.secretariat@hse.gov.uk	nhs.estates@doh.gov.uk	http://www.open.gov.uk/ doh/nhsexec/acda.htm
CHAIR	Dr Brian Kirby	Professor Andrew Lowe	Dr Michael Crumpton	Mr Alan Milburn MP, Minister of State	Sir William Reid
SECRETARY	Mr Leslie Whitbread	Ms Frances Millichip	DH SECRETARY: Mrs Eileen Lawrence; HSE SECRETARY: Dr Mark Bale	Mr Julian Garthwaite	Mr Sean Kirwan
TERMS OF REFERENCE	To give advice on safety and quality in relation to any homoeopathic medicinal product for human use, in respect of which a Certificate of Registration could be granted.	To advise Health Minister and the medical professions as to whether particular substances, preparations or items should or should not be treated as drugs for the purposes of the General Medical Service Regulations.	To advise the Health and Safety Commission, Health and Safety Executive and Health and Agriculture Ministers, as required, on all aspects of hazards and risks to workers and others from exposure to pathogens.	FORMER TERMS OF REFERENCE: To advise the Secretary of State for Health on ways of promoting high standards of architecture and design quality in buildings used for the National Health Service.	To consider recommendations for distinction awards for NHS consultants and to act on behalf of the Secretaries of State for Health, and for Scotland and Wales, in deciding which consultants should receive awards.
a	–	–	–	–	–
b	–	–	–	–	–
c	Body	NP	NP	NP	Body
d	–	–	–	–	–
e	–	–	–	–	–
f	–	–	–	–	–
g	£0.036m	£0.044m	£0.099m	£0.002m	£0.178m
h	–	–	–	–	–
i	1M, 200pm	1M	1M	†	1M, £20,925
j	1M, £160pm	1M	–	–	1M, £25,775*
k	7M, 3F, £160pm	6M, 3F	11M, 5F	–	26M, 5F
l	–	–	–	–	–
m	–	–	–	–	–

* Joint DH/HSE Advisory Committee.

* This body was abolished in June 1998.
† Chairman is a Minister.

* Medical Director.

DEPARTMENT OF HEALTH

Advisory NDPBs

	14 Advisory Committee on Genetic Testing	15 Advisory Committee on the Micro-biological Safety of Food	16 Advisory Committee on NHS Drugs	17 Advisory Group on Hepatitis	18 British Pharmacopoeia Commission
Address	Room 401, Wellington House, 133–155 Waterloo Road, London SE1 8UG	Skipton House, 80 London Road, London SE1 6LW	Department of Health, Richmond House, 79 Whitehall, London SW1A 2NS	Department of Health, Room 725, Wellington House, 133–155 Waterloo Road, London SE1 8UG	Market Towers, 1 Nine Elms Lane, London SW8 5NQ
TEL	0171 972 4017	0171 972 5048	0171 210 5642	0171 972 4479	0171 273 0559
FAX	0171 972 4196	0171 972 5558	0171 210 5585	0171 972 4559	0171 273 0566
EMAIL	mstraugh@doh.gov.uk http://www.open.gov.uk/doh/genetics.htm	phayer@doh.gov.uk			http://www.pharmacopoeia.co.uk
CHAIR	Reverend Dr John Polkinghorne	Professor Douglas Georgala	Dr Jeremy Metters	Dr Jeremy Metters	Professor Derek Calam
SECRETARY	Mr Anthony Taylor	Dr Judith Hilton	Mr Michael Cummins	Dr Hugh Nicholas	Dr Robin Hutton
TERMS OF REFERENCE	To provide advice to Ministers on developments in testing for genetic disorders and to advise on testing individuals for genetic disorders.	To assess the risk to humans of micro-organisms which are used, or occur, in or on food; and to advise Ministers on the exercise of powers in the Food Safety Act, relating to the Micro-biological safety of food.	To ensure all the real clinical needs of NHS patients can be provided as economically as possible under the National Health Service.	To advise the Chief Medical Officers of the Health Departments of the UK on appropriate policies for the prevention and control of viral hepatitis in the community and in health care settings, but excluding advice on the microbiological safety of blood and tissues for transplantation, and of health care equipment.	To publish any compendium or new edition of and/or amendment to the British Pharmacopoeia, and British Pharmacopoeia (Veterinary), together with establishment and publication of British Approved Names. This provides publicly available specifications and standards that apply to any medicinal product, at any time during its shelf-life.
a	–	–	–	–	–
b	–	–	–	–	–
c	Body	Body	NP	NP	TSO
d	–	–	–	–	–
e	–	–	–	–	–
f	–	–	–	–	–
g	£0.080m	£0.148m	£0.071m	£0.005m	£0.040m
h	–	–	–	–	–
i	1M, £163pm	1M, £104pm	*	*	1M, £200pm
j	–	–	1M, £100pm	–	1M, £160pm
k	7M, 6F, £131pm	12M, 3F, £84pm	15M, 4F, £100pm	10M, 3F	10M, 1F, £160pm 1 vacancy
l	–	–	–	–	–
m	–	–	–	–	–

* Chairman is a civil servant. (columns 16 and 17)

DEPARTMENT OF HEALTH

Advisory NDPBs

19
Clinical Standards Advisory Group

Room 320
Wellington House
133 Waterloo Road
London SE1 8UG
TEL : 0171 972 4918
FAX : 0171 972 4930
CHAIR : Professor Martin Harris
SECRETARY : Mr Paul Marshall
TERMS OF REFERENCE : To provide independent advice to Health Ministers and National Health Service bodies on standards of clinical care, and on the access and availability of services to NHS patients.

20
Committee on Carcinogenicity of Chemicals in Food, Consumer Products and the Environment

Skipton House
80 London Road
London
SE1 6LH
TEL : 0171 972 5020
FAX : 0171 972 5134
kmistry@doh.gov.uk
WEB : http://www.open.gov/doh.gov.uk/coc.htm
CHAIR : Professor Peter Blain
SECRETARY : Khandu Mistry
TERMS OF REFERENCE : To advise the Chief Medical Officer on carcinogenicity of chemicals in food, consumer products and the environment.

21
Committee on Medical Aspects of Food and Nutrition Policy

Skipton House
80 London Road
London
SE1 6LH
TEL : 0171 972 5907
FAX : 0171 972 5413
a.refearn@doh.gov.uk
CHAIR : Professor Sir John Grimley Evans
TERMS OF REFERENCE : To consider and advise the Chief Medical Officer and the Government on the medical and scientific aspects of nutrition and health in relation to policy.

22
Committee on the Medical Effects of Air Pollutants

Room 679D, Skipton House
80 London Road
London SE1 6LH
TEL : 0171 972 5130
FAX : 0171 972 5167
EMAIL : jcumberl@doh.gov.uk
CHAIR : Professor Stephen Holgate ; SECRETARY : Ms Julie Cumberlidge
TERMS OF REFERENCE : To assess and advise Government on the effects upon health of air pollutants, both outdoor and indoor air, and to assess the adequacy of the available data and the need for further research. To co-ordinate the assessment of the effects of exposure to air pollutants and the associated risks to health.

23
Committee for Monitoring Agreements on Tobacco Advertising and Sponsorship

PO Box 3982
London
SE1 8YJ

TEL : 0171 972 4203
FAX : 0171 972 4218
CHAIR : Sir Clive Whitmore
SECRETARY : Miss Luisa Stewart
TERMS OF REFERENCE : To monitor and report on the operation of the voluntary agreement on tobacco advertising and promotion and sports sponsorship.

	19	20	21	22	23
a	–	–	–	–	–
b	–	–	–	–	–
c	NP	TSO	Body	NP	Body
d	–	–	–	–	–
e	–	–	–	–	–
f	–	–	–	–	–
g	£0.384m	£0.041m	£0.089m	£0.010m	£0.010m
h	–	–	–	–	–
i	1M	1M, £105pm*	1M, £105pm	1M, £105pm	1M, £3,000
j	–	–	–	1F	–
k	11M, 8F	10M, 2F, £84pm*	7M, 2F, £84pm	16M, 3F, £84pm	{5M, 2F}*
l	–	–	–	–	–
m	–	–	–	–	–

* Per meeting

* Membership consists of representatives from the Tobacco Industry and departmental officials, none of whom are public appointments.

DEPARTMENT OF HEALTH

Advisory NDPBs

24

Committee on Medical Aspects of Radiation in the Environment

Room 682D
Skipton House
80 London Road
London SE16LW
TEL : 0171 972 5123
FAX : 0171 972 5135
http://www.open.gov.uk/doh/comare.htm
CHAIR : Professor Bryn Bridges
SECRETARY : Dr Roy Hamlet
TERMS OF REFERENCE : To assess and advise Government on the health effects of natural and man-made radiation in the environment; and to assess the adequacy of the available data and the need for further research.

25

Committee on Mutagenicity of Chemicals in Food, Consumer Products and the Environment

Skipton House
80 London Road
London
SE1 6LH
TEL : 0171 972 5020
FAX : 0171 972 5134
kmistry@doh.gov.uk
http://www.open.gov.uk/doh/com.htm
CHAIR : Professor Jim Parry
SECRETARY : Khandu Mistry
TERMS OF REFERENCE : To advise the Chief Medical Officer on the mutagenicity of chemicals in food, consumer products and the environment.

26

Committee on the Safety of Medicines

Market Towers
1 Nine Elms Lane
London
SW8 5NQ
TEL : 0171 273 0451/0477
FAX : 0171 273 0453
lesliewhitbread@mca.gov.uk
http://www.open.gov.uk/mca/mcahome.htm
CHAIR : Professor Michael Rawlins ; SECRETARY : Mr Leslie Whitbread
TERMS OF REFERENCE : To give advice on safety, quality and efficiency in relation to human use of any substance or article to which any provision of the Medicines Act 1968 is applicable.

27

Committee on Toxicity of Chemicals in Food, Consumer Products and the Environment

Skipton House
80 London Road
London
SE16LW
TEL : 0171 972 5018
FAX : 0171 972 5134
EMAIL : jlighthi@doh.gov.uk
http://www.open.gov.uk/doh/cot.htm
CHAIR : Professor Frank Woods
SECRETARIES : Dr J Grieg and Mr J Lighthill
TERMS OF REFERENCE : To assess and advise the Chief Medical Officer on the toxic risks to people of chemicals in food, consumer products and the environment.

28

Dental Rates Study Group*

Room 311, Department of Health, Richmond House
79 Whitehall
London
TEL : 0171 210 5767
FAX : 0171 210 5913
CHAIR : Mr Clive Monks
TERMS OF REFERENCE : To fix times for each dental operation as could reasonably be taken by the average dentist, and to determine gross fees for each of the operations.

	24	25	26	27	28
a	–	–	–	–	–
b	–	–	–	–	–
c	TSO	Body	Body	Body	NP
d	–	–	–	–	–
e	–	–	–	–	–
f	–	–	–	–	–
g	£0.140m	£0.033m	£0.196m	£0.149m	–
h	–	–	–	–	–
i	1M, £131pm	1M, £105pm*	1M, £200pm	1M, £105pm	–
j	–	–	1M, £160pm	–	–
k	13M, 4F, £84pm	8M, £84pm*, 1 vacancy	22M, 5F, £160pm	12M, 4F, £84pm	–
l	–	–	–	–	–
m	–	–	–	–	–

* Per meeting.

* The Group has not met for four years and has no members though its chairman's tenure has still to run its course. The sponsor branch is shortly to seek (and expects to receive) ministers' approval to abolish the group. There will be no appointments made to the group but it does still formally exist.

DEPARTMENT OF HEALTH

Advisory NDPBs

29
Doctors' and Dentists' Review Body

Office of Manpower Economics
Oxford House
76 Oxford Street
London W1N 9FD
TEL : 0171 467 7244
FAX : 0171 467 7248
CHAIR : Mr Brandon Gough
SECRETARY : Miss Susan Haird
TERMS OF REFERENCE : To advise on the remuneration of doctors and dentists taking any part in the NHS, in accordance with their terms of reference.

30
Expert Advisory Group on AIDS

HP3C, Room 724
Wellington House
135–155 Waterloo Road
London SE1 8UG
TEL : 0171 972 4378
FAX : 0171 972 2000
CHAIR : Dr Jeremy Matters
MEDICAL SECRETARY : Ms Susan Turnbull
TERMS OF REFERENCE : To provide advice on such matters relating to AIDS as may be referred to it by the Chief Medical Officers of the Health Departments of the United Kingdom.

31
Gene Therapy Advisory Committee

HP4E, Room 401
Wellington House
135–155 Waterloo Road
London SE1 8UG
TEL : 0171 972 4021
FAX : 0171 972 4196
mstraugh@doh.gov.uk
http://www.open.gov.uk/doh/genetics.htm
CHAIR : Professor Norman Nevin
SECRETARY : Mr Anthony Taylor
TERMS OF REFERENCE : To consider proposals for gene therapy research on ethical grounds, and to advise Ministers on their acceptibility, taking account of their scientific merits and of the potential benefits and risks involved.

32
Joint Committee on Vaccination and Immunisation

Room 707
Wellington House
135–155 Waterloo Road
London SE1 8UG
TEL : 0171 972 4488
FAX : 0171 972 4468
CHAIR : Professor Sir David Hull
SECRETARY : Dr David Sainsbury
TERMS OF REFERENCE : To advise the Secretaries of State for Health, Scotland, Wales and Northern Ireland on matters relating to communicable disease, preventable and potentially preventable through immunisation.

33
Medical Workforce Standing Advisory Committee

c/o Room 2N35B
Quarry House
Quarry Hill
Leeds LS2 7UE
TEL : 0113 254 5866
FAX : 0113 254 6350
EMAIL : lmallett@doh.gov.uk
CHAIR : Professor Sir Colin Campbell ; SECRETARY : Mr Bill Urry
TERMS OF REFERENCE : To advise the Secretary of State for Health on future developments in the balance of medical workforce supply and demand in the United Kingdom.

	29	30	31	32	33
a	–	–	–	–	–
b	–	–	–	–	–
c	Cm	NP	Body	TSO*	NP
d	–	–	–	–	–
e	–	–	–	–	–
f	–	–	–	–	–
g	£0.500m*	£0.023m	£0.072m	£0.026m	£0.100m
h	–	–	–	–	–
i	1M	*	1M, £163pm	1M	1M
j	–	–	–	–	–
k	4M, 3F	{10M, 6F}	9M, 7F, £131pm	11M, 3F	9M, 3F
l	–	–	–	–	–
m	–	–	–	–	–

* Secretariat provided by the Office of Manpower Economics (OME) part of the Department of Trade and Industry (DTI). The costs of the OME are borne on the DTI Vote.

* Chairman is a civil servant.

* No annual report published but bi-annual publication 'Immunisation Against Infectious Diseases' contains the body's advice on immunisation matters.

DEPARTMENT OF HEALTH

Advisory NDPBs

34 Medicines Commission

c/o Market Towers
1 Nine Elms Lane
London
SW8 5NQ
TEL : 0171 273 0652
FAX : 0171 273 0020
CHAIR : Professor David Lawson
SECRETARY : Mrs Sue Jones
TERMS OF REFERENCE : To advise Health and Agriculture Ministers on general policy or matters relating to the Medicines Act.

a	–
b	–
c	TSO
d	–
e	–
f	–
g	£0.074m
h	–
i	1M, £200pm
j	1F, £160pm
k	16M, 4F, £160pm
l	–
m	–

35 Microbiology Advisory Committee

Medical Devices Agency
Hannibal House
Elephant and Castle
London SE1 6YQ
TEL : 0171 972 8000
FAX : 0171 972 8108
nmoore@doh.gov.uk
WEB : http://www.medical-devices.gov.uk
CHAIR : Dr G Ridgway ;
SECRETARY : Mr Nathan Moore
TERMS OF REFERENCE : To advise on the preparation and ratification of Departmental guidance on microbiological aspects of equipment used and intended to be used in the Health Service.

a	–
b	–
c	NP
d	–
e	–
f	–
g	£0.011m
h	–
i	1M
j	–
k	9M, 2F
l	–
m	–

36 Nurses', Midwives' and other NHS Professions' Review Body

Office of Manpower Economics
Oxford House
76 Oxford Street
London W1N 9FD
TEL : 0171 467 7244
FAX : 0171 467 7248
CHAIR : Professor Clive Booth
SECRETARY : Miss Susan Haird
TERMS OF REFERENCE : To advise on the remuneration of nurses, midwives and health visitors employed in the NHS; and physiotherapists, radiographers, occupational therapists, chiropodists, dieticians and related grades employed in the NHS, in accordance with their terms of reference.

a	–
b	–
c	Cm
d	–
e	–
f	–
g	£0.500m*
h	–
i	1M
j	–
k	4M, 3F
l	–
m	–

* Secretariat provided by the Office of Manpower Economics (OME) part of the Department of Trade and Industry (DTI). The costs of the OME are borne on the DTI Vote.

37 Pharmacists' Review Panel

Office of Manpower Economics
Oxford House
76 Oxford Street
London W1N 9FD
TEL : 0171 467 7244
FAX : 0171 467 7248
CHAIR : Mr Jimmy Keir
SECRETARY : Miss Susan Haird
TERMS OF REFERENCE : To advise the Health Secretary on any aspect relating to the gross remuneration of chemist contractors producing services under Part II of the National Health Act.

a	–
b	–
c	NP
d	–
e	–
f	–
g	*
h	–
i	1M
j	–
k	2M, 1F
l	–
m	–

* Secretariat provided by the Office of Manpower Economics (OME) part of the Department of Trade and Industry (DTI). The costs of the OME are borne on the DTI Vote.

38 Royal Commission on Long Term Care for the Elderly

5th Floor
Hannibal House
Elephant and Castle
London SE1 6TE
TEL : 0171 972 2400
FAX : 0171 972 22020/22021
http://www.open.gov.uk/doh/elderly.htm
CHAIR : Sir Stewart Sutherland
SECRETARY : Mr Alan Davey
TERMS OF REFERENCE : To examine options for a sustainable system of funding of long term care for elderly people, both in their own homes and in other settings; and within twelve months, to recommend how, and in what circumstances, the cost of such care should be apportioned between public funds and individuals.

a	–
b	–
c	NP
d	–
e	–
f	–
g	£0.037m
h	–
i	1M
j	–
k	6M, 5F
l	–
m	–

Advisory NDPBs

DEPARTMENT OF HEALTH

39
Scientific Committee on Tobacco and Health*

Department of Health
Room 725, Wellington House
135–155 Wellington Road
London SE1
TEL : 0171 972 4026
FAX : 0171 972 4218
EMAIL : dmilner@doh.gov.uk
CHAIR : Professor David Poswillo (Retired April 1998)
SECRETARY : Dr Dawn Milner
TERMS OF REFERENCE : To provide advice to the Chief Medical Officer on scientific matters concerning tobacco and health; in particular, to review scientific and medical evidence on such areas, including behavioural aspects of tobacco use.

40
Standing Committee on Postgraduate Medical and Dental Education

1 Park Square West
London
NW1 4LJ

TEL : 0171 935 3916
FAX : 0171 935 8601
secretary@scopmc.org.uk
http://www.scopme.org.uk/get/reports/
CHAIR : Professor Dame Barbara Clayton ; SECRETARY : Dr Jolyon Oxley
TERMS OF REFERENCE : To advise the Secretary of State on the delivery of postgraduate and continuing medical and dental education.

41
Standing Dental Advisory Committee

Department of Health
Richmond House
79 Whitehall
London SW1A 2NS
TEL : 0171 210 5763
FAX : 0171 210 5774
CHAIR : Mr John Renshaw
SECRETARY : Ms Andrea Goring
TERMS OF REFERENCE : To advise the Secretary of State on dental matters and to respond to any question referred to the Committee by him.

42
Standing Medical Advisory Committee

Room 320
Wellington House
133–155 Waterloo Road
London SE1 8UG
TEL : 0171 972 4919
FAX : 0171 972 4930
EMAIL : mhart@doh.gov.uk
CHAIR : Professor Alan Johnson
SECRETARY : Mr Paul Marshall
TERMS OF REFERENCE : To advise the Secretary of State for Health on matters relating to medical services; and to respond to any question referred to the Committee by him.

43
Standing Nursing and Midwifery Advisory Committee

Room 320
Wellington House
133–155 Waterloo Road
London SE1 8UG
TEL : 0171 972 4919
FAX : 0171 972 4930
mhart@doh.gov.uk
CHAIR : Mr Tony Bell
SECRETARY : Ms Mellisa Hart
TERMS OF REFERENCE : To advise the Secretary of State for Health on matters relating to nursing and midwifery services, and to respond to any questions referred to the Committee by the Secretary of State.

	39	40	41	42	43
a	–	–	–	–	–
b	–	–	–	–	–
c	NP	Body	NP	NP	NP
d	–	–	–	–	–
e	£0.057m	–	–	–	–
f	–	–	–	–	–
g	£0.055m	£0.021m*	£0.004m	£0.026m	£0.026m
h	–	–	–	–	–
i	{1 vacant, £105pm}	1F	1M	1M	1M
j	–	1M	1F	1F	1F
k	{9M, 1F, 2 vacancies £84pm}	13M, 4F	12M, 3F	10M, 6F	6M, 18F
l	–	–	–	–	–
m	–	–	–	–	–

* SCOTH is temporarily dormant.
* Receives grant-in-aid of £0.324m.

DEPARTMENT OF HEALTH

Advisory NDPBs

44
Standing Pharmaceutical Advisory Committee

Department of Health
Richmond House
79 Whitehall
London SW1A 2NS
TEL : 0171 210 5117
FAX : 0171 210 5483
CHAIR : Mr William Darling
SECRETARY : Miss Catherine Dewsbury
TERMS OF REFERENCE : To advise Health Ministers in England and Wales on technical pharmaceutical matters which bear upon the provision of effective and efficient pharmaceutical services.

45
Steering Committee on Pharmacy Postgraduate Education

School of Pharmacy & Pharmaceutical Sciences,
University of Manchester, Oxford Road, Manchester M13 9PL
TEL : 0161 275 2324
FAX : 0161 275 2419
EMAIL : cppe@man.ac.uk
CHAIR : Mr Bryan Hartley
SECRETARY : Dr Peter Wilson
TERMS OF REFERENCE : To advise the Department of Health on the continuing education and vocational training needs of hospital and community pharmacists who provide NHS pharmaceutical services.

46
UK Advisory Panel for Health Care Workers Infected with Bloodborne Viruses

Room 724
Wellington House
133–155 Waterloo Road
London SE1 8UG
TEL : 0171 972 4378
FAX : 0171 972 4559
CHAIR : Vacant
SECRETARY : Dr Susan Turnbull
TERMS OF REFERENCE : To establish and update as necessary, criteria for local advice on modifying working practices.

47
United Kingdom Xenotransplantation Interim Regulatory Authority

Room 311/2
Wellington House
133–155 Waterloo Road
London SE1 8UG
TEL : 0171 972 4822
FAX : 0171 972 4852
http://www.open.gov.uk/doh/ukxira.htm
CHAIR : Rt Rev Lord Habgood of Calverton ; SECRETARY : Ms Rachel Arrundale
TERMS OF REFERENCE : To advise the Government on the action necessary to regulate xenotransplantation.

48
Unrelated Live Transplant Regulatory Authority

Room 311/2
Wellington House
133–155 Waterloo Road
London SE1 8UG
TEL : 0171 972 4822
FAX : 0171 972 4852
CHAIR : Professor Martin Bobrow CBE ; SECRETARY : Mr William Kent MBE
TERMS OF REFERENCE : To consider all cases where it is proposed to transplant organs between living persons who are not related.

	44	45	46	47	48
a	–	–	–	–	–
b	–	–	–	–	–
c	NP	Body	NP	Body	NP
d	–	–	–	–	–
e	–	–	–	–	–
f	–	–	–	–	–
g	£0.003m	£0.007m	£0.009m	£0.065m	£0.025m
h	–	–	–	–	–
i	1M	*	1M	1M, £163pm	1M
j	1F	–	1M	–	–
k	4M, 6F	7M, 5F	9M, 4F, 2 vacancies	4M, 4F, £131pm	6M, 4F
l	–	–	–	–	–
m	–	–	–	–	–

* Chairman is a civil servant.

Advisory NDPBs

Tribunal NDPBs

49
Wider Health Working Group

Department of Health
Room 534/5, Wellington House, 135–155 Waterloo Road, London SE1 8UG
TEL : 0171 972 4123
FAX : 0171 972 4469
TERMS OF REFERENCE : To implement and take forward the wider dimensions of the 'Health of the Nation' strategy in England, as set out in the 1992 White Paper.

50
Mental Health Review Tribunal

London North,
Canons Park, Govt Buildings Honeypot Lane, Stanmore Middlesex HA7 1AY
TEL : 0171 972 3754
FAX : 0171 972 3731
REGIONAL CHAIR : Mr M J Christie
BUSINESS MANAGER : Mrs K Vale
TERMS OF REFERENCE : Mental Health Review Tribunals are statutorily independent judicial bodies which operate under the Mental Health Act 1983. The members of the tribunal are responsible for considering whether there is a need for a patient to continue to be detained in hospital under the Mental Health Act 1983.

51
National Health Service Tribunal

East Hookers, Bolney Chapel Road, Twineham,
Nr Haywards Heath,
West Sussex RH17 5NN
TEL : 01444 881345
FAX : 01444 881342
CHAIR : Mr Adrian Whitfield QC
TERMS OF REFERENCE : To protect the NHS family services by ensuring they are not brought into disrepute by the continued practice of FHS practitioners who prejudice their efficiency.

52
Registered Homes Tribunals

Social Care 2A, Room 624, Wellington House
135–155 Waterloo Road
London SE1 8UG
TEL : 0171 972 4034
FAX : 0171 972 4525
SECRETARIAT : Michelle Haywood
TERMS OF REFERENCE : To hear appeals under the Registered Homes Act 1984.

	49	50	51	52
a	–	4	–	–
b	–	–	–	–
c	NP	Body	NP	NP
d	–	–	–	–
e	–	–	–	–
f	–	–	–	–
g	–	£1.35m	£0.077m	£0.116m*
h	–	–	–	–
i	–	1M, £239pd*	1M, £265pd	{5M, 3F}, £254pd
j	–	–	1M, 1F, £265pd	–
k	14M, 6F, 1 vacancy	88M, 62F, £48.50–£340pd £97.00pd–£48.50hd £226.00pd–£113.00hd £239.00pd–£340pd	30M, 9F, £119pd lay members £165pd, prof members*	{25M, 15F, £162pd}
l	–	14,946	6	73
m	–	12,110	5	72

* Chairmen receive retainer fees of £18,000 per annum.

* The clerk receives £60 per hour.

* Additional staff costs of £0.132m

DEPARTMENT OF HEALTH : NHS BODIES

Department of Health NHS Bodies

Quarry House, Quarry Hill,
Leeds LS2 7UE

Enquiries   Nick Hope
Telephone   0113 254 5644
Facsimile   0113 254 5670
E-mail   nhope@doh.gov.uk

GTN   5134 5644

National Health Service Bodies

Health Authorities and Trusts

53 National Health Service Trusts

Addresses throughout England

TERMS OF REFERENCE : Responsible for providing health care services to patients, either in hospitals, health centres clinics, in the community or as ambulance services. They work with HAs, GPs, local people and other agencies to deliver integrated health care services to meet national and local needs.

54 Health Authorities (HAs)

Addresses throughout England

TEL : 0113 254 5644

TERMS OF REFERENCE : Responsible for implementing national policy on public health and health care within the area served by the Authority. They work with GPs, hospital and community services, local people and other agencies to meet national and local priorities for health and health care.

Special HAs

55 The Ashworth Hospital Authority

1–4 Parkbourne
Park Lane
Mughill
Merseyside L31 1HW

TEL : 0151 473 0303
FAX : 0151 473 6603
CHAIR : Mr Paul Lever
CHIEF EXECUTIVE : Mr P Clarke

TERMS OF REFERENCE : One of three special hospitals which provide psychiatric services for the whole of England and Wales, for patients who require treatment under conditions of high security.

		53 NHS Trusts	54 HAs	55 Ashworth
a.	Number if a multiple body/system (1.4.98)	402	100	–
b.	Number of staff employed by the body (1.4.98)	668,840*	15,350*	1,451
c.	Annual Report	Body	Body	Body
d.	Audit arrangements	–	–	–
e.	Total gross expenditure of body (1997/98)	£22,973m†‡	£25,230m†	£46.819m
f.	Amount funded by government (1997/98)	§	£23,230m†‡	£45.418m
g.	Other expenditure by sponsoring dept (1997/98)	–	–	–
h.	Chief Executive's Remuneration (1997/98)	£75,000†¶	£77,750†¶	£122,000*
i.	Chairman/President (Appointments and Remuneration 1.9.98)	261M, 120F, £15,125–£19,285, 11 vacancies	57M, 40F, £15,125–£19,285, 3 vacancies	1M, £17,415
j.	Deputy	–	–	–
k.	Members	966M, 871F, £5,000, 138 vacancies	251M, 216F, £5,000, 52 vacancies	1M, 2F, £5,000, vacancies
l.	Tribunal cases received	–	–	–
m.	Tribunal cases disposed of	–	–	–

* Non-medical workforce census at (30.9.97) for NHS Hospital and Community Health Services. Excludes medical/dental staff and agency nurses.
† Source : 1996/97 NHS (England) Summarised Accounts.
‡ Total operating expenses.
§ Not directly funded. Funding via Health Commissioners.
¶ Includes basic salary and performance bonuses only.

* Non-medical workforce census at (30.9.97) for NHS Hospital and Community Health Services. Excludes medical/dental staff and agency nurses.
† Source : 1996/97 NHS (England) Summarised Accounts.
‡ Final cash limits March 1997.
¶ Includes basic salary and performance bonuses only.

* Total paid for 2 Chief Executives who held post during year.

National Health Service Bodies

Special Health Authorities

	56	57	58	59	60
	The Broadmoor Hospital Authority	**Dental Vocational Training Authority**	**Family Health Services Appeal Authority**	**Health Education Authority**	**Mental Health Act Commission**
	Crowthorne Berkshire RG45 7EG	Masters House, Temple Grove Compton Place Eastbourne BN20 8AD	30 Victoria Avenue Harrogate HG1 5PH	Trevelyan House 30 Great Peter Street London SW1P 2HW	Maid Marion house 56 Hounds Gate Nottingham NG1 6BG
TEL	01344 773111	01323 431189	01423 530280	0171 222 5300	0115 943 7100
FAX	01344 754388	01323 433432	01423 522034	0171 413 8900	0115 943 7101
				http://www.hea.org.uk	
CHAIR	Ms Sheila Drew Smith	Mr Colin Forsyth	Mr Alan Crute	Mr Tony Close	Viscountess Runciman
		SECRETARY: Ms Jane Verity	CHIEF EXECUTIVE: Mr David Laverick	CHIEF EXECUTIVE: Mr Seymour Fortescue	CHIEF EXECUTIVE: Mr William Bingley
TERMS OF REFERENCE	One of three special hospitals which provide psychiatric services for the whole of England and Wales for patients who require treatment under conditions of high security.	To allocate dental vocational training numbers on behalf of health authorities in England and Wales.	To deal with appeals against decisions of Health Authorities under the NHS (Pharmaceutical) Regulations and the NHS (Service Committee) Regulations.	Advises the Secretary of State for Health on Health Education; public campaigns; sponsoring research; publishing material; providing a national centre of information and health education	To protect the interests of patients detained under the Mental Health Act in England and Wales.
a	–	–	–	–	–
b	1,080	2	16	249	24
c	Body	Body	Body	Body	Body*
d	–	–	–	–	–
e	£42.229m	£0.074m	£1.344m	£36.452m	£2.804m
f	£41.349m	£0.074m	£1.245m	£33.872	£2.755m
g	–	–	–	–	–
h	£78,000	–	£74,000	£96,283	£54,000
i	1F, £17,145	1F, £183.50pm	1M, £10,085	1M, £20.925	1F, £199pd
j	–	–	–	–	1M, £199pd
k	3M, 2F, £5,000	20M, 3F, 17 vacancies GDPs, £183.50pm Others, £109.50pm	1M, 1F, £5,000 1 vacancy	8M, 1F, £5,000*	Commissioners: 49M, 34F, £193 or 171pd, 2 vacancies Visiting Members: 35M, 43F, £89pd 20 vacancies
l	–	–	–	–	–
m	–	–	–	–	–

* Operating with nine members but can have up to nineteen.

* Report published biennielly.

DEPARTMENT OF HEALTH : NHS BODIES

National Health Service Bodies

Special Health Authorities

61 Microbiological Research Authority

Centre for Applied Microbiology and Research
Porton Road, Salisbury
Wiltshire SP4 0JG
TEL : 01980 612100
FAX : 01980 610166
bdd@camr.org.uk
http://www.camr.gov.uk
CHAIR : Mr Jim Everitt
SECRETARY : Mr Mike Harker
TERMS OF REFERENCE : To conduct research on specified microbiological hazards, with the view to the development and production of effective diagnostic prophylactic and therapeutic products.

a	–
b	377
c	Body
d	–
e	£19.197m
f	£5.386m
g	–
h	£95,731*
i	1M, £15,125
j	–
k	4M, 1F, £5,000†
l	–
m	–

62 National Blood Authority

Oak House
Reeds Crescent
Watford
Herts WD1 1QH
TEL : 01923 486800
FAX : 01923 486801
submissions@nbs.nhs.uk
http://www.blooddonor.org.uk
CHAIR : Mr Mike Fogdon
DIRECTOR OF FINANCE & ADMINISTRATION : Mr Barry Savery
TERMS OF REFERENCE : The Authority's principal task is the strategic planning and management of the blood supplies in England. The Authority aims to ensure high standards of safety, quality and cost-efficiency.

a	–
b	4,554
c	Body
d	–
e	£207.619m*
f	£11.486m
g	–
h	£89,000
i	1M, £17,936
j	–
k	3M, 1F, £5,000 1 vacancy
l	–
m	–

63 National Health Service Litigation Authority

5 Pemberton Row
London
EC4A 3BA
TEL : 0171 936 4400
FAX : 0171 583 1920
CHAIR : Sir Bruce Martin QC
CHIEF EXECUTIVE : Mr Stephen Walker
TERMS OF REFERENCE : The Authority's principal task to administer schemes set up under Section 21 of the National Health Service and Community Care Act 1990, to handle claims for clinical negligence against NHS bodies.

a	–
b	25
c	–
d	–
e	£5.892m
f	£5.481m
g	–
h	£81,614
i	1M, £19,285
j	–
k	2M, £5,000
l	–
m	–

64 National Health Service Supplies Authority

Premier House
60 Caversham Road
Reading
RG1 7EB
TEL : 0118 980 8600
FAX : 0118 980 8650
http://www.supplies.nhs.uk
CHAIR : Mr David Hall ; CHIEF EXECUTIVE : Mr Terry Hunt CBE
TERMS OF REFERENCE : The Authority's principal role is to enable the NHS to obtain the maximum possible benefit from the money it spends on the goods and services it requires for the delivery of health care. The Authority aims to be the NHS's own supplies centre of expertise, knowledge and excellence.

a	–
b	3,345
c	Body
d	–
e	£587.949m
f	–
g	–
h	£112,000
i	1M, £21,000
j	–
k	3M, 1F, £5,000 1 vacancy
l	–
m	–

65 Prescription Pricing Authority

Bridge House
152 Pilgrim Street
Newcastle Upon Tyne
NE1 6SN
TEL : 0191 232 5371
FAX : 0191 2322480
http://www.ppa.org.uk
CHAIR : Mr J C MacFarlane CBE
CHIEF EXECUTIVE : Mr A Hilton
TERMS OF REFERENCE : The Prescription Pricing Authority (PPA) main functions: calculate sums due to dispensers for prescriptions dispensed in England; provide information on NHS prescribing; administer the NHS Low Income Scheme; detect and follow up prescription fraud.

a	–
b	1,844
c	Body
d	–
e	£43.465m
f	£42.280m
g	–
h	£68,281
i	1M, £15,125
j	–
k	3M, 3F, £5,000
l	–
m	–

* Total paid for 2 Chief Executives who held post.
† Operating with five members but can have up to ten.

* Additional Department of Health costs of £0.112m.

National Health Service Bodies

Special Health Authorities

66 Rampton Hospital Authority

Retford
Nottinghamshire
DN22 0PD

TEL : 01777 248321
FAX : 01777 248442
CHAIR : Mr Philip Champ
SECRETARY : Mrs Sheila Foley
TERMS OF REFERENCE : One of three special hospitals which provide psychiatric services for the whole of England and Wales, for patients who require treatment under conditions of high security.

a	–
b	1,368
c	Body
d	–
e	£43.149m
f	£42.047m
g	–
h	£79,000
i	1M, £17,145
j	–
k	3M, 2F, £5,000
l	–
m	–

67 United Kingdom Transplant Support Service Authority

Fox Den Road
Stoke Gifford
Bristol
BS34 8RR

TEL : 0117 975 7575
FAX : 0117 975 7577
CHAIR : Mr John Shaw
SECRETARY : Mrs Robina Balderson
TERMS OF REFERENCE : Assisting in, and facilitating or promoting, the provision of a service for the transplantation of organs.

a	–
b	95
c	Body
d	–
e	£5.953m
f	£5.591m
g	–
h	£65,923
i	1M, £10,085
j	–
k	4M, £2,500
l	–
m	–

Other NHS Bodies

68 Dental Practice Board

Compton Place Road
Eastbourne
East Sussex
BN20 8AD

TEL : 01323 417000
FAX : 1323 433517
webmaster@dentanet.org.uk
http://www.dentanet.org.uk
CHAIR : Mr Colin Forsyth
CHIEF EXECUTIVE : Mr John Taylor
TERMS OF REFERENCE : To prevent and detect fraud and abuse within the General Dental Services and to approve the payment and estimate claims received from GDS dentists.

a	–
b	497
c	Body
d	–
e	£23.229m
f	£22.628m
g	–
h	£70,651
i	1M, £28,132*
j	1M, £160pd
k	3M, 2F, £160pd
l	–
m	–

* Plus £269.87 per extra day worked.

69 Appeal Board (DVTA)

Department of Health
Room 325a, Richmond House
79 Whitehall
London SW1A 2NS

TEL : 0117 210 7563
FAX : 0117 210 5774
CHAIR : Mr Alan Parsons
SECRETARY : Mrs Andrea Goring
TERMS OF REFERENCE : To hear appeals from dentists against decisions of the Dental Vocational Trading Authority.

a	–
b	–
c	*
d	–
e	£0.0002m
f	£0.0002m
g	–
h	–
i	1M, £286pd
j	–
k	7M, 1F, 2 vacancies
l	–
m	–

* Included in the report of the Dental Vocational Training Authority.

Home Office

Room 302, Horseferry House,
Dean Ryle Street, London SW1P 2AW

Enquiries   David Williams
Telephone   0171 217 8485
Facsimile   0171 217 8180
Internet   http://www.homeoffice.gov.uk

GTN   217 8485

Executive NPDBs

1 Alcohol Education and Research Council

Room 520
Clive House
Petty France
London SW1H 9HD
TEL : 0171 271 8379
FAX : 0171 271 8877
CHAIR : Baroness Flather
SECRETARY : Mr Leonard Hay
TERMS OF REFERENCE : To administer the Alcohol Education and Research Fund which is available to finance educational and research projects within the United Kingdom relating to alcohol misuse and to provide novel forms of help to those with drinking problems.

2 Commission for Racial Equality

Elliot House
10–12 Allington Street
London
SW1E 5EH
TEL : 0171 828 7022
FAX : 0171 630 7605
CHAIR : Sir Herman Ouseley
TERMS OF REFERENCE : Working towards the elimination of racial discrimination and promoting equality of opportunity and good relations between people of different racial groups.

3 Community Development Foundation*

60 Highbury Grove
London
N5 2AG
TEL : 0171 226 5375
FAX : 0171 704 0313
106043.1620@compuserve.com
http://www.vois.org.uk/edf
CHAIR : Mr Eddie O'Hara MP
TERMS OF REFERENCE : Develops and promotes informal activity in local communities not usually reached by the agencies concerned with more formal volunteering.

		1	2	3
a.	Number if a multiple body (1.4.98)	–	–	–
b.	Number of staff employed by the body (1.4.98)	1.5	210	37
c.	Annual Report	Body	Body	Body
d.	Audit arrangements	Y	X	Y
e.	Total gross expenditure of body (1997/98)	£0.448m	£15.067m	£1.660m
f.	Amount funded by government (1997/98)	–	£14.68m*	£0.902m
g.	Other expenditure by sponsoring dept (1997/98)	£0.008m	£0.095m	£0.009m
h.	Chief Executive's Remuneration (1997/98)	–	†	£43,363
	Appointments and Remuneration (1.9.98)			
i.	Chairman/President	1F	1M, £80,490†	1M
j.	Deputy	–	1M, £9,805§	1M
k.	Members	10M, 4F	8M, 3F, £136pd	7M, 4F
l.	Tribunal cases received	–	–	–
m.	Tribunal cases disposed of	–	–	–

* Excluding pension payments to ex-chairmen.
† Chairman also acts as Chief Executive.
§ Works 1 day a week.

* Responsibility for the sponsorship of this body transferred from the Department of Culture, Media and Sport to the Home Office on 1 May 1997.

HOME OFFICE

Executive NDPBs

4
Criminal Cases Review Commission

21st Floor, Alpha Tower
Suffolk Street
Queensway
Birmingham B1 1TT
TEL : 0121 633 1800
FAX : 0121 633 1823/1804
ccrc@gtnet.gov.uk
CHAIR : Sir Frederick Crawford
CHIEF EXECUTIVE : Mrs Glenys Stacey
TERMS OF REFERENCE : To investigate suspected miscarriages of justice in England, Wales and Northern Ireland, and refer appropriate cases to the courts.

5
Criminal Injuries Compensation Authority (CICA)

Morley House
26–30 Holborn Viaduct
London
EC1A 1JQ*
TEL : 0171 842 6800
FAX : 0171 436 0804
CHIEF EXECUTIVE : Mr Peter Spurgeon
TERMS OF REFERENCE : To determine payment to victims of crimes of violence and to persons injured while attempting to apprehend an offender, attempting to prevent the committing of an offence, or assisting the police in one of the foregoing.

6
Gaming Board for Great Britain

Berkshire House
168–173 High Holborn
London
WC1V 7AA
TEL : 0171 306 6200
FAX : 0171 306 6266
CHAIR : Mr Peter Dean CBE
TERMS OF REFERENCE : The Board is the regulatory body for casinos, bingo clubs, gaming machines and for larger lotteries (including all local authority lotteries) in Great Britain.

7
Horserace Betting Levy Board

52 Grosvenor Gardens
London
SW1W 0AU
TEL : 0171 333 0043
FAX : 0171 333 0041
hblb@hblb.org.uk
http://www.hblb.org.uk
CHAIR : Mr Robert Hughes
TERMS OF REFERENCE : To assess and collect a levy on bets on horse racing; and to distribute it for the benefit of horse-racing.

8
Horserace Totalisator Board (The Tote)

Tote House
74 Upper Richmond Road
Putney
London SW15 2SU
TEL : 0181 874 6411
htb@tote.co.uk
http://www.tote.co.uk
CHAIR : Mr Peter Jones
TERMS OF REFERENCE : The Tote is a commercial betting operation whose aims are to provide a full betting service to its customers and financial support to racing. It has, by statute, the exclusive right to run pool betting on horse racing.

	4	5	6	7	8
a	–	–	–	–	–
b	47	458†	69	26	862*
c	Body	Cm	HC	Body	Body
d	X	X	X	Y	Y
e	£4.104m*	£222.466m‡	£3.431m	£57.628m	£44.078m
f	£4.104m	£222.466m	£3.318m	–	–
g	£1.891m†	£0.100m	£0.044m	£0.021m	£0.034m
h	£102,648	£57,268	£55,694	£115,680	£115,000
i	1M, £98,638	–	1M, £37,105	1M, £45,000*	1M, £78,225†
j	–	–	–	1M, £17,300	–
k	4M, £62,100 / 3M, 2F, £37,260 / 4M, £24,840	–	4M, £14,875	1M, £13,500	7M, £9,000
l	–	–	–	–	–
m	–	–	–	–	–

* For the fifteen months ended 31 March 1998 which was the commission's first accounting period.
† This figure represents start-up costs and direct expenditure on IT.

* Also at: Tay House, 300 Bath Street, Glasgow, G2 4JR.
† Includes staff working in parallel on or an earlier scheme in the Criminal Injuries Compensation Board.
‡ Includes expenditure by the Criminal Injuries Compensation Board and the Criminal Injuries Compensation Appeal Panel.

* Works 3 days a week.

* Each part-time employee has been counted as a half. Casual and supplementary employees are not included.
† Works 4 days a week.

75

HOME OFFICE

Executive NDPBs

Advisory NDPBs

9 Office of the Data Protection Registrar

Wycliffe House
Water Lane
Wilmslow
Chesire SK9 5AF
TEL : 01625 545745
FAX : 01625 524510
data@wycliffe.demon.co.uk
WEB: http://www.open.gov.uk/dpr/dprhome/htm
REGISTRAR: Mrs Elizabeth France
TERMS OF REFERENCE : Supervision and enforcement of the Data Protection Act 1984, which establishes a statutory framework for the use of computerised information about identifiable individuals.

10 Parole Board

Abell House
John Islip Street
London
SW1P 4LH
TEL : 0171 217 5314
FAX : 0171 217 5677
CHAIR : Ms Usha Prashar
CHIEF EXECUTIVE : Mr Mike Todd
TERMS OF REFERENCE : To advise the Home Secretary on the release of both determinate and life sentence prisoners and on the recall to prison of anyone so released coming to adverse notice while on license. In addition, the Board may direct the release of a discretionary life sentence prisoner, and takes decisions on the granting of parole.

11 Police Complaints Authority

10 Great George Street
London
SW1P 3AE
TEL : 0171 273 6450
FAX : 0171 273 6401
http://www.coi.gov.uk/coi/depts/deptlist.htm
CHAIR : Mr Peter Moorhouse
TERMS OF REFERENCE : The Police Complaints Authority is the independent body established to oversee public complaints against police officers.

12 Police Information Technology Organisation (PITO)

Horseferry House
Dean Ryle Street
London
SW1P 2AW
TEL : 0181 358 5367
FAX : 0181 358 5534
eva.rak@pito.org
http://www.pito.org.uk
CHAIR : Sir Trefor Morris CBE, QPM, CI Mgt ; CHIEF EXECUTIVE : Joan MacNaughton
TERMS OF REFERENCE : To develop and manage the delivery of national information technology systems in support of the police, to co-ordinate the development of local IT systems, and to provide a procurement service to police forces.

13 Advisory Board on Restricted Patients

Mental Health Unit
Home Office
50 Queen Anne's Gate
London SW1H 9AT
TEL : 0171 273 4153
FAX : 0171 273 2172
CHAIR : Judge Elisabeth Fisher
SECRETARY : Mrs Jennifer Morris
TERMS OF REFERENCE : To provide the Home Secretary with independent advice to assist with decisions about the discharge or transfer between hospitals of those patients who are subject to special restrictions and whose potential risk to public safety is thought to be particularly difficult to assess.

	9	10	11	12	13
a	–	–	–	–	–
b	108.5	44	53	325	–
c	HC	HC	HC	Body	NP
d	X	X	X	X	–
e	£3.660m	£2.5m*	£3.503m	*	–
f	£3.657m	£2.5m	£3.503m	*	–
g	£0.020m	£0.820m	£0.010m	*	£0.043m
h	–	£48,030		*	–
i	1F, £63,549	1F, £56,100	1M, £75,745	1M, £41,814	1F
j	–	1M†	1M, £54,000	–	–
k	–	62M, 32F‡	4M, 6F, £46,160	1M, £259pd 11M	2M, 3F, 2 vacancies £225 per hospital visit £450pm
l	–	–	–	–	–
m	–	–	–	–	–

* Expenditure calculated on an accruals basis.
† Vice-chairman is a serving high court judge and receives no remuneration.
‡ Includes 1 full-time member and 93 part-time members. Remuneration for full-time member, £35,654. Fees for part-time members: retired judges £332pd; psychiatrist £245pd; independents, criminologists and probation members £157pd.

* PITO took on its full range of responsibilities from 1.4.98.

76

HOME OFFICE

Advisory NDPBs

14
Advisory Council on the Misuse of Drugs

Room 243
Home Office
50 Queen Anne's Gate
London SW1H 9AT
TEL : 0171 273 2994
FAX : 0171 273 2671
CHAIR : Professor David Grahame-Smith CBE
SECRETARY : Mr Richard Rhodes
TERMS OF REFERENCE : To keep under review the problems of drug misuse in the United Kingdom and to advise Ministers on ways of dealing with them.

15
Animal Procedures Committee

Animals, Byelaws and Coroners Unit, Home Office
50 Queen Anne's Gate
London SW1H 9AT
TEL : 0171 273 2861
FAX : 0171 273 2029
CHAIR : The Reverend Professor Michael Banner ; SECRETARY : Mr Steven Wilkes
TERMS OF REFERENCE : To advise the Secretaries of State for the Home Office and Northern Ireland Offices on: the use of living animals in scientific procedures which may cause those animals pain, suffering, distress or lasting harm; and their duties under the terms of the Animals (Scientific Procedures) Act 1986.

16
Crime Prevention Agency Board*†

Room 571
Queen Anne's Gate
London
SW1H 9AT
TEL : 0171 273 3113
CHAIR : Mr Alun Michael MP‡
SECRETARY : Mr Barrie Hartley
TERMS OF REFERENCE : The Board advises Ministers on effective crime prevention strategies and co-ordinates crime prevention activities. It includes authorities and businesses.

17
Firearms Consultative Committee

Room 543
Home Office
50 Queen Anne's Gate
London SW1H 9AT
TEL : 0171 273 2184
FAX : 0171 273 4284
CHAIR : The Earl of Shrewsbury and Talbot ; SECRETARY : Mr Richard Worth
TERMS OF REFERENCE : To keep under review the controls on firearms, to make recommendations to the Home Secretary as to how these may be improved, and to advise him on matters which he may refer to Committee.

18
Metropolitan Police Committee

Room 706
Clive House
Petty France
London SW1H 9HD
TEL : 0171 271 8361
FAX : 0171 271 8369
mpc@gtnet.gov.uk
http://www.mpc.homeoffice.gov.uk/mpcar.htm
CHAIR : Sir John Quinton
SECRETARY : Mr Peter Honour
TERMS OF REFERENCE : To advise the Home Secretary on the exercise of his functions in his capacity as the Authority responsible for the Metropolitan Police.

	14	15	16	17	18
a	–	–	–	–	–
b	–	–	–	–	–
c	NP	Cm	NP	Cm	TSO
d	–	–	–	–	–
e	–	–	–	–	–
f	–	–	–	–	–
g	£0.021m	£0.020m	£0.004m	£0.033m	£0.355m
h	–	–	–	–	–
i	1M*	1M, £200pd	‡	1M	1M
j	–	–	–	–	–
k	24M, 8F†	10M, 7F	7M	12M, 1F	14M, 6F
l	–	–	–	–	–
m	–	–	–	–	–

* New membership to be appointed from 1.11.98.
† New Membership to be appointed from 1.1.99.

* Replaced the National Board for Crime Prevention in November 1995.
† The Board is currently in abeyance awaiting formal abolition.
‡ Minister of State, Home Office.

HOME OFFICE

Advisory NDPBs

Tribunal NDPBs

19 Parliamentary Boundary Commission for England

Room RG/11
1 Drummond Gate
London
SW1V 2QQ
TEL : 0171 533 5177
FAX : 0171 533 5176
gerald.tessier@ons.gov.uk
http://www.coi.gov.uk/coi/depts/gbo/gbo.html
CHAIR : Rt Hon Betty Boothroyd MP* ; JOINT SECRETARIES : Mr Robert Farrance and Mr Stephen Limpkin
TERMS OF REFERENCE : To keep under continuous review the representation of England in the House of Commons and to submit to the Home Secretary reports with recommendations for constituencies.

a	–
b	–
c	Body
d	–
e	–
f	–
g	£0.585m
h	–
i	{1F}*
j	1M
k	2M, £360pd
l	–
m	–

* Ex officio as Speaker of the House of Commons.

20 Parliamentary Boundary Commission for Wales

Room RG/11
1 Drummond Gate
London
SW1V 2QQ
TEL : 0171 533 5177
FAX : 0171 533 5176
terry.bergin@ons.gov.uk
http://www.coi.gov.uk/coi/depts/gbw/gbw.html
CHAIR : Rt Hon Betty Boothroyd MP* ; JOINT SECRETARIES : Mr Robert Farrance and Mr Stephen Limpkin
TERMS OF REFERENCE : To keep under continuous review the representation of Wales in the House of Commons and to submit to the Home Secretary reports with recommendations for constituencies and for representation of the regions in the Welsh Assembly.

a	–
b	–
c	Body
d	–
e	–
f	–
g	£0.065m
h	–
i	{1F}*
j	1M
k	1M, 1F, £360pd
l	–
m	–

* Ex officio as Speaker of the House of Commons.

21 Poisons Board

Home Office
50 Queen Anne's Gate
London
SW1H 9AT
TEL : 0171 273 3627
CHAIR : Vacant
SECRETARY : Ms Linda Ward
TERMS OF REFERENCE : To advise the Home Secretary on matters relating to non-medicinal poisons.

a	–
b	–
c	NP
d	–
e	–
f	–
g	–
h	–
i	1 vacancy*
j	–
k	*
l	–
m	–

* The Chairman retired in June 1992. A new chairman has yet to be appointed. Membership fell into abeyance during Summer 1993. The Board will be reappointed and will have 17 members.

22 Police Negotiating Board

Office of Manpower Economics
Oxford House
76 Oxford Street
London W1N 9FD
TEL : 0171 636 1742 ext 7218
CHAIR : Professor Sir Lawrence Hunter CBE ; SECRETARY : Mrs Elizabeth Santry
TERMS OF REFERENCE : To consider questions relating to hours of duty; leave; pay and allowances; pensions; on the issue, use and return of police clothing, personal equipment and accoutrements.

a	–
b	–
c	NP
d	–
e	–
f	–
g	£0.750m
h	–
i	1M, £158pd
j	1M, £126pd
k	{54M, 4F}
l	–
m	–

23 Criminal Injuries Compensation Appeals Panel (CICAP)*

5th Floor, Morley House
26–30 Holborn Viaduct
London
EC1A 1JQ
TEL : 0171 583 0870
FAX : 0171 842 6983
CHAIR : Michael Lewer QC
SECRETARY : Miss Valerie Jenson
TERMS OF REFERENCE : To determine appeals by applicants for criminal injuries compensation. The panel is concerned only with appeals from applicants to the Criminal Injuries Compensation Authority which were received on and after 1 April 1996.

a	–
b	–
c	Cm
d	–
e	–
f	–
g	£0.005m
h	–
i	1M, £37,930
j	–
k	39M, 12F, £312pd
l	2,894
m	1,436

* The Criminal Injuries Compensation Appeals Panel (CICAP) was established on 1.4.96 when the 1996 Criminal Injuries Compensation Scheme came into effect under the Criminal Injuries Compensation Act 1985. The Criminal Injuries Compensation Board administers the earlier, non-statutory scheme.

Tribunal NDPBs

24
Criminal Injuries Compensation Board (CICB)

Morley House
26–30 Holborn Viaduct
London
EC1A 1JQ*

TEL : 0171 842 6800
FAX : 0171 436 0804

CHAIR : Rt Hon Lord Carlisle of Bucklow QC

TERMS OF REFERENCE :
Established administratively in 1964. The Criminal Injuries Compensation Board deals with applications for criminal injuries compensation lodged before 1 April 1996 and provides ex-gratia payments of compensation to blameless victims of crimes of violence.

25
Data Protection Tribunal

Room 1171
Home Office
50 Queen Anne's Gate
London SW1H 9AT

TEL : 0171 273 3492
FAX : 0171 273 3205

CHAIR : Mr John Spokes QC ;
SECRETARY : Mr David Anderson

TERMS OF REFERENCE :
Established in 1985 under the Data Protection Act 1984. To determine appeals against the enforcement decisions of the Data Protection registrar.

26
Horserace Betting Levy Appeal Tribunal for England and Wales*

c/o Tavistock House South
Tavistock Square
London
WC1H 9LS

TEL : 0171 383 7111
FAX : 0171 383 7117

CHAIR : Mr Thomas Brundell QC
SECRETARY : Mr Andrew Lockhart-Mirams

TERMS OF REFERENCE : To hear appeals from bookmakers regarding the amount of levy payable to the Horserace Betting Levy Board.

27
Interception of Communications Tribunal

PO Box 12376
London
SW1P 1XU

TEL : 0171 273 4096

CHAIR : Hon Sir William Macpherson of Cluny
SECRETARY : Mr E Wilson

TERMS OF REFERENCE : To investigate complaints relating to the interceptions of communications.

28
Misuse of Drugs Advisory Board

Home Office
50 Queen Anne's Gate
London
SW1H 9AT

TEL : 0171 273 3302

CHAIR : Miss J Southworth
SECRETARY : Mr John Glaze

TERMS OF REFERENCE : To hear representations made by a practitioner against a proposed direction prohibiting him from prescribing a particular controlled drug or drugs; and to advise the Home Secretary.

	24	25	26	27	28
a	–	–	–	–	–
b	–	–	–	–	–
c	Cm	NP	NP	NP	NP
d	–	–	–	–	–
e	–	–	–	–	–
f	–	–	–	–	–
g	£0.100m	£0.019m	£0.001m	£0.022m	–
h	–	–	–	–	–
i	1M, £37,930	1M*, £377pd	1M, £265pd†	1M, £316pd	1F, £353pd
j	–	2M*, £295pd	–	1M, 316pd	–
k	43M, 5F, £312pd £35pc	23M, 8F, £212pd	1M, 1F, £169pd	3M, £316pd	£242pd*
l	–	3	–	79*	–
m	21,730†	1	–	93*	–

* Also at: Tay House, 300 Bath Street, Glasgow, G2 4JR.
† Cases resolved. Includes 11,829 cases resolved by hearing.

* Appointed by the Lord Chancellor's Department.

* Financed by the Horserace Betting Levy Board.
† Appointed by Lord Chancellor.

* 1997 Calender Year.

* These are chosen from a pool of 39 doctors.

HOME OFFICE

Tribunal NDPBs

29 Misuse of Drugs Professional Panel

Home Office
50 Queen Anne's Gate
London
SW1H 9AT
TEL : 0171 273 3302
CHAIR : Mr John Glaze
TERMS OF REFERENCE : To consider a case against a practitioner who is suspected of irresponsible prescribing.

30 Misuse of Drugs Tribunal

Home Office
50 Queen Anne's Gate
London
SW1H 9AT
TEL : 0171 273 3302
CHAIR : Mrs H Sarkany
SECRETARY : Mr John Glaze
TERMS OF REFERENCE : To consider a case against a practitioner who is suspected of contravening the regulations relating to controlled drugs or of prescribing irresponsibly.

31 Police Arbitration Tribunal

ACAS
26 Wilton Street
London
SW1X 7AZ
TEL : 0171 210 3625
CHAIR : Professor Sir John Crossley Wood CBE ; SECRETARY : Mr Simon Gouldstone
TERMS OF REFERENCE : Where the Police Negotiating Board has failed to agree on a recommendation, and where any attempt at reconciliation has not resulted in an agreed recommendation between the Staff Side and the Official Side, the dispute will, at the request of either Side, be referred to the Police Arbitration Tribunal.

32 Police Discipline Appeals Tribunal*

Police Personnel and Training Unit, Room 53 IA, The Home Office, 50 Queen Anne's Gate, London SW1H 9AT
TEL : 0171 273 4043
FAX : 0171 273 2501
TERMS OF REFERENCE : To enquire into and report on any appeal referred by the Home Secretary in respect of Police discipline against an officer.

33 Security Service Tribunal

PO Box 18
London
SE1 0TZ
TEL : 0171 273 4095
CHAIR : Rt Hon Lord Justice Simon Brown ;
SECRETARY : Mr E Wilson
TERMS OF REFERENCE : To investigate complaints about the Security Service. Any individual or organisation can complain to the Tribunal about anything they believe the Security Service has done to them or to their property.

	29	30	31	32	33
a	–	–	–	–	–
b	–	–	–	–	–
c	NP	NP	NP	–	NP
d	–	–	–	–	–
e	–	–	–	–	–
f	–	–	–	–	–
g	–	£0.018m	£0.001m	–	£0.022m
h	–	–	–	–	–
i	1, £242pd*	1F, £281pd	1M, £279pd	11M, 4F, £377pd	1M[†]
j	–	–	–	–	1M, £316pd
k	£172pd*	£242pd*	2M, £153pd	27M, 1F, £169pd	1M, £316pd
l	–	–	1	81	81*
m	–	–	–	73	73*

* These are chosen from a pool of 39 doctors. (29)
* These are chosen from a pool of 39 doctors. (30)
* Convened on an ad hoc basis. The figures in rows 'i' and 'k' are the number of individuals on the panels from which appointments are made. (32)
* 1997 Calender Year.
† Not paid. Expenses only.

Other Bodies

34
Boards of Visitors to Penal Establishments

Boards of Vistitors Secretariat
3rd Floor, Horseferry House
Dean Ryle Street
London SW1P 2AW
TEL : 0171 217 8292
FAX : 0171 217 8596
DIRECTOR : Mr Delbert Sandiford
TERMS OF REFERENCE : The role of Boards of Vistors has been described as that of independent 'watchdogs' of the prison system. Their duty is to satisfy themselves as to the state of the prison premises, their administration and the treatment of prisoners.

HOME OFFICE

a	133
b	–
c	Body
d	–
e	–
f	–
g	£0.852m
h	–
i	79M, 53F
j	80M, 52F
k	775M, 723F
l	–
m	–

INLAND REVENUE

Inland Revenue

Somerset House, Strand,
London WC2R 1LB

Enquiries	Sue Wiles
Telephone	0171 438 6059
Facsimile	0171 438 6601
Internet	http://www.inlandrevenue.gov.uk
GTN	3541 6059

Tribunal NDPBs

1
Section 706 Tribunal

VAT Tribunals
15–19 Bedford Avenue
London
WC1B 3AS
TEL : 0171 323 9156
FAX : 0171 323 9156
CHAIR : His Honour Stephen Oliver QC ; REGISTRAR : Mr Gerraint Jones OBE
TERMS OF REFERENCE : To hear appeals arising under section 706 of the Income and Corporation Taxes Act.

a.	Number if a multiple body/system (1.4.98)	–
b.	Number of staff employed by the body (1.4.98)	–
c.	Annual Report	NP
d.	Audit arrangements	–
e.	Total gross expenditure of body (1997/98)	–
f.	Amount funded by government (1997/98)	–
g.	Other expenditure by sponsoring dept (1997/98)	£0.003m
h.	Chief Executive's Remuneration (1997/98)	–
	Appointments and Remuneration (1.9.98)	
i.	Chairman/President	1M, £900*
j.	Deputy	–
k.	Members	7M, 1F, £500
l.	Tribunal cases received	1
m.	Tribunal cases disposed of	1

* £900 may be paid, but present Chairman is a member of the judiciary in receipt of a full-time salary and therefore cannot receive fees for other part-time judicial appointments.

DEPARTMENT FOR INTERNATIONAL DEVELOPMENT

Department for International Development

94 Victoria Street, London SW1E 5JL

Enquiries David Richards
Telephone 0171 917 0833
Facsimile 0171 917 0686
E-mail d-richards@dfid.gtnet.gov.uk
Internet http://www.dfid.gov.uk

GTN 3535 0833

Public Corporations

1 Commonwealth Development Corporation

1 Bessborough Gardens
London
SW1V 2JQ
TEL : 0171 828 4488
FAX : 0171 828 6505
rbagley@cdc.co.uk
http://www.cdc.co.uk
CHAIR : Rt Hon Earl Cairns CBE
CHIEF EXECUTIVE : Dr Roy Reynolds
TERMS OF REFERENCE : The Corporation is the UK's leading international development finance institution charged with the task of assisting overseas countries in the development of their economies.

Executive NDPBs

2 Commonwealth Scholarship Commission in the United Kingdom

John Foster House
36 Gordon Square
London
WC1H 0PF
TEL : 0171 387 8572
FAX : 0171 387 2655
awards@acu.ac.uk
http://www.acu.ac.uk
CHAIR : Mr Geoffrey Caston CBE
DEPUTY CHAIR : Professor Berrick Saul CBE
TERMS OF REFERENCE : The Commission was set up under the Commonwealth Scholarship Act 1959 as the body responsible for the United Kingdom's participation in the Commonwealth. Scholarship and Fellowship Plan.

3 Crown Agents Holding and Realisation Board

St Nicholas House
St Nicholas Road
Sutton
Surrey SM1 1EL
TEL : 0181 643 3311
FAX : 0181 643 6518
CHAIR : Mr David Probert
SECRETARIAT : Mrs Heather Kent
TERMS OF REFERENCE : The Board is a statutory corporation established under the Crown Agents Act 1979 to manage the orderly rundown of certain own-account activities of the Crown Agents prior to their incorporation.

		1	2	3
a.	Number if a multiple body/system (1.4.98)	–	–	–
b.	Number of staff employed by the body (1.4.98)	–	–	–
c.	Annual Report	Body	DFID	Body
d.	Audit arrangements	–	Y	X
e.	Total gross expenditure of body (1997/98)	–	£0.086m	£0.015m
f.	Amount funded by government (1997/98)	–	£0.086m	–
g.	Other expenditure by sponsoring dept (1997/98)	–	–	–
h.	Chief Executive's Remuneration (1997/98)	£153,762	–	–
	Appointments and Remuneration (1.9.98)			
i.	Chairman/President	1M, £30,000	1M	1M
j.	Deputy	1M, £9,000	1M	–
k.	Members	6M, 1F, £7,500	8M, 3F	2M
l.	Tribunal cases received	–	–	–
m.	Tribunal cases disposed of	–	–	–

DEPARTMENT FOR INTERNATIONAL DEVELOPMENT

Advisory NDPBs

4 Advisory Committee on Overseas Economic and Social Research

ESCOR
94 Victoria Street
London
SW1E 5JL
TEL : 0171 917 0432
FAX : 0171 917 0636
a-stirton@dfid.gtnet.gov.uk
http://www.dfid.gov.uk
CHAIR : Dr Andrew Goudie
SECRETARY : Ms Alfreda Stirton
TERMS OF REFERENCE : To provide research grants for high quality research activities, reflecting DFID's priorities. This involves the generation of new knowledge, informing policy and practice in, and develop partnerships with, the developing and transitional countries.

5 Development Awareness Working Group

c/o Information Department, DFID, Abercrombie House, Eaglesham Road, East Kilbride, Glasgow G75 8EA
TEL : 01355 843509
FAX : 01355 843539
f-burns@dfid.gtnet.gov.uk
CHAIR : Mr George Foulkes MP
TERMS OF REFERENCE : To advise DFID on how to increase its work in promoting awareness of development issues, both through the formal education sector and more broadly within society.

6 Indian Family Pensions Funds Body of Commissioners

c/o Overseas Pensions Dept, DFID, Abercrombie House, Eaglesham Road, East Kilbride, Glasgow G75 8EA
TEL : 01355 843515
FAX : 01355 843636
n-baxter@dfid.gtnet.gov.uk
CHAIR : Mr Richard Plumb
SECRETARY : Mr Nick Baxter
TERMS OF REFERENCE : To represent the interests of the subscribers and beneficiaries of the Indian Family Pensions (Transferred) (United Kingdom) Scheme 1985.

7 Know-How Fund Advisory Board

20 Victoria Street
London
SW1H 0NF
TEL : 0171 210 0079
FAX : 0171 210 0010
j-tudor@dfid.gtnet.gov.uk
CHAIR : Rt Hon Clare Short
SECRETARY : Mr Jeff Tudor
TERMS OF REFERENCE : The Know-How Fund (KHF) is Britain's programme of bilateral assistance to the countries of central and Eastern Europe and central Asia. The KHF Advisory Board advises on KHF policies and strategies for different countries and sectors.

8 Overseas Service Pensions Scheme Advisory Board

c/o Overseas Pensions Dept, DFID, Abercrombie House, Eaglesham Road, East Kilbride, Glasgow G75 8EA
TEL : 01355 843576
FAX : 01355 843636
a-macdonald@dfid.gtnet.gov.uk
CHAIR : Mr Richard Plumb
SECRETARY : Mr Alan MacDonald
TERMS OF REFERENCE : To advise the Parliamentary Under Secretary of State for International Development on the administration of the Overseas Service Pensions Scheme 1985 and to represent the interests of members.

	4	5	6	7	8
a	–	–	–	–	–
b	–	–	–	–	–
c	NP	NP	NP	Body*	NP
d	–	–	–	–	–
e	–	–	–	–	–
f	–	–	–	–	–
g	£0.001m	£0.002m	£0.001m	£0.001m	£0.001m
h	–	–	–	–	–
i	*	*	–	†	–
j	–	–	–	–	–
k	8M, 4F	14M, 8F	6M, 2F	15M, 4F	3M, 1F
l	–	–	–	–	–
m	–	–	–	–	–

* Chairman is Dr Andrew Goudie, DFID Chief Economist.

* Chairman is George Foulkes MP, Minister of State

* Know-How Fund Annual Report published by DFID.
† Chairman is Clare Short MP, Secretary of State.

Lord Chancellor's Department

Selborne House, 54–60 Victoria Street,
London   SW1E 6QW

Enquiries   Miss J D Halliday
Telephone   0171 210 8764
Facsimile   0171 210 8566
Internet   http://www.open.gov.uk/lcd

GTN   210 8764

Executive NDPBs

1. Authorised Conveyancing Practitioners Board

TERMS OF REFERENCE: The Board was established by the Courts and Legal Services Act 1990 and came into existence in April 1991. It has been inactive since March 1992, when the then Lord Chancellor announced his decision to postpone the implementation of the Authorised Practitioners Scheme.

2. Legal Aid Board

85 Gray's Inn Road
London
WC1X 8AA

TEL: 0171 813 1000
FAX: 0171 813 8638
http://www.open.gov.uk/lcd/lcdhome.htm
CHAIR: Sir Tim Chessells
SECRETARY: Ms Anne-Marie Roberts

TERMS OF REFERENCE: To ensure that advice, assistance and representation are available within the framework of the Legal Aid Act 1988. This includes responsibility for assessing and paying bills from suppliers of civil legal aid work and criminal work in Magistrates' Courts

Advisory NDPBs

3. Advisory Board on Family Law

Lord Chancellor's Department
Selborne House
54–60 Victoria Street
London SW1E 6QW

TEL: 0171 210 0642
CHAIR: Sir Thomas Boyd-Carpenter; SECRETARY: Mr Philip Dear

TERMS OF REFERENCE: To monitor the implementation of the Family Law Act 1996; and to advise the Lord Chancellor on matters arising from its implementation. The Board also maintains an overview of the working of the policies contained in the Children Act 1989 within the family court system.

		1. Authorised Conveyancing Practitioners Board	2. Legal Aid Board	3. Advisory Board on Family Law
a.	Number if a multiple body (1.4.98)	–	–	–
b.	Number of staff employed by the body (1.4.98)	–	1,358	–
c.	Annual Report	HC	Cm	Body
d.	Audit arrangements	Y	Y	–
e.	Total gross expenditure of body (1997/98)	–	£1,670m*	–
f.	Amount funded by government (1997/98)	–	£1,235m	–
g.	Other expenditure by sponsoring dept (1997/98)	–	£0.036m	£0.028m
h.	Chief Executive's Remuneration (1997/98)	–	£99,288	–
	Appointments and Remuneration (1.9.98)			
i.	Chairman/President	–	1M, £32,183	1M, £250pd
j.	Deputy	–	1M, £10,726	–
k.	Members	–	4M, 3F, £10,726†	5M, 6F
l.	Tribunal cases received	–	–	–
m.	Tribunal cases disposed of	–	–	–

* Expenditure on the Legal Aid Fund incurred by the Legal Aid Board and the Legal Aid Board's administration budget (£58m).
† Excludes two executive members (including the Chief Executive).

LORD CHANCELLOR'S DEPARTMENT

Advisory NDPBs

4
Advisory Committees on General Commissioners of Income Tax

c/o Selborne House
54–60 Victoria Street
London
SW1E 6QW
TEL : 0171 210 8990
FAX : 0171 210 0660

OFFICE OF THE SECRETARY OF COMMISSIONS : Miss Janet Skeates

TERMS OF REFERENCE : To select, for the Lord Chancellor's consideration, candidates with the qualities necessary for appointment as a General Commissioner of Income Tax. There are 76 Advisory Committees on General Commissioners of Income Tax covering England and Wales.

a	76
b	–
c	NP
d	–
e	–
f	–
g	£0.008m
h	–
i	69M, 6F
j	–
k	355M, 122F
l	–
m	–

5
Advisory Committees on General Commissioners of Income Tax (NI)

Northern Ireland Court Service, Windsor House,
9–15 Bedford Street,
Belfast BT2 7LT
TEL : 01232 328594
FAX : 01232 439110

ASSISTANT SECRETARY OF COMMISSIONS (NI) : Mrs Christine Doherty

TERMS OF REFERENCE : To select for the Lord Chancellor's consideration, candidates with the qualities necessary for appointment as a General Commissioner of Income Tax. There are two advisory Committees on General Commissioners of Income Tax covering Northern Ireland.

a	2
b	–
c	NP
d	–
e	–
f	–
g	£0.002m
h	–
i	2M
j	–
k	11M, 3F
l	–
m	–

6
Advisory Committees on Justices of the Peace in England and Wales

c/o Selborne House
54–60 Victoria Street
London
SW1E 6QW
TEL : 0171 210 8990
FAX : 0171 210 0660

OFFICE OF THE SECRETARY OF COMMISSIONS : Miss Janet Skeates

TERMS OF REFERENCE : To advise the Lord Chancellor on the appointment of Justices of the Peace in England and Wales. There are 94 Advisory Committees on Justices of the Peace in England and Wales.

a	94
b	–
c	NP
d	–
e	–
f	–
g	£0.379m
h	–
i	74M, 20F
j	–
k	490M, 428F
l	–
m	–

7
Advisory Committees on Justices of the Peace (Northern Ireland)

Northern Ireland Court Service, Windsor House,
9–15 Bedford Street,
Belfast BT2 7LT
TEL : 01232 328594
FAX : 01232 439110

ASSISTANT SECRETARY OF COMMISSIONS (NI) : Mrs Christine Doherty

TERMS OF REFERENCE : To advise the Lord Chancellor on the appointment of Justices of the Peace in Northern Ireland. There are eight Advisory Committees on Justices of the Peace in Northern Ireland.

a	8
b	–
c	NP
d	–
e	–
f	–
g	£0.010m
h	–
i	8M
j	–
k	32M, 14F
l	–
m	–

8
Advisory Committee on Juvenile Court Lay Panel (Northern Ireland)

Northern Ireland Court Service, Windsor House,
9–15 Bedford Street,
Belfast BT2 7LT
TEL : 01232 328594
FAX : 01232 439110

ASSISTANT SECRETARY OF COMMISSIONS (NI) : Mrs Christine Doherty

TERMS OF REFERENCE : To select for the Lord Chancellor's consideration candidates with the necessary judicial qualities for appointment as Juvenile Court lay panel members.

a	–
b	–
c	NP
d	–
e	–
f	–
g	£0.008m
h	–
i	1M
j	–
k	5M, 5F
l	–
m	–

LORD CHANCELLOR'S DEPARTMENT

Advisory NDPBs

	9	10	11	12	13
	Advisory Committee on Legal Education and Conduct	**Advisory Council on Public Records**	**Civil Justice Council**	**Civil Procedure Rule Committee**	**Council on Tribunals***
	8th Floor Millbank Tower Millbank London SW1P 4QU	Public Record Office Kew Richmond Surrey TW9 4DU	Selborne House 54–60 Victoria Street London SW1E 6QW	Selborne House 54–60 Victoria Street London SW1E 6QW	22 Kingsway London WC2B 6LE
	TEL : 0171 217 4280/4256 FAX : 0171 217 4283	TEL : 0181 876 3444 x2351 FAX : 0181 392 5295 tim.padfield@pro.gov.uk	TEL : 0171 210 8654	TEL : 0171 210 0730 FAX : 0171 210 0725	TEL : 0171 936 7045 FAX : 0171 936 7044
	CHAIR : Lord Justice Potter SECRETARY : Mr Rael Zackon	CHAIR : Rt Hon Lord Woolf (Master of the Rolls) SECRETARY : Mr Tim Padfield	CHAIR : Rt Hon Lord Woolf (Master of the Rolls) SECRETARY : Mrs Leanne Hedden	CHAIR : Rt Hon Lord Woolf (Master of the Rolls) COMMITTEE SECRETARY : Mr Michael Kron	CHAIR : Rt Hon Lord Archer of Sandwell PC QC ; SECRETARY : Mr Alastair Twort
	TERMS OF REFERENCE : Following the provision of advice to applicant bodies, the Committee advises the Lord Chancellor on applications from professional or other bodies seeking authorisation to grant to their members rights of audience or the right to conduct litigation.	TERMS OF REFERENCE : To advise the Lord Chancellor on matters concerning public records in general and, in particular, on those aspects of the work of the Public Record Office which affect members of public who make use of its facilities.	TERMS OF REFERENCE : To keep the Civil Justice system under review; to consider how to make the system more accessible, fair, and efficient: and to make recommendations.	TERMS OF REFERENCE : To make rules of procedure for the civil division of the Court of Appeal, the High Court and county courts. The Committee is at present operating concurrently with, but is intended to supersede, the Supreme Court Rule Committee and County Court Rule Committee.	TERMS OF REFERENCE : To advise on and keep under review the constitution and working of administrative tribunals, as well as to consider and report on administrative procedures involving statutory inquiries.
a	–	–	–	–	–
b	–	–	–	–	–
c	Cm	HC	*	NP	HC
d	–	–	–	–	–
e	–	–	–	–	–
f	–	–	–	–	–
g	£0.885m	£0.014m	£0.001m	£0.019m	£0.650m
h	–	–	–	–	–
i	1M	*	†	*	1M, £37,447 1M, £18,724
j	–	–	1M	–	–
k	11M, 3F, 366pd	10M, 6F	14M, 4F	9M, 3F	11M, 3F, £8,563 4F, £6,813
l	–	–	–	–	–
m	–	–	–	–	–

* Chairman is Master of the Rolls.
* At time of going to press the Council has not yet decided how to make available its Annual Report.
† Chairman is Master of the Rolls.
* Chairman is Master of the Rolls.
* Includes Scottish Committee of Council.

LORD CHANCELLOR'S DEPARTMENT

Advisory NDPBs

	14 County Court Rule Committee	15 Crown Court Rule Committee	16 Family Proceedings Rule Committee	17 Honorary Investment Advisory Committee	18 Insolvency Rules Committee*
Address	Selborne House, 54–60 Victoria Street, London SW1E 6QW	Selborne House, 54–60 Victoria Street, London SW1E 6QW	Selborne House, 54–60 Victoria Street, London SW1E 6QW	Public Trust Office, Stewart House, 24 Kingsway, London WC2B 6JX	c/o The Insolvency Service, PO Box 203, 21 Bloomsbury Street, London WC1B 3QW
TEL	0171 210 0730	0171 210 8835	0171 210 0730	0171 664 7143	0171 291 6747
FAX	0171 210 0725		0171 210 0725		0171 291 6746
CONTACT		Ms Sarah Jameson			
COMMITTEE SECRETARY	Mr Michael Kron				
SECRETARY			Mr Michal Kron	Mr Hugh Stevenson	Mr Eamon Murphy
CHAIR					Hon Mr Justice Evans-Lombe
TERMS OF REFERENCE	To make rules of procedure for the county courts. See also terms of reference of Civil Procedure Rule Committee.	Crown Court Rules were developed in 1982; and the Committee's function is to examine proposed amendments to those rules. Amendments are usually necessary to supplement new primary legislation.	To make rules of court for the purpose of family proceedings.	To give advice in general on the investment of monies coming within the care of the Public Trust Office and the Court of Protection.	Section 413 of the Insolvency Act requires the Lord Chancellor to consult the Committee before making any rules under Section 411 (Company insolvency rules) or section 412 (Individual insolvency rules).

	14	15	16	17	18
a	–	–	–	–	–
b	–	–	–	–	–
c	NP	NP	NP	NP	NP
d	–	–	–	–	–
e	–	–	–	–	–
f	–	–	–	–	–
g	£0.001m	£0.001m	£0.001m	£0.005m	£0.001m
h	–	–	–	–	–
i	–	–	–	–	1M
j	–	–	–	–	–
k	4M, 3F	3M, 3F*	6M, 3F	4M	6M, 1F
l	–	–	–	–	–
m	–	–	–	–	–

* Also three ex-officio members. (15)

* Serviced by the Insolvency Service. (18)

LORD CHANCELLOR'S DEPARTMENT

Advisory NDPBs

19 Judicial Studies Board

9th Floor
Millbank Tower
Millbank
London SW1P 4QU
TEL : 0171 217 4762/3/4/5
FAX : 0171 217 4779
jsboard@compuserve.com
CHAIR : Rt Hon Lord Justice Henry ; BOARD SECRETARY : Mr Edward Adams
TERMS OF REFERENCE : To assess training requirements and provide training for judges, to set syllabuses for, provide advice on and monitor the provision of training for lay magistrates on behalf of the Lord Chancellor; to provide help and guidance for the development of chairmen and members of tribunals.

a	–
b	–
c	Body
d	–
e	–
f	–
g	£3.280m
h	–
i	1M
j	–
k	1M, 2F, £120pd 6M, 1F
l	–
m	–

20 Land Registration Rule Committee

HM Land Registry
Lincoln's Inn Fields
London
WC2A 3PH
TEL : 0171 917 5994
FAX : 0171 917 5966
CHAIR : Sir William Blackburne
CONTACT : Mr Oliver Christopherson
TERMS OF REFERENCE : To give advice and assistance to the Lord Chancellor on the making of new or revised rules for the various purposes referred to in Section 144 of the Land Registration Act 1925.

a	–
b	–
c	NP
d	–
e	–
f	–
g	£0.002m
h	–
i	1M
j	–
k	1M, 1F
l	–
m	–

21 Law Commission

Conquest House
37–38 John Street
Theobalds Road
London WC1N 2BQ
TEL : 0171 453 1220
FAX : 0171 453 1297
lawcomm@gtnet.gov.uk
http://www.open.gov.uk/lawcomm/homepage.htm
CHAIR : Hon Mrs Justice Arden DBE ; SECRETARY : Mr Michael Sayers
TERMS OF REFERENCE : To keep the law under review and to make recommendations for reform.

a	–
b	–
c	HC
d	–
e	–
f	–
g	£3.831m
h	–
i	1F*, £116,045
j	–
k	3M, 1F, £78,713
l	–
m	–

22 Legal Aid Advisory Committee (Northern Ireland)

Northern Ireland Court Service
Windsor House
9–15 Bedford Street
Belfast BT2 7LT
TEL : 01232 328594
FAX : 01232 439110
CHAIR : His Honour Judge Smyth QC ; COMMITTEE SECRETARY : Mrs Helen Fullerton
TERMS OF REFERENCE : To receive the annual report of the Law Society of Northern Ireland on the operation and finance of legal aid in Northern Ireland and to comment and advise the Lord Chancellor.

a	–
b	–
c	HC
d	–
e	–
f	–
g	£0.015m
h	–
i	1M
j	–
k	8M, 3F
l	–
m	–

23 Supreme Court Rule Committee

Selborne House
54–60 Victoria Street
London
SW1E 6QW
TEL : 0171 210 0730
FAX : 0171 210 0725
SECRETARY : Mr Michal Kron
TERMS OF REFERENCE : To make rules of procedure for the Supreme Court. See also Civil Procedure Rule Committee.

a	–
b	–
c	NP
d	–
e	–
f	–
g	£0.001m
h	–
i	–
j	–
k	4M
l	–
m	–

* High Court Judge.

LORD CHANCELLOR'S DEPARTMENT

Tribunal NDPBs§

24

General Commissioners of Income Tax (GCIT)*

c/o Selborne House
54–60 Victoria Street
London
SW1E 6QW

TEL : 0171 210 0670

CONTACT : Mrs J Hartley

TERMS OF REFERENCE : To determine, postpone or adjourn appeals against tax assessments in relation to Income Tax, Corporation Tax, Capital Gains Tax and certain matters concerning National Insurance contributions, and to determine appeals against penalties and surcharges arising from Self Assessment.

a	–
b	–
c	–
d	–
e	–
f	–
g	£4.180m
h	–
i	†
j	–
k	2,671M, 563F
l	†
m	208,824‡

* Responsibility for payment of Clerks to GCITs transferred from Inland Revenue on 1.4.94.
† Information not availabe.
‡ Number of appeals on which substantive decisions were made. It includes 89,427 cases concluded at hearings not attended by appellants or their representatives, and 12,039 concluded where appellants or their represenatatives did attend.
§ Figures exclude those tribunals which are part of the Court Service.

NORTHERN IRELAND : NORTHERN IRELAND OFFICE

Northern Ireland Office

11 Millbank, London SW1P 4QE
Telephone   0171 210 6470

128 Stormont House Annex,
Stormont Estate, Belfast BT4 3ST
Telephone   01232 527066

Executive NDPBs

	1	2	3
	Police Authority for Northern Ireland	**Probation Board for Northern Ireland**	**Juvenile Justice Board** *
	River House 48 High Street Belfast BT1 2DR TEL : 01232 230111 FAX : 01232 245098 information.pani@nics.gov.uk http://www.pani.org.uk CHAIR : Mr Pat Armstrong SECRETARY : Mr Joe Stewart TERMS OF REFERENCE : It is charged with securing the maintenance of an adequate and efficient police force.	80–90 North Street Belfast BT1 1LD TEL : 01232 262400 FAX : 01232 262436 pbni@nics.gov.uk http://www.nics.gov.uk/pbni/index.htm CHAIR : Mr Sean Curran OBE SECRETARY : Mr Peter Moss TERMS OF REFERENCE : To provide an adequate and efficient Probation Service in Northern Ireland.	Rathgael Centre 169 Rathgael Road Bangor County Down BT19 1TA TEL : 01247 454276 FAX : 01247 271579 CHAIR : Mr Jon McCartney[‡] TERMS OF REFERENCE : To provide residential accommodation at Rathgael and Lisnevin Training Schools for children found guilty of offences and given custodial sentences. It is also responsible for community provision at Whitefield House and the Applied Psychology and Research Unit (APRU).
a. Number if a multiple body/system (1.4.98)	–	–	–
b. Number of staff employed by the body (1.4.98)	16,106*	341*	94.5
c. Annual Report	Body	Body	NP
d. Audit arrangements	X	X	Y
e. Total gross expenditure of body (1997/98)	£662.741m	£11.265m	£2.360m[†]
f. Amount funded by government (1997/98)	£657.350m	£11.241m	£2.360m[†]
g. Other expenditure by sponsoring dept (1997/98)	£1.539m	£0.078m	£0.100m
h. Chief Executive's Remuneration (1997/98)	£70,565	£66,645	£38,000
Appointments and Remuneration (1.9.98)			
i. Chairman/President	1M, £35,260[†]	1M, £11,460[†]	‡
j. Deputy	1M, £17630	1M, £27.70–£54.40hd	‡
k. Members	3M, 2F, £6,465 7M, 5F, £4,850	8M, 6F, £20.78–£41.56hd	‡
l. Tribunal cases received	–	–	–
m. Tribunal cases disposed of	–	–	–

* 3,315 civilians, 8,475 Royal Ulster Constabulary, 2,958 full-time Royal Ulster Constabulary Reservists and 1,358 part-time Royal Ulster Constabulary Reservists.
[†] Part time appointment.

* Includes 1 civil servant on secondment and 53 casual/seasonal staff.
[†] Part time appointment.

* Formerly Rathgael and Whiteabbey Training Schools Management Board.
[†] The £3.032m reduction on last year's figure reflects the transfer of care pupil facilities to the Health and Social Trust on 4.11.96.
[‡] As a tempory arrangement only, the new Board is made up of NIO officials with responsibility for juvenile justice matters.

NORTHERN IRELAND : NORTHERN IRELAND OFFICE

Executive NDPBs

4

The Independent Commission for Police Complaints for Northern Ireland

22 Great Victoria Street
Belfast
BT2 7LP

TEL : 01232 244821
FAX : 01232 248563
icpc@nics.gov.uk
CHAIR : Mr Paul Donnelly
CHIEF EXECUTIVE : Mr Brian McClelland
TERMS OF REFERENCE : The Commission has a duty to supervise the investigation of any complaint alleging that the conduct of a police officer resulted in the death of or serious injury to some other person. In the public interest it may also supervise any other cases.

Advisory NDPBs

5

Boundary Commission for Northern Ireland

c/o Northern Ireland Office
Millbank
London
SW1P 4QE

TEL : 0171 210 6569
FAX : 0171 2106537
CHAIR : Rt Hon Betty Boothroyd MP (Speaker of the House of Commons)
SECRETARY : Ms C Marson
TERMS OF REFERENCE : To keep under review the number, names and boundaries of the parliamentary constituencies into which Northern Ireland is divided and to make recommendations to the Secretary of State.

6

Standing Advisory Commission on Human Rights*

Temple Court
39 North Street
Belfast
BT1 1NA

TEL : 01232 243987
FAX : 01232 247844
sachr@nics.gov.uk
CHAIR : Mr Michael Lavery QC
SECRETARY : Mr D McGoran
TERMS OF REFERENCE : To advise the Secretary of State on the adequacy and effectiveness of the law in preventing, discrimination on the grounds of religious belief or political opinion in Northern Ireland.

Other NDPBs

7

Boards of Visitors and Visiting Committees

128 Stormont House Annex
Stormont Estate
Belfast
BT4 3ST

TEL : 01232 525202
FAX : 01232 524843
nips@nics.co.uk
http://www.nio.gov.uk
TERMS OF REFERENCE : To visit the prison regularly and report to the Secretary of State on the conditions of imprisonment and the treatment of prisoners.

	4	5	6	7
a	–	–	–	4
b	18	–	–	–
c	HC	NP*	HC	NP
d	X	–	–	–
e	£0.876m	–	–	–
f	£0.876m	–	–	–
g	–	£0.007m	£0.276m	£0.114m
h	£47,659	–	–	–
i	1M, £63,010*	{1F}†	1M, £9,115	1M, 3F
j	1M, £47,325*	1M	–	2M, 2F
k	1M, £21,725 / 1F, £17,380 / 3M, 1F, £8,690	2 vacancies	8M†, 4F†, £85pd or £42.50hd	31M, 22F, 10 vacancies
l	–	–	–	–
m	–	–	–	–

* Full time appointments.

* Periodic reports published as Command Papers.
† The Chairman of the Boundary Commission is the Speaker of the House of Commons (under Schedule 1 of the Parliamentary Constituencies Act 1986).

* To be replaced by Human Rights Commission in December 1998.
† Includes 2M and 1F ex officios who do not receive fees.

Northern Ireland Department of Agriculture

Dundonald House
Upper Newtonards Road
Belfast BT4 3SB

Executive NDPBs

1 Agricultural Research Institute of Northern Ireland

Large Park
Hillsborough
County Down
BT26 6DR
TEL : 01846 682484
FAX : 01846 689594
http://www.arini.ac.uk
CHAIR : Mr Walter Smyth OBE
DIRECTOR : Professor Fred Gordon
TERMS OF REFERENCE : The Agricultural Research Institute of Northern Ireland conducts research into animals and crops.

2 Agricultural Wages Board for Northern Ireland

Dundonald House
Upper Newtonards Road
Belfast
BT4 3SB
TEL : 01232 524521
FAX : 01232 524456
jim.o'hare@dani.gov.uk
http://www.nics.gov.uk/dani/awb.htm
CHAIR : Mrs Gwen Savage MBE
SECRETARY : Mr Michael McKillen
TERMS OF REFERENCE : To set the minimum rates of wages, and certain other related entitlement such as holiday pay and the value of benefits in lieu of cash, for agricultural workers.

3 Fisheries Conservancy Board for Northern Ireland

1 Mahon Road
Portadown
Craigavon
County Armagh BT62 3EE
TEL : 01762 334666
FAX : 01762 338912
CHAIR : Dr Jasper Parsons
CHIEF EXECUTIVE : Mr William Smith
TERMS OF REFERENCE : The conservation and protection of salmon and inland fisheries of Northern Ireland (apart from the fisheries in the Foyle catchment area).

		1	2	3
a.	Number if a multiple body/system (1.4.98)	–	–	–
b.	Number of staff employed by the body (1.4.98)	99	–	42
c.	Annual Report	Body	TSO	Body
d.	Audit arrangements	Y	–	–
e.	Total gross expenditure of body (1997/98)	£3.480m	†	£0.808m*
f.	Amount funded by government (1997/98)	£2.601m	–	£0.404m†
g.	Other expenditure by sponsoring dept (1997/98)	–	–	–
h.	Chief Executive's Remuneration (1997/98)	–	–	£30,557
	Appointments and Remuneration (1.9.98)			
i.	Chairman/President	1M*	1F, £202pd	1M, £3,715
j.	Deputy	–	–	1F, £2,870
k.	Members	{8M}*	1F, 1M, £103pd {9M, 3F}*	18M, 2F
l.	Tribunal cases received	–	–	–
m.	Tribunal cases disposed of	–	–	–

* Travel expenses only.

* Travel expenses only.
† Expenditure forms part of the total Northern Ireland Department of Agriculture (NIDA) expenditure. Accounts for NIDA are audited by the Comptroller and Auditor General.

* Relates to FCBNI financial year which ended on 31 December 1997. From audited accounts.
† This expenditure relates to agency services provided by the board.

NORTHERN IRELAND : DEPARTMENT OF AGRICULTURE

Executive NDPBs

Advisory NDPBs

	4 Foyle Fisheries Commission	5 Livestock and Meat Commission for Northern Ireland	6 Northern Ireland Fishery Harbour Authority	7 Pig Production Development Committee	8 Drainage Council for Northern Ireland
	8 Victoria Road Londonderry BT47 2AB	57 Malone Road Belfast BT9 6SA	3 St Patrick's Avenue Downpatrick County Down BT30 6DW	Pig Testing Station 14 Kirby's Lane Antrim BT41 4PP	c/o Rivers Agency Hydebank 4 Hospital Road Belfast BT8 8JP
	TEL : 01504 342100 FAX : 01504 342720 danderson.ffc@dnet.co.uk CHAIR : Maurice Mullan CHIEF EXECUTIVE : Mr Derick Anderson TERMS OF REFERENCE : The conservation, protection, improvement and development of the fisheries of the Foyle area.	TEL : 01232 590000 FAX : 01232 590001 lmcbelfast@btinternet.com http://www.nibeefandlamb.com CHAIR : Mr Gerald Lowe SECRETARY : Mr H D Ritchie TERMS OF REFERENCE : Marketing of beef and sheepmeat in Northern Ireland, Great Britain and overseas (mainly the European Union).	TEL : 01396 613844 FAX : 01396 617128 CHAIR : Mr Robert Ferris CHIEF EXECUTIVE : Mr Chris Warnock TERMS OF REFERENCE : The Authority is responsible for the fishing ports of Kilkeel, Ardglass and Portavogie. This includes the management, maintenance and improvement of the harbour; the operation of facilities provided at the harbour; and the maintenance of entrances and channels to the harbours.	TEL : 01849 464137 FAX : 01849 460471 p.i.g@netmatters.co.uk http://www.users.netmatters.co.uk/p.i.g/ CHAIR : Mr Derek Telford SECRETARY : Miss Lynne Martin TERMS OF REFERENCE : To provide services and facilities intended to benefit persons engaged in the production of pigs in Northern Ireland.	TEL : 01232 253357 FAX : 01232 253455 CHAIR : Mrs Dinah Browne SECRETARY : Miss Hazel Campbell TERMS OF REFERENCE : To decide which watercourses and sea defences should be maintained by the Rivers Agency at public expense and to consider the Department's proposals in relation to drainage schemes.
a	–	–	–	–	–
b	24	70	24	–	–
c	Body	Body	Body	Body	NP
d	–	–	Y	–	–
e	£0.745m*	£2.784m	£1.427m	–	–
f	£0.568m†	–	£0.347m	–	–
g	–	–	–	–	£0.020m
h	£43,000	£52,279	£28,951	–	–
i	–	1M, £13,645	1M, £4,815	1M*	1F
j	‡	–	1F, £2,905	–	1M
k	{2M}‡	4M, 2F, £5,105	4M, 2F, £2,905	7M	12M, 2F
l	–	–	–	–	–
m	–	–	–	–	–

* Relates to FFC Financial Year ending 30.9.97. From draft audited accounts.
† Part funded by ROI Government. £0.14m of this expenditure relates to agency services provided by the Commission (Bailiffing and Water Pollution Control).
‡ All members of the FFC are civil servants – two appointed by DANI and two appointed by the Department of the Marine and Natural Resources (ROI). Only Northern Ireland appointees shown.

* Travel expenses only.

Northern Ireland Department of Economic Development

Finance Branch
Netherleigh,
Massey Avenue
Belfast BT4 2JP

Executive NDPBs

	1	2	3
	Commission for Racial Equality for Northern Ireland*	**Construction Industry Training Board**	**Enterprise Ulster**
	Scottish Legal House 65–67 Chichester Street Belfast BT1 4JT TEL : 01232 315996 FAX : 01232 315993 creni.user@btinternet.com CHAIR : Mrs Joan Harbison CBE CHIEF EXECUTIVE : Ms Sheila Rogers TERMS OF REFERENCE : To promote equality of opportunity and good relations between persons of different racial groups generally.	17 Dundrod Road Crumlin County Antrim BT29 4SR TEL : 01232 825466 FAX : 01232 825693 citb@psilink.co.uk http://www.citbni.org.uk CHAIR : Mr William Gillespie OBE CHIEF EXECUTIVE : Mr Allan McMullen TERMS OF REFERENCE : To encourage the adequate training of people employed in, or intending to be employed in, the construction industry.	The Close Ravenhill Reach Belfast BT6 8RB TEL : 01232 736400 FAX : 01232 736404 xcp06@dial.pipex.com http://www.enterpriseulster.co.uk CHAIR : Mr Len O'Hagan TERMS OF REFERENCE : To create or provide quality training for employment in Northern Ireland.
a. Number if a multiple body/system (1.4.98)	–	–	–
b. Number of staff employed by the body (1.4.98)	5	62	171
c. Annual Report	HC	TSO	Body
d. Audit arrangements	Y	–	Y
e. Total gross expenditure of body (1997/98)	£0.402m*	£2.831m*	£7.052m
f. Amount funded by government (1997/98)	£0.402m*	£0.400m†	£6.386m
g. Other expenditure by sponsoring dept (1997/98)	£0.035m	£0.027m	£0.032m
h. Chief Executive's Remuneration (1997/98)	£40,303	£40,000‡	£43,496
Appointments and Remuneration (1.9.98)			
i. Chairman/President	1F, 17,500†	1M, £8,280‡	1M, £15,850
j. Deputy	1M, £3,855	–	–
k. Members	2M, 3F, £3,855	15M§	3M, 4F, £129pm
l. Tribunal cases received	–	–	–
m. Tribunal cases disposed of	–	–	–

* Commission was established in August 1997, therefore 1997/98 costs represent only an 8 month period.
† Chairman's remuneration does not include superannuation.

* Latest figures available (year ending 31 August 1997).
† Grants and payments to run specific prograammes and projects ie Priority Skills Initiative and the Job Training Programme.
‡ Remuneration is paid through levy and there is no financial implication for the public purse.
§ Remuneration limited to reimbursement of travel and related expenses.

NORTHERN IRELAND : DEPARTMENT OF ECONOMIC DEVELOPMENT

Executive NDPBs

	4	5	6	7	8
	Equal Opportunities Commission for Northern Ireland	**Fair Employment Commission for Northern Ireland**	**General Consumer Council for Northern Ireland**	**Labour Relations Agency**	**Local Enterprise Development Unit**
	Chamber of Commerce House 22 Great Victoria Street Belfast BT2 7BA	Andras House 60 Great Victoria Street Belfast BT2 7BB	Elizabeth House 116 Holyrood Road Belfast BT4 1NY	2–8 Gordon Street Belfast BT1 2LG	Ledu House Upper Gallway Belfast BT8 6TB
	TEL : 01232 242752 FAX : 01232 331047 info@eocni.org.uk http://www.eocni.org.uk	TEL : 01232 240020 FAX : 01232 331544 robert.cooper.fec@nics.gov.uk http://www.fec-ni.org	TEL : 01232 672488 FAX : 01232 657701 gcc@nics.gov.uk http://www.nics.gov.uk	TEL : 01232 321442 FAX : 01232 330827 lra@dnet.co.uk http://www.lra.org.uk	TEL : 01232 491031 FAX : 01232 691432 ledu@nics.gov.uk http://www.ledu-ni.gov.uk
	CHAIR AND CHIEF EXECUTIVE : Mrs Joan Smyth CBE	CHAIR : Sir Robert Cooper CBE CHIEF EXECUTIVE: Mr Harry Goodman	CHAIR : Mrs Joan Whiteside OBE DIRECTOR : Mrs Maeve Bell	CHAIR : Professor Desmond Rea OBE ; CHIEF EXECUTIVE : Mr William Patterson	CHAIR : Mr Eamon McElroy SECRETARY : Dr Alan Neville
	TERMS OF REFERENCE : To enforce legislation on sex discrimination and equal pay and to promote equality of opportunity between women and men.	TERMS OF REFERENCE : To promote equality of opportunity in employment in Northern Ireland.	TERMS OF REFERENCE : To promote and safeguard the interests of consumers; and to campaign for the best possible standards of service and protection.	TERMS OF REFERENCE : To improve industrial relations in Northern Ireland.	TERMS OF REFERENCE : To assist in the profitable growth of client businesses and to increase the number of business start-ups, with particular emphasis on those with export growth potential.
a	–	–	–	–	–
b	31	74	9.5	44	191.5
c	HC	HC	Body	Body	Body
d	Y	Y	Y	Y	Y
e	£1.535m	£2.752m	£0.451m	£1.756m	£29.286m
f	£1.535m	£2.752m	£0.440m	£1.756m	£29.286m
g	£0.035m	£0.035m	£0.025m	£0.035m	£0.057m
h	*	£58,233	£38,412*	£67,165	£79,733
i	1F, £55,702*	1M, £68,074	1F, £12,154	1M, £20,757	1M, £19,000
j	1F, £4,880	–	1M, £105pd	–	1F, £6,085
k	2M, 3F, £3,855 2 vacancies	5M, 3F, £5,010	5M, 6F†, 1 vacancy	4M, 5F, £3,855	6M, 1F, £6,085 1 vacancy
l	–	–	–	–	–
m	–	–	–	–	–

* Chair is also Chief Executive.

* Director.
† Members receive £73pd for Council meetings, and £61pd for Group meetings. These fees are currently under review.

NORTHERN IRELAND : DEPARTMENT OF ECONOMIC DEVELOPMENT

Executive NDPBs

Advisory NDPBs

9
Northern Ireland Commissioner for Protection Against Unlawful Industrial Action

Scottish Legal House
65–67 Chichester Street
Belfast
BT1 4JT
TEL : 01232 233640
FAX : 01232 237787
CHAIR : Mrs Margaret-Ann Dinsmore QC
TERMS OF REFERENCE : To provide, where appropriate, assistance to people who are actual or prospective parties to certain legal proceedings.

10
Northern Ireland Commissioner for the Rights of Trade Union Members

Scottish Legal House
65–67 Chichester Street
Belfast
BT1 4JT
TEL : 01232 233640
FAX : 01232 237787
CHAIR : Mrs Margaret-Ann Dinsmore QC
TERMS OF REFERENCE : To provide assistance to a trade union member who is taking or contemplating taking action against his union or an official or trustee of the union.

11
Northern Ireland Tourist Board

St Anne's Court
59 North Street
Belfast
BT1 1NB
TEL : 01232 231221
FAX : 01232 240960
general.enquiries.nitb@nics.gov.uk
http://www.ni-tourism.com
CHAIR : Mr Roy Bailie
CHIEF EXECUTIVE : Mr Ian Henderson
TERMS OF REFERENCE : To optimise the tourist industry's potential as a significant creator of wealth and jobs by marketing and developing Northern Ireland as a high quality, competitive tourist destination through pro-active partnerships

12
Ulster Supported Employment Ltd*

88–136 Lawnbrook Avenue
Belfast
BT13 2QD
TEL : 01232 322881
FAX : 01232 331038
CHIEF EXECUTIVE : Mr Mitchel Wylie ; SECRETARY : Mr David Macedo
TERMS OF REFERENCE : To create jobs for disabled people by direct manufacturing employment or through third party employment.

13
Health and Safety Agency for Northern Ireland

83 Ladas Drive
Belfast
BT6 9FJ
TEL : 01232 243249
FAX : 01232 235383
CHAIR : Mrs Ann Shaw
TERMS OF REFERENCE : To review and make recommendations on measures for securing the health, safety and welfare of people at work and protecting all other people against risks to their health and safety arising from work related activities.

	9	10	11	12	13
a	–	–	–	–	–
b	0.5*	0.5*	127	82	–
c	Body	Body	Body	Body	Body
d	X	X	X	Y	Y
e	£0.015m	£0.037m	£15.162m	£5.007m	–
f	£0.015m	£0.037m	£13.730m	£2.641m	–
g	£0.004m	£0.005m	£0.057m	£0.010m	£0.570m
h	–	–	£57,631	£41,297	£53,273
i	1F, £4,755	1F, 7,925	1M, £9,888	1M, £131pd	1F, £11,683
j	–	–	1F, £5,392	–	–
k	–	–	3M, 3F, £5,392 1 vacancy	3M, 2F, £105pd	6M, 3F, £3,930*
l	–	–	–	–	–
m	–	–	–	–	–

* Member of staff on part-time secondment from sponsor Department.

* Member of staff on part-time secondment from sponsor Department.

* Known as Ulster Sheltered Employment Ltd until 16.9.98.

* From 1.10.97 the basis for remuneration was changed from a daily fee to an annual fee.

97

NORTHERN IRELAND : DEPARTMENT OF ECONOMIC DEVELOPMENT

Advisory NDPBs

Tribunal NDPBs

14
Industrial Development Board for Northern Ireland

IDB House
64 Chichester Street
Belfast
BT1 4JX
TEL : 01232 233233
FAX : 01232 545000
idb@nics.gov.uk
http://www.idbni.co.uk
CHAIR : Dr Alan Gillespie
CHIEF EXECUTIVE : Mr Bruce Robinson
TERMS OF REFERENCE : To attract new inward investment and encourage the development of internationally competitive companies in the manufacturing and tradeable service sectors.

15
Industrial Research and Technology Unit (Advisory Board)

17 Antrim Road
Lisburn
County Antrim
BT28 3AL
TEL : 01846 623000
FAX : 01846 676054
b.ohare@irtu.dedni.gov.uk
http://www.nics.gov.uk/irtu
CHAIR : Professor Peter McKie
BOARD SECRETARY : Ms Bernadette O'Hare
TERMS OF REFERENCE : To provide advice on policy and delivery of programmes and services, in furtherance of the Agency's objective of improving the competitiveness of NI industry through innovation and R&D; and to link the Agency with industry and academia.

16
Statistics Advisory Committee

Statistics Research Branch,
Department of Economic Development, Massey Avenue,
Belfast BT4 2JP
TEL : 01232 529588
FAX : 01232 529459
hepper@dedni.gov.uk
CHAIR : Mr Ronnie Foreman
SECRETARY : Mrs Norah McCorry
TERMS OF REFERENCE : To advise relevant Northern Ireland Departments on the conduct of statistical enquiries.

17
Training and Employment Agency (Advisory Board)

39–49 Adelaide Street
Belfast
BT2 8FD
TEL : 01232 257777
FAX : 01232 257778
CHAIR : Mr Bill McGinnis
BOARD SECRETARY : Mr John Murray
TERMS OF REFERENCE : To help secure strong collaboration and co-operation between the Agency and the private sector; and to assist in the development of training and employment services.

18
Fair Employment Tribunal

Long Bridge House
20–24 Waring Street
Belfast
BT1 2EB
TEL : 01232 327666
FAX : 01232 230184
PRESIDENT : Mr John Maguire CBE ; SECRETARY : Mrs Patricia McVeigh
TERMS OF REFERENCE : To hear employment disputes and resolve employment matters, on the grounds of religious belief or political opinion.

	14	15	16	17	18
a	–	–	–	–	–
b	–	–	–	–	–
c	TSO	HC	NP	Body	NP
d	–	–	–	–	–
e	–	–	–	–	–
f	–	–	–	–	–
g	£0.138m	£0.080m	£0.002m	£0.119m	*
h	–	–	–	–	–
i	1M, £34,125	1M, £7,976	1M*	1M, £23,035	†
j	–	1M, £3,513	–	–	1F, £317pd‡
k	5M, 2F, £6,330, 1 vacancy	7M, 2F, £3,513	3M, 4F*, 2 vacancies	7M, 4F, £4,300 1 vacancy	35M, 19F, £123pd
l	–	–	–	–	612
m	–	–	–	–	614

* Remuneration limited to reimbursement of travelling and related expenses.

* Costs included in the figure for Industrial Tribunals.
† The President is also the President of the Industrial Court and the Industrial Tribunals.
‡ The Vice-President and full-time Chairmen are also the Vice-President and full-time Chairmen of the Industrial Tribunals.

NORTHERN IRELAND : DEPARTMENT OF ECONOMIC DEVELOPMENT

Tribunal NDPBs

19
Northern Ireland Industrial Court

Long Bridge House
20–24 Waring Street
Belfast
BT1 2EB
TEL : 01232 327666
FAX : 01232 230184
PRESIDENT : Mr John Maguire CBE
TERMS OF REFERENCE : To enforce, by hearing appeals from trade unions, the requirement on employers to provide trade unions with information relevant to collective bargaining.

20
Northern Ireland Industrial Tribunals

Long Bridge House
20–24 Waring Street
Belfast
BT1 2EB
TEL : 01232 327666
FAX : 01232 230184
PRESIDENT : Mr John Maguire CBE ; SECRETARY : Mrs Patricia McVeigh
TERMS OF REFERENCE : To hear employment disputes and resolve employment matters.

21
Scheme of Compensation for Loss of Employment through Civil Unrest*

Room 52
Netherleigh
Massey Avenue
Belfast BT4 2JP
TEL : 01232 529344
FAX : 01232 529485
CHAIR : Dr James McQuitty
SECRETARY : Mr Gary Swenarton
TERMS OF REFERENCE : To provide compensation for employees who suffer loss of employment through circumstances connected with the disturbances in Northern Ireland.

	19	20	21
a	–	–	–
b	–	–	–
c	NP	NP	NP
d	–	–	–
e	–	–	–
f	–	–	–
g	*	£1.665m*	£0.007m
h	–	–	–
i	†	1M, £113,309	1M, £317pd
j	–	1F, £99,810 / 2F, £83,403 / 14M, 7F, £317pd	–
k	9M, 2F, £123pd / 1 vacancy	106M, 46F, £123pd / –	1M, £117pd / 3 vacancies
l	–	3,885	8
m	–	4,137	6

* Costs included in the figure for Industrial Tribunals.
† The President is also the President of the Fair Employment Tribunal and the Industrial Tribunals.

* Includes costs for all administrative and support staff plus electricity and heating costs.

* Scheme ends 31.12.98.

NORTHERN IRELAND : DEPARTMENT OF EDUCATION

Northern Ireland Department of Education

Rathgael House
Balloo Road
Bangor
Co Down BT19 7PR

Executive NDPBs

1
Arts Council of Northern Ireland

MacNeice House
77 Malone Road
Belfast
BT9 6AQ
TEL : 01232 385200
FAX : 01232 661715
CHAIR : Professor Brian Walker
CHIEF EXECTIVE : Mr Brian Ferran
TERMS OF REFERENCE : To develop and improve the knowledge, appreciation and practice of the arts, and to increase public access to, and, participation in, the arts.

2
Council for Catholic Maintained Schools

160 High Street
Holywood
County Down
BT18 9HT
TEL : 01232 426972
FAX : 01232 424255
info.ccms@nics.gov.uk
CHAIR : Bishop Michael Dallat
TERMS OF REFERENCE : To provide an upper tier of management for the Catholic maintained sector; and to raise standards within that sector. It employs all teachers in Catholic maintained schools.

3
Northern Ireland Council for the Curriculum, Examinations and Assessment (NICCEA)

Clarendon Dock
29 Clarendon Road
Belfast
BT1 3BG
TEL : 01232 261200
FAX : 01232 261234
info@ccea.org.uk
http://www.ccea.org.uk
CHAIR : Dr Alan Lennon
CHIEF EXECUTIVE : Mrs Catherine Coxhead
TERMS OF REFERENCE : To keep all aspects of the curriculum, examinations and assessment under review, to publish and disseminate curriculum, examinations and assessment materials, and to conduct examinations and assessment.

	1	2	3
a. Number if a multiple body/system (1.4.98)	–	–	–
b. Number of staff employed by the body (1.4.98)	37	47	230*
c. Annual Report	Body	Body	TSO[†]
d. Audit arrangements	X	Y	X
e. Total gross expenditure of body (1997/98)	£8.112m*[‡]	£1.712m*	£13.223m[‡]
f. Amount funded by government (1997/98)	£7.324m	£1.710m	£8.850m
g. Other expenditure by sponsoring dept (1997/98)	£0.082m	£0.029m	£0.056m
h. Chief Executive's Remuneration (1997/98)	£55,078[†]	£49,599[†]	£54,846
Appointments and Remuneration (1.9.98)			
i. Chairman/President	1M, £8,000	{1M, £4,945}[‡]	1M, £10,731
j. Deputy	1F, £4,000	{1F}[‡]	–
k. Members	7M, 4F, 2 vacancies	6M, 2F {16M, 10F}	11M, 6F
l. Tribunal cases received	–	–	–
m. Tribunal cases disposed of	–	–	–

* Includes £68,358 charged to the national lottery for staff and premises costs.
† 20% charged to the National Lottery
‡ Estimated gross expenditure figures pending audit of 1997/98 accounts.

* Represents full gross expenditure figure of recurrent and capital figure.
† Director.
‡ Chairman and Deputy chosen from among the Council's Board Members. The total at Row 'k' does not include the Chairman or his Deputy.

* Includes 19 full-time permanent staff on fixed-term contracts (of between 1 and 2 years), 26 full-time temporary staff and 3 part-time permanent staff and 1 temporary part-time staff.
† 1st Annual Report 1997/98 will be published as one document along with the accounts for the year.
‡ Expenditure costs as per 1997/98 accounts – yet to be audited.

NORTHERN IRELAND : DEPARTMENT OF EDUCATION

Executive NDPBs

Advisory NDPBs

4
National Museums and Galleries of Northern Ireland*

Botanic Gardens
Belfast
BT9 5AB

TEL : 01232 383000
FAX : 01232 383003
CHAIR : Mrs Margaret Elliott
DIRECTOR : Mr Michael Houlihan
TERMS OF REFERENCE : Through its collections, its key functions are to promote the awareness, appreciation and understanding of i) art, history and science, ii) the culture and way of life of the people of Northern Ireland and iii) the migration and settlement of people.

5
Northern Ireland Museums Council

66 Donegall Pass
Belfast
BT7 1BU

TEL : 01232 550215
FAX : 01232 550216
museums.council@nimc.org.uk
http://www.nimc.org.uk
CHAIR : Professor T G Fraser
DIRECTOR : Mr Aidan Walsh
TERMS OF REFERENCE : To advise on information in respect of museums, museum services and collections.

6
Sports Council for Northern Ireland

House of Sport
Upper Malone Road
Belfast
BT9 5LA

TEL : 01232 381222
FAX : 01232 682757
http://www.sportscouncil-ni.org.uk
CHAIR : Mr Don Allen
SECRETARY : Mrs Elizabeth Bailie
TERMS OF REFERENCE : To further sport and recreational facilities in Northern Ireland.

7
Youth Council for Northern Ireland

Forestview
Purdy's Lane
Belfast
BT8 7AR

TEL : 01232 643882
FAX : 01232 643874
ycni@ycouncil.dnet.co.uk
CHAIR : Dr Michael Murphy
CHIEF EXECUTIVE : Mr David Guilfoyle
TERMS OF REFERENCE : To take action on issues affecting young people and to develop and enhance the quality of youth work practice in Northern Ireland. Assessment and payment of grants to headquarters voluntary youth organisations.

8
Northern Ireland Higher Education Council

Room 607B, Department of Education, Rathgael House, Balloo Road, Bangor
Co Down BT19 7PR

TEL : 01247 279333
FAX : 01247 275593
nihec.deni@nics.gov.uk
CHAIR : Sir Kenneth Bloomfield
SECRETARY : Mr John Coote
TERMS OF REFERENCE : To advise the Department of Education and, more broadly, the Government, on the planning and funding of higher education in Northern Ireland.

	4	5	6	7	8
a	–	–	–	–	–
b	330	3	56	18*	–
c	TSO	Body	Body	Body	Body
d	–	Y	X	X	–
e	*	£0.182m*	£3.428m	£2.411m†	–
f	*	£0.165m	£2.919m	£2.265m	–
g	*	£0.018m	£0.091m	£0.053m	£0.221m
h	*	£31,539†	£55,215*	£45,892‡§	–
i	1F, £8,000	1M‡	1M, £10,635	1M, £11,045	1M, £9,485
j	{1M}†	1 vacancy§	1M, £3,475	1F, £3,705	–
k	10M, 3F	1F, {11M, 1F}	8M, 5F†	7M, 5F¶, 1 vacancy	7M, 2F
l	–	–	–	–	–
m	–	–	–	–	–

* On 1.4.98, the Museums and Galleries (Northern Ireland) Order 1998 abolished the Ulster Museum and the Ulster Folk and Transport Museum and formally created a new merged body known as the National Museums and Galleries of Northern Ireland (NMGNI).
† Chosen by the Board from among its members. The total at Row 'k' does not include the Chairman or the Deputy.

* Estimated gross expenditure figures pending audit of 1997/98 accounts.
† Director.
‡ Appointed initially by Ministers. In future the Chairman will be elected by the wider membership of the body.
§ Chosen by the Board from among its members. The total at Row 'k' does not include the Chairman or his Deputy.

* 20% charged to the National Lottery.
† Does not include Chairman or Deputy.

* Includes 2 part-time staff and 1 person employed for 2 years.
† Estimated gross expenditure figures pending audit of 1997/98 accounts.
‡ Director.
§ Currently under review.
¶ Does not include Chairman or Deputy.

NORTHERN IRELAND : DEPARTMENT OF EDUCATION

Bodies which in Northern Ireland fulfil functions carried out by Local Government in Great Britain

Education and Library Boards

9	10	11	12	13
Belfast Education and Library Board	**North Eastern Education and Library Board**	**South Eastern Education and Library Board**	**Southern Education and Library Board**	**Western Education and Library Board**
40 Academy Street Belfast BT1 2NQ	County Hall 182 Galgorm Road Ballymena Co Antrim BT42 1HN	Grahansbridge Road Dundonald Belfast BT16 0HS	3 Charlemont Place The Mall Armagh BT61 9AX	1 Hospital Road Omagh Co Tyrone BT79 0AW
TEL : 01232 564000 FAX : 01232 331714	TEL : 01266 653333 FAX : 01266 46071	TEL : 01232 566200 FAX : 01232 566266/7	TEL : 01861 512200 FAX : 01861 512490	TEL : 01662 411411 FAX : 01662 411400
CHIEF EXECUTIVE : Mr T G J Moag OBE	CHIEF EXECUTIVE : Mr G Topping BA Hons	CHIEF EXECUTIVE : Mr J B Fitzsimons	CHIEF EXECUTIVE : Mrs H M McClenaghan	CHIEF EXECUTIVE : Mr P J Martin BA BD
TERMS OF REFERENCE : The Board is responsible for securing the provision of the following services: primary and secondary education; educational services for children with special needs.	TERMS OF REFERENCE : The Board is responsible for securing the provision of primary and secondary education; and educational services for children with special needs.	TERMS OF REFERENCE : The Board is responsible for securing the provision of primary and secondary education; and educational services for children with special needs.	TERMS OF REFERENCE : The Board is responsible for securing the provision of primary and secondary education; and educational services for children with special needs.	TERMS OF REFERENCE : The Board is responsible for securing the provision of primary and secondary education; and educational services for children with special needs.
a —	a —	a —	a —	a —
b 2,809*	b 3,699*	b 3,279*	b 2,517*	b 3,549*
c Body	c Body	c Body	c Body	c Body
d X	d X	d X	d X	d X
e £189.82m†	e £229.87m†	e £196.54m†	e £232.47m†	e £208.62m†
f £185.62m‡	f £221.91m‡	f £191.90m‡	f £227.95m‡	f £201.81m‡
g £0.373m¶	g £0.373m¶	g £0.373m¶	g £0.373m¶	g £0.373m¶
h £61,516	h £61,516	h £57,770	h £61,516	h £60,116
i 1F, £5,045§	i 1M, £5,045§	i 1m, £5,045§	i 1M, £5,045§	i 1M, £5,045§
j 1M§	j 1M§	j 1M§	j 1M§	j 1M§
k 26M, 7F	k 24M, 9F	k 21M, 12F	k 22M, 11F	k 22M, 8F
l —	l —	l —	l —	l —
m —	m —	m —	m —	m —

* Figures relate to non-teaching staff and are at 1.9.97 — most recent figures available.
† Estimated gross expenditure figures pending audit of 1997/98 accounts.
‡ Actual cash advanced to the Boards in 1997/98.
§ Chairman and Vice Chairman chosen by the Board from among its members. Total at Row 'k' does not include Chairman or Deputy.
¶ Total cost involved in dealing with five ELBS.

14
Staff Commission for Education and Library Boards

Lamont House
Purdy's Lane
Belfast
BT8 4TA

TEL : 01232 491461
FAX : 01232 491744

CHAIR : Mr Maurice Moroney
SECRETARY : Mrs Patricia Weir
TERMS OF REFERENCE : To oversee matters connected with the recruitment training and terms and conditions of employment of officers of Education and Library Boards.

a	–
b	5
c	Body
d	X
e	£0.190m
f	£0.190m
g	£0.008m
h	£37,337*
i	1M, £5,225†
j	1F
k	9M, 3F
l	–
m	–

* Staff Commission Secretary. Figures taken from 1997/98 unaudited accounts. The actual salary is not specified in the accounts.
† Remuneration as at 1 December 1997.

NORTHERN IRELAND : DEPARTMENT OF THE ENVIRONMENT

Northern Ireland Department of the Environment

Clarence Court
10–18 Adelaide Street
Belfast BT2 8GB

Executive NDPBs

1 Laganside Corporation

Clarendon Building
15 Clarendon Road
Belfast
BT1 3BG
TEL : 01232 328507
FAX : 01232 332141
info@laganside.com
http://www.laganside.com
CHAIR : Mr Tony Hopkins
CHIEF EXECUTIVE : Mr Mike Smith
TERMS OF REFERENCE : Revitalising and rejuvenating of the Laganside area for the benefit and welfare of Belfast and Northern Ireland.

2 Northern Ireland Local Government Officers' Superannuation Committee

Templeton House
411 Holywood Road
Belfast
BT4 2LP
TEL : 01232 768025
FAX : 01232 768790
nilgosc@compuserve.com
http://ourworld.compuserve.com/homepages/nilgosc
CHAIR : Mr Frank Ledwidge
SECRETARY : Mr Richard Nesbitt
TERMS OF REFERENCE : To administer the local government pension funds in Northern Ireland.

Advisory NDPBs

3 Council for Nature Conservation and the Countryside

5–33 Hill Street
Belfast
BT1 2LA
TEL : 01232 235000
FAX : 01232 543111
hmb.ehs@nics.gov.uk
CHAIR : Mr Robert Hanna CBE JP
TERMS OF REFERENCE : To advise the Department on the exercise of its nature conservation and countryside responsibilities.

		1	2	3
a.	Number if a multiple body/system (1.4.98)	–	–	–
b.	Number of staff employed by the body (1.4.98)	19.5	26	–
c.	Annual Report	Body	Body	NP*
d.	Audit arrangements	Y*	*	–
e.	Total gross expenditure of body (1997/98)	£11.000m	£56.600m	–
f.	Amount funded by government (1997/98)	£7.800m	–	–
g.	Other expenditure by sponsoring dept (1997/98)	£0.027m	–	£0.029m
h.	Chief Executive's Remuneration (1997/98)	£60,432†	–	–
	Appointments and Remuneration (1.9.98)			
i.	Chairman/President	1M, £23,445	1M†	1M, £7,420
j.	Deputy	–	–	1M, £4,965
k.	Members	5M, 5F, £7,815	9M, 7F‡	8M, 9F†
l.	Tribunal cases received	–	–	–
m.	Tribunal cases disposed of	–	–	–

* Audited by Commercial Aditors; NIAO have access rights.
† Acting Chief Executive at 31.3.98 Chief Executive cost has been aggregated for year.

* Audited by Local Government Auditors.
† Annual Allowance of £8,070 expenses.
‡ Expenses only.

* Report produced every 3 years.
† Expenses only.

NORTHERN IRELAND : DEPARTMENT OF THE ENVIRONMENT

Advisory NDPBs

4
Historic Buildings Council

5–33 Hill Street
Belfast
BT1 2LA

TEL : 01232 235000
FAX : 01232 543111
hmb.ehs@nics.gov.uk
CHAIR : Mrs Primrose Wilson
TERMS OF REFERENCE : To advise the Department on the exercise of its powers under the 1991 Order.

5
Historic Monuments Council

5–33 Hill Street
Belfast
BT1 2LA

TEL : 01232 235000
FAX : 01232 543111
hmb.ehs@nics.gov.uk
CHAIR : Mr Campbell Tweed
TERMS OF REFERENCE : To advise the Department on the exercise of its powers under the 1995 Order.

6
Northern Ireland Advisory Committee on Travellers

c/o Special Programmes Branch, Brookmount Buildings, 42 Fountain Street,
Belfast BT1 5EE
TEL : 01232 251910
FAX : 01232 541828
CHAIR : Mr William J Newburn
SECRETARY : Mr Terry Neill
TERMS OF REFERENCE : To advise and make practical recommendations in relation to Travellers' issues.

7
Northern Ireland Building Regulations Advisory Committee

Cawood House
24–26 Arthur Street
Belfast
BT1 4GF

TEL : 01232 246898
FAX : 01232 313178
CHAIR : *
SECRETARY : Mr Gerald Coulter
TERMS OF REFERENCE : To advise the Department of the Environment on the amendment of building regulations; and on any other matter arising out of or connected with the operation of building regulations.

8
Northern Ireland Construction Industry Advisory Council[‡]

4th Floor, Clarence House
10–18 Adelaide Street
Belfast
BT2 8GB

TEL : 01232 540045
FAX : 01232 540840
CHAIR : Lord Dubs
SECRETARY : Mr Hugh Murray
TERMS OF REFERENCE : To consider and advise government on matters affecting the building and civil engineering industry in Northern Ireland, other than matters relating to wages and conditions of employment.

	4	5	6	7	8
a	–	–	–	–	–
b	–	–	–	–	–
c	NP	NP	NP*	NP	NP
d	–	–	–	–	–
e	–	–	–	–	–
f	–	–	–	–	–
g	£0.020m	£0.003m	£0.010m	£0.034m[†]	£0.040m[†]
h	–	–	–	–	–
i	1F*	1M*	1M	*	*
j	–	–	–	*	*
k	8M, 6F*	6M, 8F	12M, 7F	*	6M
l	–	–	–	–	–
m	–	–	–	–	–

* Expenses only.

* Expenses only.

* Report produced at end of every 3 year term.

* No membership at 1.9.98. Committee not due to be reconstituted until October 1998.
† Estimated figure.

* Chairman is Lord Dubs, Parliamentary Under-Secretary.
† Estimated figure.
‡ The future of the Council is under review.

NORTHERN IRELAND : DEPARTMENT OF THE ENVIRONMENT

Advisory NDPBs

Tribunal NDPBs

9 Northern Ireland Water Council

Clarence Court
10–18 Adelaide Street
Belfast
BT2 8GB
TEL : 01232 540540
FAX : 01232 541156
CHAIR : Mr John Kelly
JOINT SECRETARIES : Mr David Walker (DOE) and Miss Hazel Campbell (Rivers Agency)
TERMS OF REFERENCE : To act as a public watchdog over DANI and DOE exercising their statutory functions in relation to Water and Sewerage matters and to assist both Departments in achieving a balance between conflicting interests in such matters.

a	–
b	–
c	NP
d	–
e	–
f	–
g	£0.003m
h	–
i	1M
j	1F
k	6M, 6F
l	–
m	–

10 Housing Benefit Review Boards

c/o Client Services, Northern Ireland Housing Executive, The Housing Centre, 2 Adelaide Street, Belfast BT2 8PB
TEL : 01232 2405888
FAX : 01232 240588
TERMS OF REFERENCE : To consider representations about decisions made by the Housing Executive and the Rate Collection Agency on individual claims for housing benefit. It should be noted that, while certain panel members are designated to chair Review Board hearings, there is no 'chairman' as such.

a	–
b	–
c	NP
d	–
e	–
f	–
g	–
h	–
i	{11M, 4F}, £41pm
j	–
k	{12M, 19F}, £32pm
l	104*
m	98*

* Cases received and disposed of between 1 April 1997 and 31 January 1998 (latest figures available).

11 Northern Ireland Review Body (Operator and Vehicle Licensing)

148–158 Corporation Street
Belfast
BT1 3DH
TEL : 01232 540540
FAX : 01232 254111
CHAIR : Mr Max Hale
SECRETARY : Mrs Helen McIlwaine
TERMS OF REFERENCE : The body reviews cases of those who have been refused Road Freight Operator and Vehicle Licenses and Road Service Licenses. It also considers appeal cases in respect of Approved Driving Instructors who have been removed from the Driving Instructors Register.

a	–
b	–
c	NP
d	–
e	–
f	–
g	£0.003m
h	–
i	1M, £101.20pd
j	–
k	4M, 1F, £50.60pd
l	14
m	14

12 Planning Appeals Commission

Park House
87–91 Great Victoria Street
Belfast
BT2 7AG
TEL : 01232 244710
FAX : 01232 312536
CHAIR : Mr Roy Hawthorne
SECRETARY : Mrs Marlene Hempton
TERMS OF REFERENCE : To make decisions on all appeals against decisions and to hold public enquiries and report to the Department on a wide range of matters including planning applications, enforcement notices, listed buildings and advertisement consents.

a	–
b	–
c	Body
d	–
e	–
f	–
g	£0.883m
h	–
i	1M, £63,458*
j	1M, £61,017†
k	5M, 2F, 3 vacancies £26,939–£51,871 1M, 1F, £165pd
l	290
m	279

* Joint post of Planning and Water Appeals Commissioner.
† Deputy and two members also hear Water Appeals.

13 Rent Assessment Panel (RAP)

Room 413A, Clarence Court
10–18 Adelaide Street
Belfast
BT2 8GB
TEL : 01232 540540
FAX : 01232 541117
RENT OFFICER FOR NORTHERN IRELAND : Mrs Joan McCrum
TERMS OF REFERENCE : To determine appropriate rents for private rented tenancies which are registered with the Department of the Environment for Northern Ireland.

a	–
b	–
c	NP
d	–
e	–
f	–
g	£0.066m
h	–
i	1F, £250pd
j	–
k	10M, 6F, £150pd*
l	113
m	118

* Members receive £230pd when acting as committee Chairperson.

NORTHERN IRELAND : DEPARTMENT OF THE ENVIRONMENT

Tribunal NDPBs

Public Corporation

Bodies which in Northern Ireland fulfil functions carried out by Local Government in Great Britain

14 Water Appeals Commission

Park House
87–91 Great Victoria Street
Belfast
BT2 7AG
TEL : 01232 244710
FAX : 01232 312536
CHAIR : Mr Roy Hawthorne
SECRETARY : Mrs Marlene Hempton
TERMS OF REFERENCE : The conduct of appeals, independent inquiries and hearings relating to water supply and sewerage, water pollution control, fisheries licensing and water recreation.

15 Northern Ireland Transport Holding Company

Chamber of Commerce House
22 Great Victoria Street
Belfast
BT2 7LX
TEL : 01232 243456
FAX : 01232 333845
CHAIR : Mr Ian Doherty
TERMS OF REFERENCE : The control and management of public transport, within Northern Ireland. It is the parent company of all publicly owned bus and rail companies.

16 Fire Authority for Northern Ireland

Brigade HQ
1 Seymour Street
Lisburn
BT27 4SX
TEL : 01846 664221
FAX : 01846 677402
bhg@nifb.btinternet.com
http://www.nifb.org.uk
CHAIR : Mr Errol Gaynor
CHIEF EXECUTIVE AND CHIEF FIRE OFFICER : Mr J McClelland
TERMS OF REFERENCE : To make provision for fire fighting services and for the protection of life and property in case of fire.

17 Local Government Staff Commission

Commission House
18–22 Gordon Street
Belfast
BT1 2LG
TEL : 01232 313200
FAX : 01232 313151
staff@nics.gov.uk
CHAIR : Mr Sid McDowell
CHIEF EXECUTIVE : Mr Adrian Kerr
TERMS OF REFERENCE : Oversight of matters connected with the recruitment, training and terms and conditions of employment of council officers; and to make recommendations to councils on such matters.

18 Northern Ireland Housing Executive (NIHE)

The Housing Centre
2 Adelaide Street
Belfast
BT2 8PB
TEL : 01232 240588
FAX : 01232 240588
CHAIR : Mr Sid McDowell
TERMS OF REFERENCE : To examine housing conditions and housing requirements on a regular basis.

	14	15	16	17	18
a	–	–	–	–	–
b	–	–	2,078*	11	3,253*
c	NP	Body	Body	Body	Body
d	–	–	Y†	Y*	Y†
e	–	–	£47.074	£0.411m	£560.591m
f	–	–	£42.954m	£0.033m	£193.019m
g	£0.001m	–	£0.124m‡	–	£47.085m‡
h	–	£113,000	£65,031§	£49,946	£71,427
i	1M*	1M, £24,520	1M, £16,800	1M, £8,505	1M, £31,585
j	–	–	1M, £8,400	–	1M, £12,640
k	1M, 2F†	6M, 2F, £8,190	9M, 5F, 1 vacancy¶	10M, 4F	3M, 2F, £5,230§
l	26	–	–	–	–
m	6	–	–	–	–

* Joint post of Planning and Water Appeals Chief Commissioner
† Joint post of Planning and Water Appeals Commissioner.

* 895 full-time firemen; 993 part-time; 306 administration control and ancillary staff.
† Audited by Local Government Auditors.
‡ £0.066m on storage and maintenance of fire fighting appliances; £25,000 on fire prevention publicity; £15,000 on Fire Service Inspection Costs; and £18,000 on Legal Costs and miscellaneous items.
§ Chief Fire Officer.

* Audited by Local Government Auditors.

* 2,829 Administration; 324 Industrial staff.
† Audited by Local Government Auditors.
‡ Borrowed from Consolidated Fund.
§ 3 members are nominated by the Northern Ireland Housing Council. There are 3 vacancies at 1 September 1998.

Northern Ireland Department of Finance & Personnel

Rathgael House
Bangor
Co Down

Advisory NDPBs

1 Law Reform Advisory Committee for Northern Ireland

Lancashire House
5 Linenhall Street
Belfast
BT2 8AA
TEL : 01232 542900
FAX : 01232 542909
michael.foster@dfpni.gov.uk
CHAIR : Mr Justice Paul Girvan
SECRETARY : Mr Michael Foster
TERMS OF REFERENCE : To keep the civil law of Northern Ireland under review and make recommendations for its reform.

2 Northern Ireland Economic Council

Bulloch House
2 Linenhall Street
Belfast
BT2 8BA
TEL : 01232 232125
FAX : 01232 331250
info@niec.org.uk
http://www.niec.org.uk
CHAIR : Vacant
SECRETARY : Mr Roy Boreland
TERMS OF REFERENCE : To provide independent advice to the Secretary of State on the development of economic policy for Northern Ireland.

3 Statute Law Committee for Northern Ireland

Statutory Publications Office
2nd Floor, Parliament Buildings
Belfast
BT4 3SW
TEL : 01232 521211
FAX : 01232 521525
Christine.scott@dfpni.gov.uk
CHAIR : Rt Hon Sir Robert Carswell, Lord Chief Justice for Northern Ireland.
SECRETARY : Mrs Christine Scott
TERMS OF REFERENCE : To oversee the publication of the annual volumes and indices of the Statute Law of Northern Ireland and make recommendations with respect to its consolidation and revision.

		1	2	3
a.	Number if a multiple body/system (1.4.98)	–	–	–
b.	Number of staff employed by the body (1.4.98)	–	–	–
c.	Annual Report	Body	Body	NP
d.	Audit arrangements			
e.	Total gross expenditure of body (1997/98)	–	–	–
f.	Amount funded by government (1997/98)	–	–	–
g.	Other expenditure by sponsoring dept (1997/98)	£0.021m	£0.470m	–
h.	Chief Executive's Remuneration (1997/98)	–	–	–
	Appointments and Remuneration (1.9.98)			
i.	Chairman/President	1M*	1M, £19,075	1M
j.	Deputy	1M*	–	–
k.	Members	4M, 4F, £2,360	11M, 3F, £3,830	5M, 5F
l.	Tribunal cases received	–	–	–
m.	Tribunal cases disposed of	–	–	–

* Holds judicial office and does not receive an honorarium.

Northern Ireland Department of Health & Social Services

Office of the Permanent Secretary
Castle Buildings, Stormont
Belfast BT4 3PP

Executive NDPBs

1
Mental Health Commission for Northern Ireland

Elizabeth House
118 Holywood Road
Belfast
BT4 1NY
TEL: 01232 651157
FAX: 01232 471180
CHAIR: Mr Gerard Duffy
SECRETARY: Mr Francis Walsh
TERMS OF REFERENCE: To monitor the care and treatment of the mentally disordered.

2
National Board for Nursing, Midwifery and Health Visiting for Northern Ireland

Centre House
79 Chichester Street
Belfast
BT1 4JE
TEL: 01232 238152
FAX: 01232 333298
enquiries@nbni.n-i.nhs.uk
http://hpssweb.n-i.uk/nbni
CHAIR: Mr Robert Bowman
CHIEF EXECUTIVE: Professor Oliver Slevin
TERMS OF REFERENCE: To approve educational institutions and courses in relation to the provision of courses in nursing, midwifery and health visiting.

3
Northern Ireland Council for Postgraduate Medical and Dental Education

5 Annadale Avenue
Belfast
BT7 3JH
TEL: 01232 491731
FAX: 01232 642279
paddy.lynch@dhssni.gov.uk
CHAIR: Professor Gary Love
TERMS OF REFERENCE: To facilitate the provision and development of high quality postgraduate and continuing medical and dental education within Northern Ireland, through the organisation and funding of training grades; co-ordinating, accrediting and reviewing programmes; and monitoring of quality and standards.

		1	2	3
a.	Number if a multiple body/system (1.4.98)	–	–	–
b.	Number of staff employed by the body (1.4.98)	8*	27.5	55.5
c.	Annual Report	TSO	Body	Body
d.	Audit arrangements	X†	X*	Y
e.	Total gross expenditure of body (1997/98)	£0.362m	£14.383m	£15.784m
f.	Amount funded by government (1997/98)	£0.362m	£12.287m	£15.593m
g.	Other expenditure by sponsoring dept (1997/98)	–	–	–
h.	Chief Executive's Remuneration (1997/98)	‡	£51,000	£75,797
	Appointments and Remuneration (1.9.98)			
i.	Chairman/President	1M, £11,325	1M, £6,000	1M
j.	Deputy	1M, £162pd	1F	1M
k.	Members	6M, 7F, £162pd	3M†, 3F, 1 vacancy	2M*, 3F, {17M, 6F}†
l.	Tribunal cases received	–	–	–
m.	Tribunal cases disposed of	–	–	–

* The Secretariat are Civil Servants seconded from the Department.
† The primary audit is carried out by auditors appointed by the Department with a secondary audit undertaken by the Comptroller and Auditor General (NI).
‡ No Chief Executive Post.

* The primary audit is carried out by auditors appointed by the Department with a secondary audit undertaken by the Comptroller and Auditor General (NI).
† Two executive members appointed by DHSS to the body.

* Includes 2 ex-officio members.
† 23 members appointed by the executive body.

NORTHERN IRELAND : DEPARTMENT OF HEALTH AND SOCIAL SERVICES

Advisory NDPBs

4 Charities Advisory Committee

Castle Buildings
Stormont
Belfast
BT4 3SL
TEL : 01232 522203
FAX : 01232 523302
CHAIR : Mr Frank Ledwidge OBE
SECRETARY : Mr Trevor Campbell
TERMS OF REFERENCE : To advise the Department of Health and Social Services on investment matters.

5 Disability Living Allowance Advisory Board for Northern Ireland

Castle Court
Royal Avenue
Belfast
BT1 1DS
TEL : 01232 336916
FAX : 01232 542112
CHAIR : Dr Agnes McKnight
BOARD SECRETARY : Dr Martin Donnelly
TERMS OF REFERENCE : To advise the Department of Health and Social Services on matters relating to Disability Living Allowance, including on specific cases and questions referred to it.

6 Distinction and Meritorious Service Awards Committee

Room 4A, Dundonald House
Upper Newtownards Road
Belfast
BT4 3SF
TEL : 01232 524319
FAX : 01232 524437
paddy.lynch@dhssni.gov.uk
CHAIR : Sir Brian Kerr
SECRETARY : Mr Paddy Lynch
TERMS OF REFERENCE : The HSS Distinction and Meritorious Service Awards Scheme is designed to award individual medical and dental consultants for outstanding work under the HSS in Northern Ireland; and the committee makes recommendations for awards under the scheme.

7 Northern Ireland Disability Council (NIDC)

Room C4.8
Castle Buildings
Stormont
Belfast BT4 3PP
TEL : 01232 520775/520528
FAX : 01232 520529
pat.osborne@dhss.ni.gov.uk
CHAIR : Mr Harry McConnell
SECRETARY : Mrs Pat Osborne
TERMS OF REFERENCE : To advise Government on the elimination of discrimination against disabled people and on the operation of the Disability Discrimination Act.

8 Poisons Board

Health Protection, Annex 4
Castle Buildings
Stormont
Belfast BT4 3SJ
TEL : 01232 522111
FAX : 01232 523270
michael.kelly2@dhssni.gov.uk
CHAIR : Mr Timothy Ferris
SECRETARY : Mr Michael Kelly
TERMS OF REFERENCE : To advise the Department of Health and Social Services on substances which are to be treated as non-medicinal poisons and on matters concerning the sale, supply and storage of non-medical poisons.

	4	5	6	7	8
a	–	–	–	–	–
b	–	–	–	–	–
c	Body	Body	Body	*	NP
d	–	–	–	–	–
e	–	–	–	–	–
f	–	–	–	–	–
g	£0.039m	£0.038m	£0.053m	£0.173m	*
h	–	–	–	–	–
i	1M	1F, £273pd/£137.50pm	1M, £2,125*	1M, £250pd	1M
j	–	–	–	–	–
k	2M, 2F	4M, 2F, £237pd/£119pm* 3M, 5F, £126pd/£63pm† 1 vacancy	6M, 2F†	7M, 6F, £122pd	9M, 1F
l	–	–	–	–	–
m	–	–	–	–	–

5:
* Medical member.
† Lay member.

6:
* The Chairman is entitled to an annual Honorarium but has declined to accept it.
† The Medical Director of the Committee receives £102hd or £201pd. Three members receive the Retired Members fee of £103pd and the remaining 4 members receive no remuneration.

7:
* NIDC has a statutory duty to prepare an annual report which has to be laid before the Assembly.

8:
* Board incurs minimal expenditure on travel to meetings.

NORTHERN IRELAND : DEPARTMENT OF HEALTH AND SOCIAL SERVICES

Tribunal NDPBs

9 Child Support Appeal Tribunals (CSATs)

Cleaver House
3 Donegall Square North
Belfast
BT1 5GA
TEL : 01232 539900
FAX : 01232 313112
CHAIR : Various
SECRETARY : Miss Ann Loney
TERMS OF REFERENCE : To consider and hear appeals following the decision of Child Support Officers. The tribunal is the responsibility of the Independent Tribunal Service.

10 Disability Appeal Tribunals (DATs)

Cleaver House
3 Donegall Square North
Belfast
BT1 5GA
TEL : 01232 539900
FAX : 01232 313112
CHAIR : Various
SECRETARY : Miss Ann Loney
TERMS OF REFERENCE : To decide on Disability Living Allowance, Working Allowance and Attendance Allowance cases, where appeals have been made on disability questions. This tribunal is the responsibility of the Independent Tribunal Service.

11 Medical Appeal Tribunals (MATs)

Cleaver House
3 Donegall Square North
Belfast
BT1 5GA
TEL : 01232 539900
FAX : 01232 313112
CHAIR : Various
SECRETARY : Miss Ann Loney
TERMS OF REFERENCE : To consider, on appeal by a claimant or by reference of the Department, the decisions of adjudication medical authorities, arising out of claims for Industrial Injuries Benefits and Severe Disablement Allowance. The tribunal is the responsibility of the Independent Tribunal Service.

12 Mental Health Review Tribunal for Northern Ireland

Room 105
Dundonald House
Upper Newtownards Road
Belfast BT4 3SF
TEL : 01232 485550
FAX : 01232 524615
bernie.gray@dhssni.gov.uk
CHAIR : Mr Frazer Elliott QC
SECRETARY : Mrs Marion Hobson
TERMS OF REFERENCE : To hear appeals against detention for treatment, or against guardianship, under the Order; and to review, periodically, patients who are detained or subject to guardianship.

13 Registered Homes Tribunal

Room 115
Dundonald House
Upper Newtownards Road
Belfast BT4 3SF
TEL : 01232 524731
FAX : 01232 524733
stuart.baxter@dhssni.gov.uk
CHAIR : Mr Kenneth Irvine
SECRETARY : Mr Stuart Baxter
TERMS OF REFERENCE : To consider an appeal against the decision of a Health and Social Services Board cancelling the registration of a person in respect of a home or varying or imposing an additional condition in respect of a home.

	9	10	11	12	13
a	–	–	–	–	–
b	–	–	–	–	–
c	NP	NP	NP	Body	NP
d	–	–	–	–	–
e	–	–	–	–	–
f	–	–	–	–	–
g	£0.037m	£0.704m	£0.082m	£0.125m	–
h	–	–	–	–	–
i	1 President* Chairmen 4M, 10F†, £131.50pm	1 President* Chairmen 10M, 7F†, £131.50pm	1 President* Chairmen 4M, 4F†, £159.50pm§	1M, £251pd* + £375†	1M, £253pd 1 vacancy*
j	–	–	–	1M, £251pd*	–
k	{48M, 33F}‡	{59M, 73F}‡ £98pm§ £60.50pm¶ £120pm#	{21M, 2F}‡ £145.50pm†	7M, 1F, £251pd* 5M, 3F, £238pd 2M, 6F, £102pd	12M, 15F, £162pd
l	274	6,931	426	228	1
m	262	8,992	654	198	1

* There is one President (M) for CSATs, DATs, MATs and SSATs. He receives a salary of £86,801.
† Appointments are made by the Lord Chancellor's Department.
‡ Members appointed by the President of the respective Appeals Tribunal.

* There is one President (M) for CSATs, DATs, MATs and SSATs. He receives a salary of £86,801.
† Appointments are made by the Lord Chancellor's Department.
‡ Members appointed by the President of the respective Appeals Tribunal.
§ Medical member.
¶ Other member.
# Consultant.

* There is one President (M) for CSATs, DATs, MATs and SSATs. He receives a salary of £86,801.
† Appointments are made by the Lord Chancellor's Department.
‡ Members appointed by the President of the respective Appeals Tribunal.
§ MAT Chairman and Members' fee includes preparation fee.

* Appointments are made by the Lord Chancellor's Department.
† Annual retainer.

* Appointments are made by the Lord Chancellor's Department.

NORTHERN IRELAND : DEPARTMENT OF HEALTH AND SOCIAL SERVICES

Tribunal NDPBs

Health and Personal Social Services NDPBs

Health and Social Services Boards

14 Social Security Appeal Tribunals (SSATs)

Cleaver House
3 Donegall Square North
Belfast
BT1 5GA
TEL : 01232 539900
FAX : 01232 313112
CHAIR : Various
SECRETARY : Miss Ann Loney
TERMS OF REFERENCE : To consider and hear appeals in relation to decisions made by adjudication officers on Social Security benefits. To decide on matters of adjudication referred by an adjudication officer. This tribunal is the responsibility of the Independent Tribunal Service.

15 Tribunal Under Schedule 11 to the Health and Personal Social Services (NI) Order 1972

Room 436
Dundonald House
Upper Newtownards Road
Belfast BT4 3SF
TEL : 01232 524980
FAX : 01232 524863
CHAIR : Mr Alan Comerton QC
CLERK TO THE TRIBUNAL : Vacant
TERMS OF REFERENCE : To inquire into cases where representations are made by a Health and Social Services Board or other persons for the continued inclusion of persons.

16 Eastern

12–22 Livenhall Street
Belfast
BT2 8BS
TEL : 01232 321313
FAX : 01232 321520
enquiry@ehssb.n-i.nhs.uk
http://www.n-i.nhs.uk/board/index.html
CHAIR : Mr Daniel Thompson CBE ; CHIEF EXECUTIVE : Dr Paula Kilbane
TERMS OF REFERENCE : Planning and commissioning health and personal services for their resident populations.

17 Northern

County Hall
182 Galgorm Road
Ballymena
BT42 1QB
TEL : 01266 653333
FAX : 01266 643094
pr@nhssb.n-i.nhs.uk
CHAIR : Mr Robert Hanna CBE
CHIEF EXECUTIVE : Mr Stuart MacDonnell
TERMS OF REFERENCE : Planning and commissioning health and personal services for their resident population.

18 Southern

Tower Hill
Armagh
BT61 5QD
TEL : 01861 410041
FAX : 01861 414550
shirlemc@shssb.n-i.nhs.uk
http://www.shssb.org
CHAIR : Mr William Gillespie OBE
CHIEF EXECUTIVE : Mr Brendan Cunningham
TERMS OF REFERENCE : Planning and commissioning health and personal services for their resident population.

	14	15	16	17	18
a	20	–	–	–	–
b	–	–	232	168.5	134
c	NP	NP	Body	Body	Body
d	–	–	–	–	–
e	–	–	£644.931m	£372.409	£283.792m
f	–	–	£661.937m	£373.359m†	£284.617m†
g	£0.889m	–	–	–	–
h	–	–	£86,000	£67,000	£69,000
i	1 President* Chairmen 31M, 16F†, £131.50pm	{1M, £256pd}*	1M, £22,660	1M, £14,835	1M, £14,835
j	–	1M, £256pd	–	–	–
k	{141M, 77F}‡ Medical Assessors§ {61M, 18F}, £98pm	9M, 3F, £118pd† £191pd‡	4M, 2F, £5,000	3M, 2F, 1 vacancy, £5,000	3M, 3F, £5,000
l	9,964	–	–	–	–
m	11,338	–	–	–	–

* There is one President (M) for CSATs, DATs, MATs and SSATs. He receives a salary of £86,801.
† Appointments are made by the Lord Chancellor's Department.
‡ Members appointed by President of respective Appeals Tribunal.
§ Medical Assessors appointed from SSAT by the President (not a member of tribunal as they do not make decisions. They are advisors on medical issues).

* Chairman is appointed by the Lord Chief Justice.
† Lay member.
‡ Professional member.

† Surplus made by this Board during the year.

NORTHERN IRELAND : DEPARTMENT OF HEALTH AND SOCIAL SERVICES

Health and Personal Social Services NDPBs

Health and Social Services Councils

19 Western	20 Eastern	21 Northern	22 Southern	23 Western
15 Gransha Park Clooney Road Londonderry BT47 1TG	19 Bedford Street Belfast BT2 7EJ	8 Broadway Avenue Ballymena BT43 7AA	Quaker Buildings High Street Lurgan BT66 8BB	'Hilltop', Tyrone and Fermanagh Hospital Omagh BT79 0NS
TEL : 01504 860086 FAX : 01504 860311 gormleym@whssb.n-i.nhs.uk CHAIR : Mr Robert Toland GENERAL MANAGER : Mr Tom Frawley TERMS OF REFERENCE : Planning and commissioning health and personal services for their resident population.	TEL : 01232 321230 FAX : 01232 321750 ecouncil@ehssc.n-i.nhs.uk CHAIR : Mrs Pat Stout CHIEF OFFICER : Ms Jane Graham TERMS OF REFERENCE : Representing the interests of the public in the health and social services in their Health and Social Services Board Area; and providing an independent oversight of the activities of the Board.	TEL : 01266 655777 FAX : 01266 655112 CHAIR : Mr Hugh Ewing CHIEF OFFICER : Mr Noel Graham TERMS OF REFERENCE : Representing the interests of the public in the health and social services in their Health and Social Services Board Area; and providing an independent oversight of the activities of the Board.	TEL : 01762 349900 FAX : 01762 349858 nancyds@shssb.n-i.nks.uk CHAIR : Mrs Fionnuela Cook CHIEF OFFICER : Mr Seamus Magee TERMS OF REFERENCE : Representing the interests of the public in the health and social services in their Health and Social Services Board Area; and providing an independent oversight of the activities of the Board.	TEL : 01662 252555 FAX : 01662 252544 CHAIR : Mr Francis Hughes SECRETARY : Mr Stanley Millar OBE TERMS OF REFERENCE : Representing the interests of the public in the health and social services in their Health and Social Services Board Area; and providing an independent oversight of the activities of the Board.
a —	a —	a —	a —	a —
b 97.5*	b 8	b 6	b 4.5	b 3
c Body	c Body	c Body	c Body	c Body
d —	d —	d —	d —	d —
e £260.004m	e £0.252m‡	e £0.140m‡	e £0.177m‡	e £0.080m‡
f £263.342m‡	f £0.252m‡	f £0.140m‡	f £0.177m‡	f £0.080m‡
g —	g —	g —	g —	g —
h £81,000	h §	h §	h §	h §
i 1M, £14,835	i 1F¶	i 1M¶	i 1F¶	i 1M¶
j —	j —	j —	j —	j —
k 3M, 3F, £5,000	k 12M, 12F, 5 vacancies	k 15M, 6F, 2 vacancies	k 10M, 10F, 3 vacancies	k 15M, 8F
l —	l —	l —	l —	l —
m —	m —	m —	m —	m —

* Staff previously employed by the Western Health and Social Services Board have transferred to Foyle Health and Social Services Trust to provide services for the trusts and are included under the trusts figure.

* Staff previously employed by the Western Health and Social Services Board have transferred to Foyle Health and Social Services Trust to provide services for the trusts and are included under the trusts figure.

† Surplus made by this Board during the year.

‡ Expenditure and funding for each of the four Health and Social Services Councils is also included in the expenditure figures for each of the four Health and Social Service Boards.

§ No Chief Executive.

¶ Elected from members.

NORTHERN IRELAND : DEPARTMENT OF HEALTH AND SOCIAL SERVICES

Health and Personal Social Services NDPBs

24 Health and Social Services Trusts

Dundonald House
Upper Newtownards Road
Belfast
BT4 3SF
TEL : 01232 520500
TERMS OF REFERENCE : To own and/or provide hospitals or other establishments or facilities formerly provided by Health and Social Services Boards for the purpose of providing services under the health and personal social services, and in some cases to exercise statutory functions by virtue of formal authorisations under article 3(1) of the Health and Personal Social Services (NI) Order 1994.

25 Northern Ireland Blood Transfusion Service Agency

Belfast City Hospital Complex
Lisburn Road
Belfast
BT9 7TS
TEL : 01232 321414
FAX : 01232 439017
CHAIR : Dr Lucinda Blakiston Houston ; CHIEF EXECUTIVE/ MEDICAL DIRECTOR : Dr W H McClelland
TERMS OF REFERENCE : To supply blood and blood products to all hospitals and clinical units in Northern Ireland.

26 Northern Ireland Central Services Agency (NICSA)

25 Adelaide Street
Belfast
BT2 8SH
TEL : 01232 324431
FAX : 01232 232304
CHAIR : Mr Brian Carlin
CHIEF EXECUTIVE : Mr Stephen Hodkinson
TERMS OF REFERENCE : To administer certain services for the health and personal social services, which are provided most effectively on a regional basis. The services include legal advice; regional supplies; general medical, opthalmic, dental and pharmaceutical services.

27 Northern Ireland Guardian Ad Litem Agency (NIGALA)

Centre House
Chichester Street
Belfast
BT1 4JE
TEL : 01232 316550
FAX : 01232 319811
ann@nigala.n-i.nhs.uk
CHAIR : Ms Corinne Philpott QC
EXECUTIVE DIRECTOR : Mr Ronnie Williamson
TERMS OF REFERENCE : To recruit and manage a panel of persons from whom courts in Northern Ireland shall appoint Guardians ad litem for the purposes of specified proceedings under the Children (Northern Ireland) Order 1995 and adoption proceedings under the Adoption (Northern Ireland) Order 1987.

28 Northern Ireland Health Promotion Agency

18 Ormeau Avenue
Belfast
BT2 8HS
TEL : 01232 311611
FAX : 01232 311711
hpani@hpa.n-i.nhs.uk
http://www.healthpromotionagency.org.uk
CHAIR : Mr Douglas Smyth OBE
CHIEF EXECUTIVE : Dr Brian Gaffney
TERMS OF REFERENCE : To advise the Department of Health and Social Services on matters relating to health promotion.

	24	25	26	27	28
a	19	–	–	–	–
b	40,746	154	312.5	27	31
c	Body	Body	Body	Body	Body
d	–	–	–	–	–
e	1,321.393m	£9.835m	£34.558m*	£0.919m	£1.843m
f	*	*	£1.677m	£0.729m	£1.502m
g	–	–	–	–	–
h	†	£72,228†	£63,462	£36,993	£69,596
i	16M, 3F, £15,125–£19,285	1F, £6,000	1M, £12,000	1F, £6,000	1M, £7,220
j	–	–	–	–	–
k	51M, 36F, £5,000 7 vacancies	2M, £1,500	3M, £3,500	1M, 1F, £2,500	4M, 4F, 1 vacancy
l	–	–	–	–	–
m	–	–	–	–	–

* Not directly funded. Funding via service level agreements with commissioners.
† HSS Trusts are required to include in their published annual report details of their Chief Executive's remuneration.

* Not directly funded. Funding via service level agreements with commissioners.
† Includes merit award and additional sessions.

* Balance of expenditure is funded via commissioners.

NORTHERN IRELAND : DEPARTMENT OF HEALTH AND SOCIAL SERVICES

29
Northern Ireland Regional Medical Physics Agency (NIRMPA)

12–22 Linenhall Dtreet
Belfast
BT2 8BS

TEL : 01232 314535
FAX : 01232 313040
heather.mcvea@mpa.n-i.nhs.uk

CHAIR : Mr Albert Sherrard OBE
CHIEF EXECUTIVE : Professor Peter Smith

TERMS OF REFERENCE : To provide a service to clinicians and other professional staff in the health and personal social services in scientific measurement and control of high technology equipment used for the safe clinical investigation and treatment of patients.

a	–
b	63
c	Body
d	–
e	£2.444m
f	*
g	–
h	£53,659
i	1M, £6,000
j	–
k	1M, £1,500
l	–
m	–

* Not directly funded. Funding via service level agreements with commissioners.

115

NORTHERN IRELAND : OFFICE FOR THE REGULATION OF ELECTRICITY & GAS

Office for the Regulation of Electricity & Gas

Brookmount Buildings
42 Fountain Street
Belfast BT1 5EE

Advisory NDPBs

1
Northern Ireland Consumer Committee for Electricity

Brookmount Buildings
42 Fountain Street
Belfast
BT1 5EE
TEL : 01232 311575
FAX : 01232 311740
CHAIR : Mrs Nuala O'Loan
SECRETARY : Mrs Anne McMinnis
TERMS OF REFERENCE : To pursue the interests of electricity consumers in Northern Ireland; and to consider how best the needs of customers are met.

		1
a.	Number if a multiple body/system (1.4.98)	–
b.	Number of staff employed by the body (1.4.98)	–
c.	Annual Report	TSO
d.	Audit arrangements	–
e.	Total gross expenditure of body (1997/98)	–
f.	Amount funded by government (1997/98)	–
g.	Other expenditure by sponsoring dept (1997/98)	£0.015m
h.	Chief Executive's Remuneration (1997/98)	–
	Appointments and Remuneration (1.9.98)	
i.	Chairman/President	{1F, £18,582}*
j.	Deputy	–
k.	Members	{5M, 4F}*†
l.	Tribunal cases received	–
m.	Tribunal cases disposed of	–

* Appointed by the Director General of Electricity Supply for Northern Ireland.
† Members receive expenses and loss of earnings (not more than four hours; £23pd; in excess of four hours; £47pd).

OFFICE FOR NATIONAL STATISTICS

Office for National Statistics

1 Drummond Gate,
London SW1V 2QQ

Enquiries	Guy Goodwin
Telephone	0171 533 6210
Facsimile	0171 533 6219
E-mail	guy.goodwin@ons.gov.uk
Internet	http://www.ons.gov.uk
GTN	3042 6210

Advisory NDPBs

1 Statistics Advisory Committee

Office for National Statistics
1 Drummond Gate
London
SW1V 2QQ

TEL : 0171 533 6210
FAX : 0171 533 6219
guy.goodwin@ons.gov.uk
http://www.ons.gov.uk
CHAIR : Dr D (Tim) Holt
SECRETARY : Mr Guy Goodwin
TERMS OF REFERENCE : The Statistics Advisory Committee advises the Director of the Office for National Statistics (ONS) on the statistical work of ONS, on annual ONS corporate targets and on his responsibilities as Head of the Government Statistical Service.

a.	Number if a multiple body (1.4.98)	a —
b.	Number of staff employed by the body (1.4.98)	b —
c.	Annual Report	c NP
d.	Audit arrangements	d —
e.	Total gross expenditure of body (1997/98)	e —
f.	Amount funded by government (1997/98)	f —
g.	Other expenditure by sponsoring dept (1997/98)	g £0.001m
h.	Chief Executive's Remuneration (1997/98)	h —
	Appointments and Remuneration (1.9.98)	
i.	Chairman/President	i *
j.	Deputy	j —
k.	Members	k {13M, 5F}† 1 vacancy
l.	Tribunal cases received	l —
m.	Tribunal cases disposed of	m —

* The Director of the Office for National Statistics is the Chairman.
† Appointments are made by the Director of ONS, with the approval of the Chancellor of the Exchequer (ONS Framework Document)

Office of the Rail Regulator

1 Waterhouse Square, Holborn Bars,
138–142 Holborn, London EC1N 2SU

Enquiries   Kevin Gargan
Telephone   0171 282 2079
Facsimile   0171 282 2044
E-mail   orr@dial.pipex.com
Internet   http://www.rail-reg.gov.uk

Executive NDPBs

	1. Central Rail Users' Consultative Committee (CRUCC)*†	2. Rail Users' Consultative Committee for Eastern England	3. Rail Users' Consultative Committee for the Midlands
Address	Clements House, 14–18 Gresham Street, London, EC2V 7NL	Crescent House, 46 Priestgate, Peterborough, PE1 1LF	77 Paradise Circus, Queensway, Birmingham, B1 2DT
TEL	0171 505 9090	01733 312188	0121 212 2133
FAX	0171 505 9004	01733 891286	0121 236 6945
CHAIR	Mr David Bertram	Mr Stewart Francis	Dr Peris Jones
ACTING NATIONAL DIRECTOR	Mr Jonathan Carter		
SECRETARY		Mr Guy Dangerfield	Ms Gillian James
TERMS OF REFERENCE	The CRUCC deals with issues affecting rail users nationally and co-ordinates the work of the eight Rail Users' Consultative Committees (RUCCs).	The Rail Users' Consultative Committee (RUCC) for Eastern England (one of the eight RUCCs) are collectively the statutory watchdog protecting and promoting the interests of rail users. Membership is made up of regular rail users who act as a focus for passengers' views in their areas.	The Rail Users' Consultative Committee (RUCC) for the Midlands (one of the eight RUCCs) are collectively the statutory watchdog protecting and promoting the interests of rail users. Membership is made up of regular rail users who act as a focus for passengers' views in their areas.
a. Number if a multiple body (1.4.98)	–	–	–
b. Number of staff employed by the body (1.4.98)	31	–	–
c. Annual Report	Body	–	–
d. Audit arrangements	Y	Y	Y
e. Total gross expenditure of body (1997/98)	£1.55m‡	–	–
f. Amount funded by government (1997/98)	£1.55m‡	–	–
g. Other expenditure by sponsoring dept (1997/98)	–	–	–
h. Chief Executive's Remuneration (1997/98)	–	–	–
Appointments and Remuneration (1.9.98)			
i. Chairman/President	1M, £8,831	1M, £6,646	1M, £6,646
j. Deputy	–	–	–
k. Members	6M, 2F, £6,646; 1M§; 3M, 1F	{9M, 4F}	{9M, 4F}*
l. Tribunal cases received	–	–	–
m. Tribunal cases disposed of	–	–	–

* ORR is directly financed by money voted by Parliament to cover its expenditure, including the costs of the Rail Users' Consultative Committees.

† CRUCC comprised from RUCC and London Rail Passengers Committee (LRPC) Chairmen as well as independent members.

‡ Figures in Rows 'b' to 'f' refer to CRUCC and Regional RUCCs.

§ LRPC Chairman salary paid by DETR.

* Members appointed by the Rail Regultor. (columns 2 and 3)

OFFICE OF THE RAIL REGULATOR

Executive NDPBs

Rail Users' Consultative Committees

	4	5	6	7	8
	Rail Users' Consultative Committee for North Eastern England	**Rail Users' Consultative Committee for North Western England**	**Rail Users' Consultative Committee for Scotland**	**Rail Users' Consultative Committee for Southern England**	**Rail Users' Consultative Committee for Wales**
	Hilary House 16 St Saviours Place York YO1 2PL	Bolton House 17–21 Chorlton Street Manchester M1 3HY	249 West George Street Glasgow G2 4QE	4th Floor 35 Old Queen Street London SW1H 9JA	St Davids House Wood Street Cardiff CF1 1ES
TEL	01904 625615	0161 228 6247	0141 221 7760	0171 222 0391	01222 227247
FAX	01904 643026	0161 236 1476	0141 221 3393	0171 222 0392	01222 223992
CHAIR	Mr Jim Beale	Mr Brendan O'Friel	Mrs Helen Millar	Ms Wendy Toms	Mr Charles Hogg
SECRETARY	Mr Ernie Preston	Mr John Moorhouse	Mr Bill Ure	Mr Mike Hewitson	Mr Clive Williams
TERMS OF REFERENCE	The Rail Users' Consultative Committee (RUCC) for North Eastern England (one of the eight RUCCs) are collectively the statutory watchdog protecting and promoting the interests of rail users. Membership is made up of regular rail users who act as a focus for passengers' views in their areas.	The Rail Users' Consultative Committee (RUCC) for North Western England (one of the eight RUCCs) are collectively the statutory watchdog protecting and promoting the interests of rail users. Membership is made up of regular rail users who act as a focus for passengers' views in their areas.	The Rail Users' Consultative Committee (RUCC) for Scotland (one of the eight RUCCs) are collectively the statutory watchdog protecting and promoting the interests of rail users. Membership is made up of regular rail users who act as a focus for passengers' views in their areas.	The Rail Users' Consultative Committee (RUCC) for Southern England (one of the eight RUCCs) are collectively the statutory watchdog protecting and promoting the interests of rail users. Membership is made up of regular rail users who act as a focus for passengers' views in their areas.	The Rail Users' Consultative Committee (RUCC) for Wales (one of the eight RUCCs) are collectively the statutory watchdog protecting and promoting the interests of rail users. Membership is made up of regular rail users who act as a focus for passengers' views in their areas.
a	–	–	–	–	–
b	–	–	–	–	–
c	–	–	–	–	–
d	Y	Y	Y	Y	Y
e	–	–	–	–	–
f	–	–	–	–	–
g	–	–	–	–	–
h	–	–	–	–	–
i	1M, £6,646	1M, £6,646	1M, £6,646	1M, £6,646	1M, £6,646
j	–	–	–	–	–
k	{11M, 1F}*	{7M, 4F}*	{10M, 2F}*	{7M, 4F}*	{12M, 2F}*
l	–	–	–	–	–
m	–	–	–	–	–

* Members appointed by the Rail Regulator.

OFFICE OF THE RAIL REGULATOR

Executive NDPBs

RUCCs

9

Rail Users' Consultative Committee for Western England

Tower House
Fairfax Street
Bristol
BS1 3BN
TEL : 0117 926 5703
FAX : 0117 929 4140
CHAIR : Mr Kevin Small
SECRETARY : Mr Sean O'Neill
TERMS OF REFERENCE : The Rail Users' Consultative Committee (RUCC) for Western England (one of the eight RUCCs) are collectively the statutory watchdog protecting and promoting the interests of rail users. Membership is made up of regular rail users who act as a focus for passengers' views in their areas.

a	–
b	–
c	–
d	Y
e	–
f	–
g	–
h	–
i	1M, £6,646
j	–
k	{8M, 2F}*
l	–
m	–

* Members appointed by the Rail Regulator.

Royal Mint

Llantrisant, Pontyclun CF72 8YT

Enquiries Mr G P Dyer
Telephone 01443 623004
Facsimile 01443 623190

Advisory NDPBs

1
Royal Mint Advisory Committee on the Design of Coins, Medals, Seals and Decorations

The Royal Mint
Llantrisant
Pontyclun
CF72 8YT

TEL : 01443 623004
FAX : 01443 623190

CHAIR : HRH Prince Philip, Duke of Edinburgh ; SECRETARY : Mr Graham Dyer

TERMS OF REFERENCE : To consider new designs for United Kingdom coins and official medals.

a.	Number if a multiple body (1.4.98)	–
b.	Number of staff employed by the body (1.4.98)	–
c.	Annual Report	*
d.	Audit arrangements	–
e.	Total gross expenditure of body (1997/98)	–
f.	Amount funded by government (1997/98)	–
g.	Other expenditure by sponsoring dept (1997/98)	£0.003m
h.	Chief Executive's Remuneration (1997/98)	–
	Appointments and Remuneration (1.9.98)	
i.	Chairman/President	1M
j.	Deputy	–
k.	Members	7M, 2F
l.	Tribunal cases received	–
m.	Tribunal cases disposed of	–

* Published as part of the Royal Mint Annual Report, available from The Stationery Office.

SCOTTISH COURTS ADMINISTRATION

Scottish Courts Administration

Hayweight House, 23 Lauriston Street, Edinburgh EH3 9DQ

Enquiries   Miss M M Peattie
Telephone   0131 221 6818
Facsimile   0131 221 6895
E-mail   mpeattie@scotcourts.gov.uk

Advisory NDPBs

1 Scottish Law Commission

140 Causewayside
Edinburgh
EH9 1PR

TEL : 0131 668 2131
FAX : 0131 662 4900
CHAIR : Hon Lord Gill
SECRETARY : Mr James MacLean
TERMS OF REFERENCE : To promote the systematic reform and development of Scottish Law.

Tribunal NDPBs

2 Lands Tribunal for Scotland (LTS)

1 Grosvenor Crescent
Edinburgh
EH12 5ER

TEL : 0131 225 3595
FAX : 0131 226 4812
PRESIDENT : The Hon Lord McGhie ; CLERK TO THE TRIBUNAL : Neil M Tainsh
TERMS OF REFERENCE : The tribunal deals with land valuations and applications in connection with tenants' rights to buy their council houses.

3 Pensions Appeal Tribunal for Scotland (PATS)

20 Walker Street
Edinburgh
EH3 7HS

TEL : 0131 220 1404
FAX : 0131 225 2596
CHAIR : Mr Colin McEachran QC
SECRETARY : Mrs Lesley Young
TERMS OF REFERENCE : To arrange and organise appeal hearings; and to issue decisions following from them. Appeals arise from the refusal of applications to the Department of Social Security for entitlement or re-assessment of war pensions.

	Scottish Law Commission	Lands Tribunal for Scotland (LTS)	Pensions Appeal Tribunal for Scotland (PATS)
a. Number if a multiple body (1.4.98)	–	–	–
b. Number of staff employed by the body (1.4.98)	–	–	–
c. Annual Report	HC	NP	NP
d. Audit arrangements			
e. Total gross expenditure of body (1997/98)	–	–	–
f. Amount funded by government (1997/98)	–	–	–
g. Other expenditure by sponsoring dept (1997/98)	£1.189m	£0.353m	£0.327m
h. Chief Executive's Remuneration (1997/98)	–	–	–
Appointments and Remuneration (1.9.98)			
i. Chairman/President	1M, 116,045	{1M}*†	{1M, £282pd}*†
j. Deputy	–	–	–
k. Members	2M, £76,646	{3M, £83,523}†	{26M, 1F, £254–£282pd}†
	1M, £30,634	{1M, £33,409}†	
	1M, £30,658		
l. Tribunal cases received	–	177	1,125
m. Tribunal cases disposed of	–	107	1,316

* President of LTS is also Chairman of the Scottish Land Court.
† Appointments to LTS and PATS are made by the Lord President of the Court of Session.

* President of PATS also receives £4,230 annual administrative allowance.
† Appointments to LTS and PATS are made by the Lord President of the Court of Session.

Scottish Office

St Andrew's House, Edinburgh EH1 3DG

Enquiries	Mr Maurice Grant
Telephone	0131 244 4995
Facsimile	0131 244 2764
Internet	http://www.scotland.gov.uk
GTN	7188 4995

Public Corporations

	1 **East of Scotland Water Authority**	2 **North of Scotland Water Authority**	3 **West of Scotland Water Authority**
	Pentland Gait 597 Calder Road Edinburgh EH11 4HJ TEL : 0131 453 7500 FAX : 0131 453 7554 info@esw.co.uk http://www.esw.co.uk CHAIR : Cllr Robert Cairns TERMS OF REFERENCE : Provision of water and sewerage services to the East of Scotland (Edinburgh, Borders, Lothians, Fife, Kinross, Stirling, Falkirk, and Clackmannan) and water services to parts of East Dunbartonshire and North Lanarkshire.	Cairngorm House Beechwood Park North Inverness IV2 3ED TEL : 01463 245400 FAX : 01463 245405 CHAIR : Cllr Colin Rennie TERMS OF REFERENCE : The provision of water and sewerage services to those communities formerly served by Grampian, Highland, Tayside Regions, Orkney, Shetland and Western Isles Councils.	419 Balmore Road Glasgow G22 6NU TEL : 0141 355 5333 FAX : 0141 355 5146 customer.services@ westscotlandwater.org.uk http://www. westscotlandwater.org.uk ACTING CHAIR : Mr John Goodwin TERMS OF REFERENCE : The provision of water and sewerage services to those communities formerly served by Dumfries and Galloway and Strathclyde Regional Councils.
a. Number if a multiple body/system (1.4.98)	–	–	–
b. Number of staff employed by the body (1.4.98)	–	–	–
c. Annual Report	Body*	Body*	Body*
d. Audit arrangements	–	–	–
e. Total gross expenditure of body (1997/98)	–	–	–
f. Amount funded by government (1997/98)	–	–	–
g. Other expenditure by sponsoring dept (1997/98)	–	–	–
h. Chief Executive's Remuneration (1997/98)	£112,810[†]	£115,000[†]	£90,000[†]
Appointments and Remuneration (1.9.98)			
i. Chairman/President	1M, £25,908	1M, £25,908	1M, £25,214
j. Deputy	–	–	–
k. Members	8M, 2F, £6,477	8M, 2F, £6,480	8M, 1F, £6,304
l. Tribunal cases received	–	–	–
m. Tribunal cases disposed of	–	–	–

* Authority publishes its own Annual Report which is laid before both Houses of Parliament.

† Including bonuses, taxable benefits and pension contributions. Current annual salary – £86,359.

† Including bonus taxable benefits and pension contributions. Current annual salary – £86,466.

† Including taxable benefits and pension contributions. Current annual salary – £86,477.

SCOTTISH OFFICE

Nationalised Industries

4
Caledonian MacBrayne Ltd

Ferry Terminal
The Pier
Gourock
PA19 1QP
TEL : 01475 650100
FAX : 01475 638708
http://www.calmac.co.uk
CHAIR : Rear Admiral Neil Rankin CB CBE
SECRETARY : Mr Gordon W MacKenzie
TERMS OF REFERENCE : The operation of the main network of ferry services to the islands off the West coast of Scotland.

5
Highlands and Islands Airports Ltd

Inverness Airport
Inverness
IV1 2JB
TEL : 01667 462445
FAX : 01667 464216
bmacleod@hial.co.uk
CHAIR : Mr Peter Grant CBE
SECRETARY : Mr A J Burns
TERMS OF REFERENCE : It is responsible for the management and operation of ten airports in the Highlands and Islands of Scotland: Barra, Benbecula, Campbeltown, Inverness, Islay, Kirkwall, Stornoway, Sumburgh, Tiree and Wick.

6
Scottish Transport Group

57 North Castle Street
Edinburgh
EH2 3LJ
TEL : 0131 226 7491
FAX : 0131 220 2216
CHAIR : Mr Ian Irwin CBE
SECRETARY : Mr John Stark
TERMS OF REFERENCE : STG remains in place to deal with residual matters from the sale in 1990–91 of the 10 Scottish Bus Group (SBG) bus companies. STG also acts as the parent company for SBG which is the final employer for the purpose of the winding up of the 2 pension schemes.

Executive NDPBs

7
The Accounts Commission for Scotland

18 George Street
Edinburgh
EH2 2QU
TEL : 0131 447 1234
FAX : 0131 477 4567
CHAIR : Professor Ian Percy CBE
SECRETARY : Mr William Magee
TERMS OF REFERENCE : To secure the audit of the accounts of all local authorities and NHS in Scotland, and a number associated public boards.

8
Hannah Research Institute

Kirkhall
Ayr
KA6 5HL
TEL : 01292 674000
FAX : 01292 674004
EMAIL : dunlop.j@hri.sari.ac.uk
http://www.hri.sari.ac.uk
CHAIR : Professor Sir Graeme Davies ; DIRECTOR : Professor Malcolm Peaker
TERMS OF REFERENCE : The UK-wide remit of the institute is to undertake fundamental, strategic and applied research relevant to the production and utilisation of milk and to lactation in general.

	4	5	6	7	8
a	–	–	–	–	–
b	–	–	–	148	146
c	Body	Body	Body	TSO	Body
d	–	–	–	X	Y
e	–	–	–	£10.318m	£4.000m
f	–	–	–	£0.050m	£2.836m
g	–	–	–	£0.020m	£0.053m
h	£70,000*	£60,000*	–	£95,002	£55,168
i	1M, £21,000	1M, £17,611	1M, £16,300	1M, £11,076	{1M}
j	–	–	–	1M, £7,035	–
k	1M* 2M, £48,626 1M, £46,261 4M, 1F, £5,695	1M* 2M, £5,623	4M, £5,795	8M, 5F, £3,588	2M, {6M}
l	–	–	–	–	–
m	–	–	–	–	–

* Managing Director (ex-officio Board Member).

* Managing Director (ex-officio Board Member).

124

SCOTTISH OFFICE

Executive NDPBs

Agricultural Research and Biological Institutes – Governing Bodies

9. Macauley Land Use Research Institute

Craigiebuckler
Aberdeen
AB15 8QH

TEL : 01224 318611
FAX : 01224 311556
d.wilkinson@mluri.sari.ac.uk
http://www.mluri.sari.ac.uk
CHAIR : Professor Janet Sprent
DIRECTOR : Professor T J Maxwell
TERMS OF REFERENCE : To undertake research, in the context of rural land use and resource management; to assess the environmental, economic and social impact of agriculture and related land use and the consequence of change resulting from factors and influence such as policy management.

10. Moredun Research Institute

Pentlands Science Park
Bush Loan
Penkicuik
Mid Lothian EH26 0PZ

TEL : 0131 445 5111
FAX : 0131 445 6235
raby.m@mri.sari.ac.uk
CHAIR : Mr John Izat
DIRECTOR : Professor Quintin McKellar
TERMS OF REFERENCE : To conduct integrated molecular, cellular and whole-animal studies on the aetiology, epidemiology, pathogenesis, immunobiology and control of animal diseases, that undermine biological efficiency, impair welfare or threaten public health.

11. Rowett Research Institute

Greenburn Road
Bucksburn
Aberdeen
AB21 9SB

TEL : 01224 712751
FAX : 01224 715349
d.blair@rri.ari.ac.uk
http://www.rri.sari.ac.uk
CHAIR : Mr James Provan
DIRECTOR : Prof W P T James
TERMS OF REFERENCE : The Institute's remit is to advance understanding of the biochemical and physiological aspects of mammalian nutrition, growth and interaction with reproduction; to conduct applied research in farm livestock production; and to investigate aspects of human nutrition.

12. Scottish Crop Research Institute

Mylnefield
Invergowrie
Dundee
DD2 5DA

TEL : 01382 562731
FAX : 01382 562426
r.killick@scri.sari.ac.uk
http://www.scri.sari.ac.uk
CHAIR : Mr Alasdair N MacCallum ; DIRECTOR : Professor John Hillman
TERMS OF REFERENCE : To contribute to crop research; in particular to exploit the advantages and to solve the problems of crop production in northern Britain through plant breeding, improved cultural practices and improved environmentally sensitive systems of crop production and protection.

13. Crofters' Commission

4–6 Castle Wynd
Inverness
IV2 3EQ

TEL : 01463 663450
FAX : 01463 711820
crofterscommission@cali.co.uk
CHAIR : Iain MacAskill
SECRETARY : Mike Grantham
TERMS OF REFERENCE : To reorganise, develop and regulate crofting and to promote the interests of crofters.

	9 Macauley	10 Moredun	11 Rowett	12 SCRI	13 Crofters'
a	–	–	–	–	–
b	253	146	278	346	60
c	Body	Body	Body	Body	Body
d	Y	Y	Y	Y	X
e	£9.000m	£5.000m	£11.000m	£11.000m	£1.780m
f	£5.816m	£3.367m	£5.812m	£7.283m	*
g	£0.107m	£0.062m	£0.107m	£0.133m	£0.023m
h	£57,182	£52,500	£62,964	£60,810	–
i	1F	{1M}	{1M}	1M	1M, £24,300
j	–	–	–	–	1M, £12,386
k	12M, 1F, 1 vacancy	2M, 1F, {4M} 1 vacancy	2M, 1F, {12M} 1 vacancy	12M, 1F	2M, 3F, £12,386, 1 vacancy
l	–	–	–	–	–
m	–	–	–	–	–

* There is no grant-in-aid to the Crofters' Commission. Theoretically, expenditure is incurred by SOAEFD on behalf of the Commission and the expenditure is borne directly on a Scottish Office Vote.

SCOTTISH OFFICE

Executive NDPBs

14	15	16	17	18
Deer Commission for Scotland	**Highlands and Islands Enterprise**	**National Board for Nursing, Midwifery and Health Visiting for Scotland**	**National Galleries of Scotland**	**National Library of Scotland**
Knowsley 82 Fairfield Road Inverness IV3 5LH	Bridge House 20 Bridge Street Inverness IV1 1QR	22 Queen Street Edinburgh EH2 1NT	The Mound Edinburgh EH2 2EL	George IV Bridge Edinburgh EH1 1EW
TEL : 01463 231751 FAX : 01463 712931 CHAIR : Mr Patrick Gordon-Duff-Pennington OBE ; SECRETARY : Mr Andy Rinning TERMS OF REFERENCE : To further the conservation, control and sustainable management of deer in Scotland; and to keep under review all relevant matters, including the welfare of deer.	TEL : 01463 234171 FAX : 01463 244469 hie.general@hient.co.uk CHAIR : Vacant ; CHIEF EXECUTIVE : Mr Iain Robertson CBE TERMS OF REFERENCE : To prepare, co-ordinate, promote and undertake measures for the economic and social development of the Highlands and Islands.	TEL : 0131 226 7371 FAX : 0131 225 9970 http://www.nbs.org.uk CHAIR : Mrs Isobel MacKinlay TERMS OF REFERENCE : To maintain and develop standards of professional education in nursing, midwifery and health visiting in Scotland, through the approval of institutions and courses and through research and development programmes.	TEL : 0131 556 8921 FAX : 0131 220 0917 CHAIR OF THE BOARD OF TRUSTEES : Countess of Airlie DIRECTOR : Mr Timothy Clifford TERMS OF REFERENCE : To care for, preserve and add to the objects in their collections; to ensure objects are exhibited to the public, and generally promote the public's enjoyment and understanding of the fine arts.	TEL : 0131 226 4531 FAX : 0131 220 6662 enquiries@nls.uk http://www.nls.uk CHAIR OF THE BOARD OF TRUSTEES : Rt Hon Earl of Crawford and Balcarres ; LIBRARIAN : Mr Ian McGowan TERMS OF REFERENCE : It is the library of legal deposit, entitled to claim works published in the United Kingdom and Ireland. It has large collections of printed books, manuscripts and maps and has an unrivalled collection of Scottish material.
a —	a —	a —	a —	a —
b 18	b 350[†]	b 45	b 172.25*	b 229*
c TSO	c Body	c Body	c Body[†]	c Body
d X	d X	d X	d X	d X
e £0.845m	e £77.000m	e £2.952m	e £9.000m	e £12.000m
f *	f £62.900m	f £2.952m	f £8.250m	f £11.817m
g £0.020m	g £0.418m*	g £0.05m	g £0.173m	g £0.173m
h —	h £78,606	h £56,352	h £65,000[‡]	h £71,564[†]
i 1M, £20,011	i 1 vacancy	i 1F, £10,000	i 1F	i 1M
j —	j —	j 1F	j —	j {1M}
k 10M, 2F	k 9M, 2F, £8,206	k 1F*, £43,764 1M[†], £45,179 3M, 3F	k 7M, 3F, 1 vacancy	k 3M, 1F, {21M, 4F} 2 vacancies
l — m —	l — m —	l — m —	l — m —	l — m —

* There is no grant-in-aid to the Deer Commission. Theoretically, expenditure is incurred by SOAEFD on behalf of the Commission and the expenditure is borne directly on a Scottish Office Vote.

* Covers Highland and Islands Enterprise and Scottish Enterprise.
† Figures expressed in whole time equivalents and do not include seconded or casual staff.

* Executive Director of Standards.
† Executive Director of Resources.

* Figures are expressed in whole time equivalents and do not include seconded or casual staff.
† Published by Body and laid before Parliament.
‡ Remuneration taken from Published Annual Statement of Accounts 1997/1998.

* Figures are expressed in whole time equivalents and do not include seconded or casual staff.
† Remuneration taken from Published Annual Statement of Accounts 1997/1998.

SCOTTISH OFFICE

Executive NDPBs

19
National Museum of Scotland

Chambers Street
Edinburgh
EH1 1JF

TEL : 0131 225 7534
FAX : 0131 247 4308
mj@nmsac.uk
http://www.nms.ac.uk
CHAIR OF THE BOARD OF TRUSTEES : Mr Robert Smith
DIRECTOR : Mr Mark Jones
TERMS OF REFERENCE : To care for, preserve and add to the objects on their collections; ensure that the objects are exhibited to the public, and to make the collections available through research, exhibitions, education and other activities.

20
Parole Board for Scotland

Room Y1/13
Saughton House
Broomhouse Drive
Edinburgh EH11 3XD

TEL : 0131 244 8755
FAX : 0131 244 6974
CHAIR : Mr Ian McNee
SECRETARY : Mr Hugh P Boyle
TERMS OF REFERENCE : To consider whether prisoners should be granted parole and to advise the Secretary of State accordingly. The Prisoners and Criminal Proceedings Act 1993 limits the cases which the Board can consider to prisoners serving sentences of four years or more.

21
Royal Botanic Garden, Edinburgh

20A Inverlieth Row
Edinburgh
EH3 5LR

TEL : 0131 552 7171
FAX : 0131 552 0382
j.wills@rbge.org.uk
http://www.rbge.org.uk
CHAIR : Professor Malcolm Wilkins ; REGIUS KEEPER: Professor D S Ingram
TERMS OF REFERENCE : To explore and explain the plant kingdom and its importance to humanity. Its role is to pursue whole plant science, notably through research of the highest quality on the origins, diversity; relationship of plants, their significance in the environment, and their conservation.

22
Royal Commission on the Ancient and Historical Monuments of Scotland

John Sinclair House
16 Bernard Terrace
Edinburgh
EH8 9NX

TEL : 0131 662 1456
FAX : 0131 662 1477/1499
rcahms.jsh@gtnet.gov.uk
CHAIR : Sir William Fraser
CHIEF OFFICIAL : Mr Roger Mercer
TERMS OF REFERENCE : To survey and record the man-made environment of Scotland and to compile and maintain in the National Monuments Records of Scotland a record of this archaeological and historical information.

23
Scottish Agricultural Wages Board

Pentland House
47 Robb's Loan
Edinburgh
EH14 ITY

TEL : 0131 244 6392
FAX : 0131 244 6551
fay.anderson@50076.gov.uk
CHAIR : Mrs Christine Davis CBE
SECRETARY : Miss Fay Anderson
TERMS OF REFERENCE : To make Orders fixing minimum wage rates, holiday entitlements and other conditions for workers for workers employed in agricultural in Scotland.

	19 National Museum of Scotland	20 Parole Board for Scotland	21 Royal Botanic Garden	22 Royal Commission	23 Scottish Agricultural Wages Board
a	–	–	–	–	–
b	271.5*	5	204	70	–
c	Body†	Cm	Body	Body	Cm
d	X	X	X	X	X*
e	£26.000m	£0.348m	£7.000m	£3.216m	*
f	£24.144m	£0.348m	£4.755m	£3.216m	–
g	£0.173m	£0.348m	£0.089m	£0.010m	£0.073m
h	£69,904‡	–	£55,445	£44.517	–
i	1M	1M, £234pm	1M	1M	1F, £206pd
j	–	1M, £237pm; 1F, £149pm	–	–	–
k	9M, 5F	4M, 4F, £149pm; 1M, £332pm; 2M, 1F, £237pm; 2M	5M, 3F	4M, 5F	3M, 1F, £133pd, {11M, 1F}
l	–	–	–	–	–
m	–	–	–	–	–

* Figures are expressed in whole time equivalents and do not include seconded or casual staff.
† Published by Body and laid before Parliament.
‡ Remuneration taken from Published Annual Statement of Accounts 1997/1998.

* Expenditure forms part of the total Scottish Office (SO) expenditure. Accounts for SO are audited by the Comptroller and Auditor General.

SCOTTISH OFFICE

Executive NDPBs

24
Scottish Arts Council

12 Manor Place
Edinburgh
EH3 7DD

TEL : 0131 226 6051
FAX : 0131 225 9833
help.desk@artsfb.org.uk
CHAIR : Mr Magnus Linklater
DIRECTOR : Ms Seona Reid
TERMS OF REFERENCE : The Council aims to create a climate in which arts of quality flourish and are enjoyed by a wide range of people throughout Scotland.

25
Scottish Children's Reporter Administration

Ochil House
Springskerse Business Park
Stirling
FK7 7XE

TEL : 01786 459500
FAX : 01786 459532
CHAIR : Mrs Sally Kuenssberg
CHIEF EXECUTIVE/PRINCIPAL REPORTER : Mr Alan Miller
TERMS OF REFERENCE : To facilitate the performance by the Principal Reporter of his statutory functions in relation to children who may be in need of compulsory measures of care; and to provide suitable accommodation and facilities for children's hearings.

26
Scottish Community Education Council

Rosebery House
9 Haymarket Terrace
Edinburgh
EH12 5EZ

TEL : 0131 313 2488
FAX : 0131 313 6800
sce@scec.dircon.co.uk
http://www.qedi.co.uk
ACTING CHAIR : Mr Jim Stretton
TERMS OF REFERENCE : To advise the Secretary of State for Scotland on all matters relating to community education.

27
Scottish Conveyancing and Executry Services Board

Room 426 Mulberry House
16–22 Picardy Place
Edinburgh
EH1 3YT

TEL : 0131 556 1945
FAX : 0131 556 8428
CHAIR : Mr Alistair Clark
TERMS OF REFERENCE : The Board regulates the provision of conveyancing and executry services by the new profession of qualified conveyancer, independent qualified conveyancer and executry practitioner.

28
Scottish Council for Educational Technology

74 Victoria Crescent Road
Glasgow
G12 9JN

TEL : 0141 337 5000
FAX : 0141 334 5050
enquiries@scet.org.uk
http://www.scet.org.uk
CHAIR : Mr Alistair Fleming
TERMS OF REFERENCE : To promote and encourage understanding and application of educational technology in its widest sense.

	24 Scottish Arts Council	25 Scottish Children's Reporter Administration	26 Scottish Community Education Council	27 Scottish Conveyancing and Executry Services Board	28 Scottish Council for Educational Technology
a	–	–	–	–	–
b	83	320	34	1	89
c	Body	Body	NP	Body	Body
d	X	X	Y	Y	Y
e	£45.000m*	£12.608m	£1.846m	£0.100m	£3.919m
f	£27.100m	£12.608m	£0.600m	£0.100m	£1.336m
g	£0.095m	£0.103m	£0.024m	£0.053m	£0.012m
h	£50,880	£61,692	£45,399	–	£55,780
i	1M, £20,000	1F, £15,805	Vacant	1M, £468pm*	1M
j	–	1M, £5,131	1M	–	–
k	9M, 5F	1M* / 1M† / 4F, £3,687	5M, 3F, {3M, 1F}	5M, 2F, £298m*	2M, 1F, {4M, 2F} 1 vacancy
l	–	–	–	–	–
m	–	–	–	–	–

* Government grant-in-aid and distribution of National Lottery funds.

* Chief Executive (ex-officio board member).
† Receives no salary (Scottish Courts Administration).

* Figures coomprise attendance fee and preparation fee.

128

Executive NDPBs

29 Scottish Enterprise

120 Bothwell Street
Glasgow
G2 7JP

TEL : 0141 248 2700
FAX : 0141 221 3217
http://www.scotnet.co.uk
CHAIR : Sir Ian Wood
CHIEF EXECUTIVE : Mr Crawford Beveridge CBE
TERMS OF REFERENCE : To generate jobs and prosperity for the people of Scotland.

a	–
b	1,457
c	Body
d	X
e	£462.000m
f	£413.000m
g	£0.418m*
h	£111,093
i	1M, £31,567
j	1M, £16,408
k	5M, 2F, £8,206
l	–
m	–

* Covers Highlands and Islands Enterprise and Scottish Enterprise.

30 Scottish Environment Protection Agency

Erskine Court
The Castle Business Park
Stirling
FK9 4TR

TEL : 01786 457700
FAX : 01786 446885
info@sepa.org.uk
http://www.sepa.org.uk
CHAIR : Professor William Turmeau CBE ; CHIEF EXECUTIVE : Mr Alisdair Paton
TERMS OF REFERENCE : Its main duty is to protect the environment in Scotland by regulating pollution of land, air and water.

a	–
b	640
c	Body
d	Y
e	£28.000m
f	£23.500m
g	£0.140m
h	£73,903
i	1M, 37,080
j	1M, £7,500
k	2M, 1F, £11,250
	3M, 1F, £5,000
l	–
m	–

31 Scottish Further Education Unit

Argyll Court
The Castle Business Park
Stirling
FK9 4TY

TEL : 01786 892000
FAX : 01786 892001
sfeu@sfeu.demon.co.uk
http://www.sfeu.org.uk
CHAIR : Mr Michael Leech OBE
CHIEF EXECUTIVE : Ms Alison Reid
TERMS OF REFERENCE : To support provision for further education colleges and to provide advice, research and consultancy services.

a	–
b	28
c	Body
d	Y
e	£1.600m
f	£0.700m
g	£0.006m
h	£51,000
i	1M
j	1 vacancy
k	3M, 2F, {1F}*, 1 vacancy
l	–
m	–

* Chief Executive. (ex-officio board member).

32 Scottish Higher Education Funding Council

Donaldson House
97 Haymarket Terrace
Edinburgh
EH12 5HD

TEL : 0131 313 6500
FAX : 0131 313 6501
jevans@shefc.ac.uk
http://www.shefc.ac.uk/shefc/welcome.htm
CHAIR : Dr Chris Masters
SECRETARY : Mr Lawrence Howells
TERMS OF REFERENCE : Provision of grants to support teaching and research in 20 Scottish higher education institutions (ie colleges and universities).

a	–
b	53
c	Body
d	X
e	£552.000m
f	£551.718m
g	£0.125m
h	£82,620
i	1M, £14,230
j	–
k	7M, 5F, £4,550
l	–
m	–

33 Scottish Homes

Thistle House
91 Haymarket Terrace
Edinburgh
EH1 5HE

TEL : 0131 313 0044
FAX : 0131 313 2680
http://www.scot-homes.gov.uk
CHAIR : Mr John Ward CBE
TERMS OF REFERENCE : Scottish Homes is Scotland's national housing agency. Its purpose is to enable the effective provision of good quality housing and to stimulate self-motivated communities so as to enhance the quality of life, social well-being and economic competitiveness of people in Scotland.

a	–
b	745.5
c	Body*
d	X
e	£399.050m
f	£267.899m
g	£0.246m
h	£98,283[†]
i	1M, £21,160
j	–
k	4M, 4F, £7,356 {1M}[†‡]
l	–
m	–

* Published by Body and laid before Parliament and Secretary of State.
† Chief Executive (ex-officio board member).
‡ Appointed by the Board.

SCOTTISH OFFICE

Executive NDPBs

34
Scottish Hospital Endowments Research Trust

Saltire Court
20 Castle Terrace
Edinburgh
EH1 2EF

TEL : 0131 228 2811
FAX : 0131 228 8118
enquiries@turcanconnell.co.uk
CHAIR : Lord Kilpatrick of Kincraig CBE MD
CONTACT : Turcan Connell
TERMS OF REFERENCE : The Trust receives and holds endowments, donations and bequests and makes grants from these funds to promote medical research in Scotland. It engages in fund-raising activities for the purposes of the Trust and develops and exploits ideas and exploits intellectual property.

a	–
b	1.5
c	Body
d	Y
e	£1.021m*
f	–
g	£0.025m
h	–
i	1M
j	–
k	2M, 3F, 4 vacancies
l	–
m	–

* Financial year runs from 1 August to 31 July. Gross expenditure is an estimate of expenditure to 31 July 1998 based on previous year expenditure with an inflationary factor built in. Actual figures will not be available till September 1998.

35
Scottish Legal Aid Board

44 Drumsheugh Gardens
Edinburgh
EH3 7SW

TEL : 0131 226 7061
FAX : 0131 220 4878
http://www.scotlegalaid.gov.uk
CHAIR : Mrs Jean Couper
CHIEF EXECUTIVE : Dr Richard Scott
TERMS OF REFERENCE : To assess and where appropriate grant applications for legal aid; to scrutinise and pay legal aid accounts submitted by solicitors and advocates; and to advise the Secretary of State for Scotland on legal aid matter.

a	–
b	267
c	Body
d	Y
e	£152.000m*
f	£142.968m
g	£0.080m
h	£58,622†
i	1F, £23,750
j	–
k	6M, 3F, £7,000
	1M
	1M†
l	–
m	–

* In 1997–98 the Board's accounts have ben prepared on an accruals basis. It is therefore not possible to make direct comparisons between 1996–97 and 1997–98 total gross expenditure figures. All future entries will be calculated on the accruals basis.
† Chief Executive (ex-officio member).

36
Scottish Medical Practices Committee

Room D017
Trinity Park House
South Trinity House
Edinburgh EH5 3SE

TEL : 0131 552 6255
FAX : 0131 552 8651
CHAIR : Dr Graham MacIntosh
SECRETARY : Mrs Denise Booth-Alexander
TERMS OF REFERENCE : To ensure an adequate number of GPs providing general medical services in Scotland.

a	–
b	2*
c	Body
d	X†
e	†
f	–
g	£0.004m
h	–
i	1M, £14,495
j	–
k	2F, £168.40pm
	2M, 1F, £152.50pm
l	–
m	–

* Staff are provided on a service agreement by the NHS Common Service Agency.
† Expenditure forms part of the total Scottish Office (SO)expenditure. Accounts for SO are audited by the Comptroller and Auditor General.

37
Scottish Natural Heritage

12 Hope Terrace
Edinburgh
EH9 2AS

TEL : 0131 447 4784
FAX : 0131 446 2277
mairib@snh-ht.demon.co.uk
http://www.snh.org.uk
CHAIR : Magnus Magnusson KBE
SECRETARY : Ms Joanna Hardy
TERMS OF REFERENCE : Statutory adviser to the Secretary of State for Scotland and others on matters affecting the natural heritage of Scotland.

a	–
b	627.5
c	NP
d	X
e	£37.005m
f	£37.005m
g	£0.077m
h	£68,575
i	1M, £37,008
j	1M, £15,942
k	1M, £15,538
	1F, £15,942
	3M, 1F, £6,474
	3M, £6,642
	1F, £15,943
l	–
m	–

38
Scottish Screen

74 Victoria Crescent Road
Glasgow
G12 9JN

TEL : 0141 302 1700
FAX : 0141 302 1711
CHAIR : Mr James Lee
TERMS OF REFERENCE : Scottish Screen is the national body for the promotion of film culture and of the film and television industry in Scotland.

a	–
b	35
c	NP
d	Y
e	£2.600m
f	£1.905m
g	£0.012m
h	–
i	1M
j	–
k	10M, 4F
l	–
m	–

SCOTTISH OFFICE

Executive NDPBs

39
Scottish Qualifications Authority

24 Douglas Street
Glasgow
G2 7NQ

TEL : 0141 248 7900
FAX : 0141 242 2244
http://www.sqa.org.uk
CHAIR : Mr David Miller CBE
CHIEF EXECUTIVE : Mr Ron Tuck
TERMS OF REFERENCE : To develop and award qualifications in the national education system in Scotland; and also qualifications for work. It is also Scotland's national accrediting body for work-based SVQ qualifications. SQA qualifications are available in schools, colleges, training centres and the workplace.

a	–
b	500*
c	NP
d	X
e	£27.00m†
f	£1.870m
g	£0.050m
h	£65,000
i	1M, £10,965
j	–
k	15M, 6F
l	–
m	–

* Includes temporary posts.
† Approximate.

40
Scottish Sports Council

Caledonia House
South Gyle
Edinburgh
EH12 9DQ

TEL : 0131 317 7200
FAX : 0131 317 7200
CHAIR : Mr Graeme Simmers CBE
TERMS OF REFERENCE : The development of sport in Scotland. The Council is an advisory agency; but it is also responsible for distributing National Lottery funding for sports programmes in Scotland.

a	–
b	167
c	Body
d	X
e	£12.800m
f	£9.929m
g	£0.066m
h	£55,703
i	1M, £23,934
j	1M, £8,511
k	5M, 5F, {1M}
l	–
m	–

41
Scottish Tourist Board

23 Ravelson Terrace
Edinburgh
EH4 3EU

TEL : 0131 332 2433
FAX : 0131 332 4441
http://www.holiday.scotland.net
CHAIR : Lord Gordon of Strathblane CBE
SECRETARY : Sheena Craigen
TERMS OF REFERENCE : To encourage tourists to visit Scotland and to encourage the provision of tourist facilities and amenities in Scotland.

a	–
b	151.5
c	HC
d	X
e	£25.000m
f	£19.196m
g	£0.184m
h	£60,000
i	1M, £19,023
j	–
k	5M, 1F, £6,967
l	–
m	–

42
Scottish Water and Sewerage Customers Council

Ochil House
Springkerse Business Park
Stirling
FK7 7XE

TEL : 01786 430200
FAX : 01786 462018
swscc@scottishwater.co.uk
CHAIR : Mr Bill Furness
DIRECTOR : Dr Vicki Nash
TERMS OF REFERENCE : To represent the interests of customers and potential or former customers of the new water and sewerage authorities.

a	–
b	17
c	Body
d	Y
e	£1.06m
f	–
g	£0.080m
h	–
i	1M, £16,114
j	1M, £8,057
k	5M, 2F, £3,223
	2M, 1F, £5,371
l	–
m	–

Advisory NDPBs

43
Advisory Committee on Dental Establishments

Room 71
St Andrews House
Edinburgh
EH1 3DG

TEL : 0131 244 2498
FAX : 0131 244 2837
CHIEF DENTAL OFFICER : Mr Ray Watkins ; SECRETARY : Mrs Anncris Roberts
TERMS OF REFERENCE : To advise the Secretary of State for Scotland on matters relating to dental work and care. It is able to force issues and is also an advisory committee.

a	–
b	–
c	NP
d	–
e	–
f	–
g	–
h	–
i	–
j	–
k	6M, 3F
l	–
m	–

131

SCOTTISH OFFICE

Advisory NDPBs

44
Advisory Committee on Sites of Special Scientific Interest

Scottish Natural Heritage
12 Hope Terrace
Edinburgh
EH9 2AS
TEL : 0131 447 4784
FAX : 0131 446 2278
david.howell@rasdsnh.demon.co.uk
http://www.snh.org.uk
CHAIR : Mr William Ritchie
SECRETARY : Mr David Howell
TERMS OF REFERENCE : To advise Scottish Natural Heritage in cases where there are sustained objections to the notification of Sites of Special Scientific Interest.

45
Ancient Monuments Board for Scotland

Longmore House
Salisbury Place
Edinburgh
EH9 1SH
TEL : 0131 668 8764
FAX : 0131 668 8765
CHAIR : Professor Michael Lynch
SECRETARY : Mr Ron Dalziel
TERMS OF REFERENCE : The Board advises the Secretary of State for Scotland on the exercise of his functions under the Ancient Monuments and Archeological Areas Act 1979.

46
Building Standards Advisory Committee

The Development Department
Construction and Building Control Group, 2-H Victoria Quay, Edinburgh EH6 6QQ
TEL : 0131 244 7439
FAX : 0131 244 7454
bsac@so062.scotoff.gov.uk
http://www.scotland.gov.uk/better/b-main-htm
CHAIR : Ms Maud Marshall
SECRETARY : Mr Jeff Carter
TERMS OF REFERENCE : To provide advice to the Secretary of State for Scotland on questions relating to his functions under Part II of the Building (Scotland) Act 1959, in particular the regulation-making function.

47
Central Advisory Committee on Justices of the Peace (Scotland)

Spur W1(E)
Saughton House
Broomhouse Drive,
Edinburgh EH11 3XD
TEL : 0131 244 2691
FAX : 0131 244 2623
janerichardson@server50082.scotoff.gov.uk
CHAIR : The Rt Hon Lord Cullen
SECRETARY : Mrs Jane Richardson
TERMS OF REFERENCE : To advise and, where necessary, make recommendations to the Secretary of State as to the problems arising in relation to the appointment and distribution of JPs and the work of JPs in general and the district court in particular.

48
Extra Parliamentary Panel

The Scottish Office
Room 1/1
Dover House
London SW1A 2AU
TEL : 0171 270 6728
FAX : 0171 270 6834
TERMS OF REFERENCE : The Panel hears evidence for and against a draft provision order at an inquiry. It reports to the Secretary of State for Scotland, making recommendations as to whether the order should proceed, be as amended or be refused.

	44	45	46	47	48
a	–	–	–	–	–
b	–	–	–	–	–
c	NP	HC	NP	NP	NP
d	–	–	–	–	–
e	–	–	–	–	–
f	–	–	–	–	–
g	£0.005m	£0.032m	£0.043m	£0.007m*	£0.003m
h	–	–	–	–	–
i	1M, 170pd	1M	1F	1M	–
j	–	–	–	–	–
k	6M, £131pd	10M, 5F	11M, 2F	14M, 4F	13M, 7F
l	–	–	–	–	–
m	–	–	–	–	–

* Approximate.

SCOTTISH OFFICE

Advisory NDPBs

	49 General Teaching Council for Scotland	50 Health Appointments Advisory Committee	51 Hill Farming Advisory Committee for Scotland	52 Historic Buildings Council for Scotland	53 Justices of the Peace Advisory Committees
Address	Clerwood House, 96 Clerniston Road, Edinburgh EH12 6UT	The Scottish Office Department of Health, Room 181, St Andrew's House, Edinburgh EH1 3DG	c/o Room 235 Pentland House, 44 Robb's Loan, Edinburgh EH14 1TW	Longmore House, Salisbury Place, Edinburgh EH9 1SH	Secretary of Commissions for Scotland, Saughton House, Broomhouse Drive, Edinburgh EH11 3XD
TEL	0131 314 6000	0131 244 3469	0131 244 6374	0131 668 8799	0131 244 2691
FAX	0131 314 6001	0131 244 3583	0131 244 6006	0131 668 8788	0131 244 2623
CHAIR		Mr Norman Irons CBE	Mr Anthony Cameron	Sir Raymond Johnstone	
SECRETARY		Mr Martin Milarky (Committee Secretary)	Mrs Alison Quirie	Ms Sheenagh Adams — sheenagh.adams@so009.scotoff.gov.uk — http://www.historic-scotland.gov.uk	
TERMS OF REFERENCE	To keep under review standards of education, training, fitness to teach, appropriate to people entering the teaching profession; and to make recommendations to the Secretary of State for Scotland in respect of these standards and on other matters in the same field.	To advise Scottish Office Ministers on appointments to be made at non-executive level to Scottish Office Health Boards, NHS Trusts, and Health Non-Departmental Public Bodies.	To advise the Secretary of State for Scotland as to the exercise of his powers under the Hill Farming Act.	To advise and make representations to the Secretary of State for Scotland on the exercise of his functions in relation to buildings of special architectural or historic interest.	To keep under review the strength of the Commission of the Peace in its particular area and to advise the Secretary of State for Scotland on the appointment of new Justices.
a	–	–	–	–	32
b	–	–	–	–	–
c	Body	NP	NP	HC	NP
d	–	–	–	–	–
e	–	–	–	–	–
f	–	–	–	–	–
g	£0.010m	£0.025m	£0.010m	£0.012m	£0.008m*
h	–	–	–	–	–
i	{1F}	1M	1M	1M, £5,710	32M
j	{1M}	–	–	–	6M, 1F
k	4F, {30M, 13F}	3M, 1F	13M, 5F	8M, 3F	125M, 61F
l	–	–	–	–	–
m	–	–	–	–	–

* Approximate.

SCOTTISH OFFICE

Advisory NDPBs

54 Local Government Boundary Commission for Scotland

3 Drumsheugh Gardens
Edinburgh
EH3 7QJ

TEL : 0131 538 7510
FAX : 0131 538 7240
lgbcs@cablenet.co.uk
CHAIR : Lord Osborne
SECRETARY : Mr Bob Smith
TERMS OF REFERENCE : To review local Government areas and electoral arrangements, and to give advice to the Secretary of State for Scotland who decides whether to implement their proposals.

55 Local Government Property Commission

3 Drumsheugh Gardens
Edinburgh
EH3 7QJ

TEL : 0131 244 7422
FAX : 0131 538 7240
CHAIR : Professor Gordon Milne
SECRETARY : Mr Jim Brown
TERMS OF REFERENCE : To advise authorities on matters relating to property to be transferred from the former local authorities (regions and districts), to the new style-tier councils.

56 Parliamentary Boundary Commission for Scotland

Sccretariat, Spur VI
Saughton House
Broomhouse Drive
Edinburgh EH11 3XD

TEL : 0131 244 2196/2188
FAX : 0131 244 2195
CHAIR : Rt Hon Betty Boothroyd MP (Speaker of the House of Commons) ; SECRETARY : Vacant
TERMS OF REFERENCE : To keep under review the Boundaries of Parliamentary Constituencies in Scotland. To conduct a periodical general review established under the Parliamentary Constituencies Act 1968, as amended.

57 Post Qualification Education Board for Health Service Pharmacists in Scotland

The School of Pharmacy, Royal College (R4.10), University of Strathclyde, 204 George Street, Glasgow G1 1XW

TEL : 0141 552 4400 x4273/4
FAX : 0141 553 4102
CHAIR : Dr Gordon Jefferson
SECRETARY : Ms Rose Marie Parr
TERMS OF REFERENCE : To advise the Secretary of State for Scotland on the post-qualification educational requirements of all registered pharmacists in Scotland working in the National Health Service.

58 Royal Fine Art Commission for Scotland

Bakehouse Close
146 Conongate
Edinburgh
EH8 8DD

TEL : 0131 556 6699
FAX : 0131 556 6633
rfacscot@gtnet.gov.uk
CHAIR : Rt Hon Lord Cameron of Lochbroom ; SECRETARY : Mr Charles Prosser
TERMS OF REFERENCE : To advise central and local government in Scotland on the quality of planning and the design of projects of major environmental significance.

	54	55	56	57	58
a	–	–	–	–	–
b	–	–	–	–	–
c	NP	Body	Cm*	Body	Cm*
d	–	–	–	–	–
e	–	–	–	–	–
f	–	–	–	–	–
g	£0.015m	£0.012	£0.010m	£0.007m	£0.006m
h	–	–	–	–	–
i	1M	1M, £207pd	{1F}†	1M	1M
j	1M, £14,940*	–	{1F}‡	–	–
k	1M, 2F, £2,117†	2M, 1F, £125pd	2M, £353pd	6M, 5F	8M, 3F
l	–	–	–	–	–
m	–	–	–	–	–

54
* From 1 December 1998 salary will be upgraded to £15,160.
† From 1 December 1998 salary will be upgraded to £2,148.

56
* The Commission publishes its main report in the form of a command paper every 8–12 years as required by statute.
† The Speaker of the House of Commons is the Chairman of the Parliamentary Boundary Commission for Scotland.
‡ The Deputy Chair is a judge of the court of session, appointed by the Lord President of the court of session.

58
* Not always annual.

SCOTTISH OFFICE

Advisory NDPBs

59

Scottish Advisory Committee on Drug Misuse

Public Health Policy Unit
Department of Health
St Andrew's House
Edinburgh EH1 3DG
TEL : 0131 244 2174
FAX : 0131 244 2689
CHAIR : Mrs Nicola Munro
SECRETARY : Mrs Mary Cuthbert
TERMS OF REFERENCE : To advise and report to the Secretary of State for Scotland on policy, priorities and strategic planning in relation to drug misuse in Scotland.

60

Scottish Advisory Committee on the Medical Workforce

Department of Health
St Andrew's House
Edinburgh
EH1 3DG
TEL : 0131 244 2486
FAX : 0131 244 2837
CHAIR : Dr David Ewing
SECRETARY : Mrs Anncris Roberts
TERMS OF REFERENCE : To advise the Secretary of State for Scotland on all matters relating to medical workforce planning in Scotland, other than terms and conditions of service matters.

61

Scottish Agricultural Consultative Panel*

c/o Room 235
Pentland House
Edinburgh
EH14 1UQ
FORMER CHAIR : Mr Tony Cameron
FORMER TERMS OF REFERENCE : To advise on land classification.

62

Scottish Consultative Council on the Curriculum

Gardyne Road
Broughty Ferry
Dundee
DD5 1NY
TEL : 01382 455053
FAX : 01382 455046
CHAIR : Mr Neil Galbraith
TERMS OF REFERENCE : The Council is the principal advisory body to the secretary of State for Scotland on all curriculum matters relating to 3–18 year olds in Scottish schools.

63

Scottish Crime Prevention Council

c/o CB2–4
Saughton House
Broomhouse Drive
Edinburgh EH11 3XD
TEL : 0131 244 3991
FAX : 0131 244 3989
CHAIR : Mr Henry McLeish MP
SECRETARY : Mr John Rowell
TERMS OF REFERENCE : To advise the Secretary of State for Scotland on crime prevention policy.

	59	60	61	62	63
a	–	–	–	–	–
b	–	–	–	–	–
c	NP	NP	NP	Body	NP
d	–	–	–	–	–
e	–	–	–	–	–
f	–	–	–	–	–
g	£0.003m	–	£0.001m	£0.012m	£0.001m
h	–	–	–	–	–
i	1F	–	–	1M	–
j	–	–	–	1M	–
k	11M, 2F	12M, 1F	–	8M, 9F	8M, 2F
l	–	–	–	–	–
m	–	–	–	–	–

* The body was formally wound up on 31.8.98.

SCOTTISH OFFICE

Advisory NDPBs

64
Scottish Industrial Development Advisory Board

Meridian Court
5 Cadogan Street
Glasgow
G2 6AT
TEL : 0141 242 5674
FAX : 0141 242 5691
CHAIR : Mr Ian Good CBE
TERMS OF REFERENCE : To advise the Secretary of State for Scotland on the exercise of his powers under Section 7 of the Industrial Development Act 1982.

65
Scottish Records Advisory Council

HM Register
Edinburgh
EH1 3YY
TEL : 0131 535 1314
CHAIR : Professor Anne Crowther ; SECRETARY : Dr Donald Abbot
TERMS OF REFERENCE : To submit proposals or make representations to the Secretary of State for Scotland, the Lord Justice General or Lord President of the Court of Session on questions relating to the public records of Scotland.

66
Scottish Standing Committee for the Calculation of Residual Values of Fertilizers & Feeding Stuffs

Agriculture, Environment and Fisheries Department,
Pentland House, 47 Robb's Loan, Edinburgh EH14 1TY
TEL : 0131 244 6450
FAX : 0131 244 6259
CHAIR : Professor David Atkinson ; SECRETARY : Mr Andrew McKean
TERMS OF REFERENCE : To calculate annually the values to be attached in Scotland to unexhausted manures, fertilizers and feeding stuffs.

67
Scottish Studentship Selection Committee

Gyleview House
3 Redheughs Rigg
Edinburgh
EH12 9HH
TEL : 0131 244 5846
FAX : 0131 244 5887
CHAIR : Professor D Harding
SECRETARY : Mrs Anne Hampson
TERMS OF REFERENCE : The Committee offers up to 75 new studentship awards each year for full time advanced postgraduate study in the Arts and Humanities to Scottish domiciled students and eligible European Union students studying in Scotland.

68
Scottish Valuation and Rating Council

LG3A-Area 3-J
Victoria Quay
Edinburgh
EH6 6QQ
TEL : 0131 244 7003
FAX : 0131 244 7058
CHAIR : Professor Gordon Milne
SECRETARY : Mr Peter Hancock
TERMS OF REFERENCE : The Council's remit is to advise the Secretary of State for Scotland on any matter pertaining to valuation and rating, including evaluation of representations and recommendations made to him, the identification of issues requiring consideration, and advice in the preparation of legislation.

	64	65	66	67	68
a	–	–	–	–	–
b	–	–	–	–	–
c	TSO	NP*	TSO	NP	NP
d	–	–	–	–	–
e	–	–	–	–	–
f	–	–	–	–	–
g	£0.037m	£0.001m	£0.001m	£0.016m	£0.007m
h	–	–	–	–	–
i	1M	1F	1M	1M, £210pd	1M
j	–	–	–	–	–
k	9M, 2F	9M, 1F	3M	8M, 1F, £160pd	13M
l	–	–	–	–	–
m	–	–	–	–	–

* Annual Report submitted to the Secretary of State.

SCOTTISH OFFICE

Advisory NDPBs

69
Secretary of State for Scotland's Advisory Group on Sustainable Development

c/o Forward Scotland
Scottish Power
St Vincent Crescent
Glasgow G3 8LT
TEL : 0141 567 4334
FAX : 0141 567 4339
forward.Scotland@virgin.net
http://www.sustainable.scotland.gov.uk
CHAIR : Dr John Markland
SECRETARY : Mr Raymond Young OBE
TERMS OF REFERENCE : To advise the Secretary of State for Scotland on policy issues and practical challenges for Scotland as a consequence of adopting the principles of sustainable development.

70
Secretary of State for Scotland's Advisory Committee on Scotland's Travelling People

c/o Room 1–F
Victoria Quay
Edinburgh
EH6 6QQ
TEL : 0131 244 5577
FAX : 0131 244 5596
Rona.tatler@scotoff.gov.uk
CHAIR : Mr Ron Ashton
SECRETARY : Mrs Rona Tatler
TERMS OF REFERENCE : To advise the Secretary of State for Scotland on issues relating to travelling people.

71
Secretary of State for Scotland's Advisory Panel of Economic Consultants

3rd Floor, Meridian Court
5 Cadogan Street
Glasgow G2 6AT

TEL : 0141 248 2855
FAX : 0141 242 5579
graemestorie@so049.scotoff.gov.uk
http://www.scotland.gov.uk
CHAIR : Rt Hon Donald Dewar MP (Secretary of State)
SECRETARY : Mr Graeme Storie
TERMS OF REFERENCE : The Panel provides advice on the Scottish economy to the Secretary of State for Scotland and Scottish Office Ministers.

72
Secretary of State (Electricity) for Scotland's Fisheries Committee

R411, Pentland House
47 Robb's Loan
Edinburgh
EH14 1TY
TEL : 0131 244 6229
FAX : 0131 244 6313
enquiries@scet.org.uk
http://www.scet.org.uk
CHAIR : Mr Robert McGillivray
SECRETARY : Mrs Lynn Goodbourn
TERMS OF REFERENCE : The Committee's statutory function is to advise and assist the Secretary of State for Scotland and any person engaging in, or proposing to engage in the generation of hydro-electric power on any question relating to the effect of hydro-electric works on fisheries or stocks of fish.

Tribunal NDPBs

73
Children's Panel*

SWSG 3/3
James Craig Walk
Edinburgh
EH1 3BA
TEL : 0131 244 5444
FAX : 0131 244 3547
CONTACT : Mrs A Snedden
TERMS OF REFERENCE : The Children's Panel is a tribunal constituted under the Children (Scotland) Act 1995. It makes decisions on children who offend or are at risk.

	69	70	71	72	73
a	–	–	–	–	32*
b	–	–	–	–	–
c	Body	*	NP	Body	NP
d	–	–	–	–	–
e	–	–	–	–	–
f	–	–	–	–	–
g	£0.068m	£0.024m	£0.004m	£0.035m	£0.580m
h	–	–	–	–	–
i	1M	1M	–	1M	11M, 21F
j	–	1F	–	–	17M, 16F
k	8M, 2F	3M, 4F	8M, 1F, £169pm	5M, 1F	894M, 1,243F
l	–	–	–	–	14,620
m	–	–	–	–	8,670

* Committee's report published at the end of its term of office, normally 3 years – this term 2 years.

* Multiple body – one per local authority.

137

SCOTTISH OFFICE

Tribunal NDPBs

National Health Service Bodies

74
Horserace Betting Levy Appeal Tribunal for Scotland

13 Coburg Place
Edinburgh
EH3 5BR

TEL : 0131 332 6820
FAX : 0131 315 2918
CHAIR : Mr Colin McEachran QC
TERMS OF REFERENCE : To consider appeals by bookmakers in Scotland against the assessments, made by the Horse Race Betting Levy Board, of the levy they should pay each year.

75
Rent Assessment Panel for Scotland

48 Manor Place
Edinburgh
EH3 7EH

TEL : 0131 226 1123
FAX : 0131 220 0110
PRESIDENT : Mr John Barton
TERMS OF REFERENCE : To provide members for Rent Assessment Committees which consider objections to fair rents set by Rent Officers under the Rent (Scotland) Act 1984 and hear appeals by tenants or landlords against rents or tenancy terms, under the Housing (Scotland) Act 1998.

76
Common Services Agency for the NHS in Scotland

Trinity Park House
South Trinity Road
Edinburgh
EH5 3SE

TEL : 0131 552 6255
FAX : 0131 552 8651
ruth.wallace@hq.csa.scot.nhs.uk
http://www.snow.scot.nhs.uk
CHAIR : Mr Geoff Scaife
SECRETARY : Mrs Ruth Wallace
TERMS OF REFERENCE : The CSA is an integral part of the NHS's supporting frontline clinical care by providing or co-ordinating essential national and regional services.

77
Health Boards

St Andrew's House
Edinburgh
EH1 3DG

TEL : 0131 244 3469
FAX : 0131 244 3583
CONTACT : Mr Martin Milarky

78
Health Education Board for Scotland

Woodburn House
Canaan Lane
Edinburgh
EH10 4SG

TEL : 0131 536 5500
FAX : 0131 536 5501
http://www.hebs.scot.nhs.uk
CHAIR : Mr David Campbell
TERMS OF REFERENCE : To undertake functions and initiatives at national level, concentrating on the priority areas of coronary heart disease, cancer, stroke, smoking, diet, physical activity, sexual health and HIV/AIDS, drug and alcohol misuse, dental health, accidents, mental health and health inequalities.

	74	75	76	77	78
a	–	–	–	15	–
b	–	–	2096.5	3,514	56.5
c	NP	NP	Body	–	Body
d	–	–	–	–	–
e	–	–	£133.000m	£4,360.916m	£7.200m
f	–	–	£124.570m	£4,271.113m	£6.860m
g	–	£0.016m	–	–	–
h	–	–	–	£56,683–£96,380*	£71,306*
i	{1M, £233pd}*	1M, £11,893	1M, £17,000	3M, £7,200; 2M, £11,960; 2M, 2F, £14,835; 2M, £17,700; 1M, 1F, £20,180; 1F, £22,660; 1M, 25,140	1M, £14,835
j	–	1F, 11,210	1F, £5,000	6M, 2F, £5,000; 2M, 2,000	–
k	2M, £149pd	9M, 14F, £239pd; 16M, 3F, £191pd; 12M, 14F, £122pd	2M, 3F, £5,000	39M, 22F, £5,000; 10M, 6F, £2,000	4M, 7F, £2,000
l	–	372	–	–	–
m	–	455	–	–	–

* Appointment made by Lord President of the Court of Session.

* Chief Executive (ex-officio board member).

* Chief Executive (ex-officio member).

SCOTTISH OFFICE

National Health Service Bodies

79
Mental Welfare Commission for Scotland

K Floor
Argyle House
3 Lady Lawson Street
Edinburgh EH3 9SH
TEL : 0131 222 6111
FAX : 0131 222 6112/3
CHAIR : Sir William Reid KCB
DIRECTOR : Dr James Dyer
TERMS OF REFERENCE : The Commission has a statutory duty to protect people who may, by reason of mental disorder, be incapable of protecting themselves or their interests adequately.

80
National Health Service Trusts

St Andrew's House
Edinburgh
EH1 3DG
TEL : 0131 244 3469
FAX : 0131 244 3583
CONTACT : Mr Martin Milarky

81
Scottish Council for Postgraduate Medical and Dental Education

4th Floor, Hobart House
80 Hanover Street
Edinburgh
EH2 1EL
TEL : 0131 225 4365
FAX : 0131 225 5891
CHAIR : Professor Peter Howie
TERMS OF REFERENCE : The Council has responsibility for the organisation and funding of postgraduate education for doctors and dentists in Scotland.

82
Scottish Hospital Trust

Saltire Court
20 Castle Terrace
Edinburgh
EH2 2EF
TEL : 0131 228 8111
FAX : 0131 228 8118
CHAIR : Mr J M Watherston CA
SECRETARY : Mr Turcan Connell
TERMS OF REFERENCE : The duties and powers of the Trust are to distribute the income from endowments transferred to it from property accepted by it (after the deduction of expenses) among Health Boards, NHS Trusts and the State Hospital Carstairs.

83
State Hospitals Board for Scotland

The State Hospital
Carstairs
Lanark
MC11 8RP
TEL : 01555 840293
FAX : 01555 840024
CHAIR : Mr Nicky James
GENERAL MANAGER : Mr Dick Manson
TERMS OF REFERENCE : The State Hospital is a secure hospital administered for the Secretary of State by a special health board, subject to the same financial regime and accountability review process as all other health boards.

	79	80	81	82	83
a	–	47	–	–	–
b	44.5*	95,175	68	–	488
c	Body	Body	Body	HC	Body
d	–	–	–	–	–
e	£1.479m	£3,263.000m	£103.000	£1.600m	£15.300m
f	£1.479m	–	£102.595m	–	£15.300m
g	–	–	–	–	–
h	£67,985†	£56,000–£102,000	£88,788	–	£69,371*
i	1M, £11,610	3M, £15,125 16M, 6F, £17,145 21M, 1F, £19,285 1 vacancy	1M, £11,657	1M	1M, £13,220
j	1F, £2,000	–	–	–	1F, £5,000
k	1M, £67,152 1F, £40,266 7M, 7F, £2,000‡ 2 vacancies	128M, 92F, £5,000 10 vacancies	13M, 4F	3M, 1F	4M, 1F, £5,000
l	–	–	–	–	–
m	–	–	–	–	–

* Includes 21 secondees all paid for by the Commission, plus 15 part-time Commissioner by Royal Appointment.
† Director.
‡ This figure relates to 15 days per year. £166 is payable for any additional days.

* General Manager.

Department of Social Security

The Adelphi, 1–11 John Adam Street, London WC2N 6HT

Enquiries	Jan Jones
Telephone	0171 962 8920
Facsimile	0171 712 2023
E-mail	jones.j@ade001.dss.gov.uk
Internet	http://www.dss.gov.uk
GTN	3912 8920

Executive NDPBs

1. Occupational Pensions Regulatory Authority (OPRA)

Invicta House
Trafalgar Place
Brighton
BN1 PDW
TEL : 01273 627600
FAX : 01273 627688
a.mallen@ade003.dss.gov.uk
CHAIR : Mr John Hayes CBE
CHIEF EXECUTIVE : Ms Caroline Johnson
TERMS OF REFERENCE : To make pensions more secure; and to give members of Occupational Pension Schemes added confidence that money put aside for their retirement is safe.

2. Pensions Compensation Board

Room 501
11 Belgrave Road
London
SW1V 1RB
TEL : 0171 828 9794
FAX : 0171 931 7239
d.bateman@ade003.dss.gov.uk
CHAIR : Dr Julian Farrand
SECRETARY : Mrs Sandra Skingley
TERMS OF REFERENCE : To administer the Pensions Compensation Scheme, which provides help to occupational pension schemes which have suffered a reduction in the value of their assets as a result of dishonesty and where the specific employer is insolvent.

Advisory NDPBs

3. Central Advisory Committee on War Pensions

c/o War & Industrial Injuries Policy, 6th Floor, The Adelphi, 1–11 John Adam Street, London, WC2N 6HT
TEL : 0171 962 8000
FAX : 0171 962 8004
c.pike@ade004.dss.gov.uk
CHAIR : Baroness Hollis of Heigham (DSS Minister responsible for War Pensions) ;
SECRETARY : Mr Colin Pike
TERMS OF REFERENCE : To advise the Social Security Minister(s) on War Pensions matters.

		1. OPRA	2. PCB	3. CACWP
a.	Number if a multiple body/system (1.4.98)	–	–	–
b.	Number of staff employed by the body (1.4.98)	162*	2	–
c.	Annual Report	Body	Body	NP*
d.	Audit arrangements	X	X	–
e.	Total gross expenditure of body (1997/98)	£7.688m	£0.640m*	–
f.	Amount funded by government (1997/98)	£7.644m	–	–
g.	Other expenditure by sponsoring dept (1997/98)	–	–	£0.031m
h.	Chief Executive's Remuneration (1997/98)	£79,983	–	–
	Appointments and Remuneration (1.9.98)			
i.	Chairman/President	1M, £85,435	1M, £8,220	†
j.	Deputy	–	–	–
k.	Members	4M, 4F, £161pd	1M, 1F, £161pd	20M, 2F
l.	Tribunal cases received	–	–	–
m.	Tribunal cases disposed of	–	–	–

* Includes 59 staff at the Pension Schemes Registry, Newcastle.

* PCB is funded via a levy on pensions schemes.

* Information obtainable from Annual Report on War Pensioners.
† Chairman is Minister with responsibility for War Pensioners.

DEPARTMENT OF SOCIAL SECURITY

Advisory NDPBs

Tribunal NDPBs

4
Disability Living Allowance Advisory Board

The Adelphi
1–11 John Adam Street
London
WC2N 6HT
TEL : 0171 962 8982
FAX : 0171 712 2507
c.cheeseman@ade004.dss.gov.uk
CHAIR : Professor Rodney Grahame CBE MD FRCP FACP
SECRETARY : Dr Mida McGrath
MEDICAL ADMINISTRATIVE MANAGER : Ms Christine Cheesman
TERMS OF REFERENCE : To advise the Secretary of State for Social Security and medical advisers on matters relating to the Disability Living Allowance and Attendance Allowance.

5
Industrial Injuries Advisory Board

6th Floor, The Adelph
1–11 John Adam Street
London
WC2N 6HT
TEL : 0171 962 8066
FAX : 0171 962 2255
g.roach@ade004.dss.gov.uk
http://www.iiac.org.uk
CHAIR : Professor Tony Newman Taylor ; SECRETARY : Mrs Anne Packer
TERMS OF REFERENCE : To advise the Secretary of State for Social Security matters relating to the industrial injuries scheme.

6
Social Security Advisory Committee

New Court
Carey Street
London
WC2A 2LS
TEL : 0171 412 1509
FAX : 0171 412 1570
ssac@nct001.dss.gov.uk
http://www.ssac.org.uk
CHAIR : Sir Thomas Boyd-Carpenter ; SECRETARY : Ms Gill Saunders
TERMS OF REFERENCE : To consider and report on Social Security Regulations referred to it by the Secretary of State for Social Security.

7
War Pensions Committees

c/o War Pensions Welfare Office, Rm 6305, North Fylde Central Offices, Norcross, Blackpool, Lancs FY5 3TA
TEL : 01253 332699
FAX : 01253 330436
a.burnham@new100.dss.gov.uk
CHAIR : There are 29 Committee Chairmen ; ADMINISTRATOR : Sandra Lloyd
TERMS OF REFERENCE : To consider complaints from claimants to war pensions, particularly about decisions which do not carry a right to appeal; and to make recommendations to the War Pensions Agency.

8
Central Adjudication Services*

Customer Services†
Quarry House
Quarry Hill
Leeds LS2 7UB
TEL : 0113 232 4854
FAX : 0113 232 4840
cas.qh@gtnet.gov.uk
http://www.open.gov.uk/cas/cashome.htm
CHIEF ADJUDICATION OFFICER AND CHIEF CHILD SUPPORT OFFICER : Mr Ernie Hazelwood
CUSTOMER SERVICES OFFICER : Nigel Watson
TERMS OF REFERENCE : To support the Chief Adjudication Officer/Chief Child Support Officer in exercising his statutory and other functions.

	4	5	6	7	8
a	–	–	–	29	–
b	–	–	–	–	–
c	*	NP	TSO*	NP*	TSO
d	–	–	–	–	–
e	–	–	–	–	–
f	–	–	–	–	–
g	£0.237m	£0.068m	£0.214m	£0.197m	£4.1m
h	–	–	–	–	–
i	1M, £273pm	1M, £210pm	1M, £263pd	26M, 2F†	1M, £55,641
j	1M, 1F, £149.90pm; 1M, £272.55pm†	–	–	24M, 3F†	–
k	7M, 1F, £237pm; 2M, 6F, £126pm	12M, 2F, £112pm	9M, 4F, £128pd	593M, 180F	–
l	–	–	–	–	–
m	–	–	–	–	–

4
* As decided by the Secretary of State.
† Only payable when member is deputising in Chariman's absence.

6
* Usually published every 18 months.

7
* Information obtainable from Annual Report on War Pensioners.
† 1 vacancy.

8
* Independent Authority responsible for adjudication on questions concerning Social Security Benefits, Income Support, Child Benefit and Family Credit and for observations on appeals to the Social Security Commissioner.
† Headquarters at 48 Carey Street, London, WC2A 2LS (Tel : 0171 412 1504, Fax : 0171 412 1505).

141

DEPARTMENT OF SOCIAL SECURITY

Tribunal NDPBs

	9	10	11	12
Independent Tribunal Service	**Child Support Appeal Tribunals**	**Disability Appeal Tribunals**	**Medical Appeal Tribunals**	**Social Security Appeal Tribunals**
The President's Office, Whittington House, 19–30 Alfred Place, London WC1 7LW	Independent Tribunal Service President's Office, Whittington House, 19–30 Alfred House, London WC1E 7LW	Independent Tribunal Service President's Office, Whittington House, 19–30 Alfred House, London WC1E 7LW	Independent Tribunal Service President's Office, Whittington House, 19–30 Alfred House, London WC1E 7LW	Independent Tribunal Service President's Office, Whittington House, 19–30 Alfred House, London WC1E 7LW
TEL : 0171 814 6500	TEL : 0171 814 6500	TEL : 0171 814 6500	TEL : 0171 814 6500	TEL : 0171 814 6500
FAX : 0171 814 6540	FAX : 0171 814 6540	FAX : 0171 814 6540	FAX : 0171 814 6540	FAX : 0171 814 6540
PRESIDENT : His Honour Judge Michael Harris; CHIEF EXECUTIVE : Mr Steven Williams	PRESIDENT : His Honour Judge Michael Harris; SECRETARY : Ms Wendy Simpson-Brown	PRESIDENT : His Honour Judge Michael Harris; SECRETARY : Ms Wendy Simpson-Brown	PRESIDENT : His Honour Judge Michael Harris; SECRETARY : Ms Wendy Simpson-Brown	PRESIDENT : His Honour Judge Michael Harris; SECRETARY : Ms Wendy Simpson-Brown
TERMS OF REFERENCE : Information on the following tribunals – Child Support, Disability, Medical, Social Security, Vaccine Damage – can be obtained from the Independent Tribunal Service.	TERMS OF REFERENCE : To consider and hear appeals following the decisions of Child Support Officers. There are 52 Child Support Appeal Tribunals.	TERMS OF REFERENCE : To decide on Disability Living Allowance, Disability Working Allowance and Attendance Allowance cases, where appeals have been made on disability questions. There are 124 Disability Appeal Tribunals.	TERMS OF REFERENCE : To review on appeal, the decisions of adjudicating medical authorities, arising out of claims for Industrial Injuries Benefits and Severe Disablement Allowance. There are 42 Medical Appeal Tribunals.	TERMS OF REFERENCE : To review on appeal, the decision of adjudication officers arising out of claims for social security benefits, including Income Support, Family Credit and Social Fund benefits. There are 142 Social Security Appeal Tribunals.
a –	a 52	a 124	a 42	a 142
b –	b –	b –	b –	b –
c TSO*	c *	c *	c *	c *
d –	d –	d –	d –	d –
e –	e –	e –	e –	e –
f –	f –	f –	f –	f –
g –	g £57.4m†	g £57.4m†	g £57.4m†	g £57.4m†
h –	h –	h –	h –	h –
i 1M† 6M, 1F, £83,523 34M, 15F, £69,793‡	i 120M, 64F, £135hd	i 242M, 87F, £135hd	i 78M, 21F, £135hd	i 439M, 191F, £135hd
j –	j –	j –	j –	j –
k –	k 324M, 283F	k 770M, 662F £101hd‡ £62hd§	k 406M, 19F, £123hd	k 1,524M, 1,044F,
l –	l 9,598	l 63,887	l 18,697	l 270,958
m –	m 8,590	m 51,989	m 16,770	m 262,795

* Reference is made to each Tribunal in the Annual Report of the Council on Tribunals available from The Stationery Office.
† President's salary is determined as recommended by the Senior Salaries Review Board.
‡ London chairmen receive £73,793.

* Reference is made to the Tribunal in the Annual Report of the Council on Tribunals available from The Stationery Office.
† £57.4m was the combined expenditure for all Tribunals.

* Reference is made to the Tribunal in the Annual Report of the Council on Tribunals available from The Stationery Office.
† £57.4m was the combined expenditure for all Tribunals.
‡ Medical members.
§ Carer members.

* Reference is made to the Tribunal in the Annual Report of the Council on Tribunals available from The Stationery Office.
† £57.4m was the combined expenditure for all Tribunals.

* Reference is made to the Tribunal in the Annual Report of the Council on Tribunals available from The Stationery Office.
† £57.4m was the combined expenditure for all Tribunals.

DEPARTMENT OF SOCIAL SECURITY

Tribunal NDPBs

13
Vaccine Damage Appeal Tribunals

Independent Tribunal Service President's Office, Whittington House, 19–30 Alfred House, London WC1E 7LW
TEL : 0171 814 6500
FAX : 0171 814 6540
PRESIDENT : His Honour Judge Michael Harris ; SECRETARY : Ms Wendy Simpson-Brown
TERMS OF REFERENCE : To decide on matters referred to them on the question of disablement – in particular, whether disablement is a result of vaccination and whether it amounts to severe disablement. There are 16 Vaccine Damage Appeal Tribunals.

14
Pensions Ombudsman

6th Floor
11 Belgrave Road
London
SW1V 1RB
TEL : 0171 834 9144
FAX : 0171 821 0065
PENSIONS OMBUDSMAN : Dr Julian Farrand ; SECRETARY : Jean Heaney
TERMS OF REFERENCE : To investigate and decide on complaints and disputes concerning occupational pension schemes. He is completely independent and acts as an impartial adjudicator.

	13	14
a	16	–
b	–	–
c	*	Body
d	–	–
e	–	–
f	–	–
g	£57.4m†	£1.386m
h	–	–
i	23M, 7F, £135hd	1M, £83,118
j	–	–
k	£123hd‡	–
l	30	2,840*
m	18	3,289

* Reference is made to the Tribunal in the Annual Report of the Council on Tribunals available from The Stationery Office.
† £57.4m was the combined expenditure for all Tribunals.
‡ Members of Vaccine Damage Tribunals drawn from members of the Medical Appeal Tribunals.

* Of these 729 were new cases acceptable for investigation of which 1,059 were cleared in 1997/98. 1,059 includes clearance of some of the cases which were in hand at the start of the year.

OFFICE OF TELECOMMUNICATIONS

Office of Telecommunication (OFTEL)

50 Ludgate Hill, London EC4M 7JJ

Enquiries	Terry Walker
Telephone	0171 634 8774
Facsimile	0171 634 8845
E-mail	actsec@acts.org.uk
Internet	http://www.oftel.gov.uk
GTN	3828 8774

Advisory NDPBs

	1 Advisory Body on Fair Trading in Telecommunications	2 Advisory Committee on Telecommunications for Disabled and Elderly People	3 Communications for Business¶
Address	50 Ludgate Hill, London EC4M 7JJ	50 Ludgate Hill, London EC4M 7JJ	50 Ludgate Hill, London EC4M 7JJ
TEL	0171 634 8747	0171 634 8773	0171 634 8774
FAX	0171 634 8949	0171 634 8845	0171 634 8845
E-mail	lknight@oftel.gov.uk	diel@acts.org.uk	cfb@acts.org.uk
Web	http://www.oftel.gov.uk	http://www.acts.org.uk	http://www.acts.org.uk
CHAIR	Mr Jeremy Lever QC	Ms Jean Gaffin	Mr Peter Calver
TERMS OF REFERENCE	To advise the Director General on the application of the Fair Trading Condition in telecommunications licenses, which prohibits the abuse of a dominant position or the making of anti-competitive agreements. A case may be referred to the ABFTT either by the Director General or by the licensee where the Director General has proposed to take formal enforcement action.	To advise the Director-General of OFTEL on any matter they consider relevant; to report to the Director-General on their activities during the year and to be an independent voice representing and promoting the needs of consumers.	To advise the Director-General of OFTEL on any matter they consider relevant; to report to the Director-General on their activities during the year and to be an independent voice representing and promoting the needs of consumers.
a. Number if a multiple body (1.4.98)	–	–	–
b. Number of staff employed by the body (1.4.98)	–	–	–
c. Annual Report	Body*	Body*	Body*
d. Audit arrangements	–	–	–
e. Total gross expenditure of body (1997/98)	–	–	–
f. Amount funded by government (1997/98)	–	–	–
g. Other expenditure by sponsoring dept (1997/98)	£0.043m	£0.061m†	£0.033m†
h. Chief Executive's Remuneration (1997/98)	–	–	–
Appointments and Remuneration (1.9.98)			
i. Chairman/President	1M, £425pd	{1F, £65pd}‡	{1M, £65pd}‡
j. Deputy	–	–	–
k. Members	{4M, 1F, £375pd}†	{7M, 3F}‡	{2M, 1F}‡
l. Tribunal cases received	–	–	–
m. Tribunal cases disposed of	–	–	–

* Statutory reports included in the Annual Report of the Director General of Telecommunications. Summary reports are available from the Secretariat.

† Appointments are made by the Director General of Telecommunications.

* Statutory Reports included in the Annual Report of the Director General of Telecommunications. Summary reports are available from the Secretariat.

† Includes an allocation of the costs of common secretarial support provided directly by OFTEL & on a repayment basis by DTI (local staff are shared with Post Office Users' Councils in Scotland, Wales & Northern Ireland).

‡ Appointments by the Director of Telecommunications.

¶ Communication for Business is the Business Advisory Committee in Telecommunications.

OFFICE OF TELECOMMUNICATIONS

Advisory NDPBs

4	5	6	7
Consumer Communications for England[§]	**Northern Ireland Advisory Committee on Telecommunications**[#]	**Scottish Advisory Committee on Telecommunications**[#]	**Welsh Advisory Committee on Telecommunications**[#]
50 Ludgate Hill London EC4M 7JJ	22 Great Victoria Street Belfast BT2 7QA	2 Greenside Lane Edinburgh EH1 3AH	Caradog House St Andrews Place Cardiff CF1 3BE
TEL: 0171 634 8774 FAX: 0171 634 8845 cce@acts.org.uk http://www.acts.org.uk	TEL: 01232 244113 FAX: 01232 247024 niact@acts.org.uk http://www.acts.org.uk	TEL: 0131 244 5576 FAX: 0131 244 5696 sacot@acts.org.uk http://www.acts.org.uk	TEL: 01222 374028 FAX: 01222 668536 EMAIL: wact@acts.org.uk WEB: http://www.acts.org.uk
CHAIR: Miss Moira Black	CHAIR: Mr Courtney Thompson	CHAIR: Vacant	CHAIR: Professor Mike Tedd
TERMS OF REFERENCE: To advise the Director-General of OFTEL on any matter they consider relevant; to report to the Director-General on their activities during the year and to be an independent voice representing and promoting the needs of consumers.	TERMS OF REFERENCE: To advise the Director-General of OFTEL on any matter they consider relevant; to report to the Director-General on their activities during the year and to be an independent voice representing and promoting the needs of consumers.	TERMS OF REFERENCE: To advise the Director-General of OFTEL on any matter they consider relevant; to report to the Director-General on their activities during the year and to be an independent voice representing and promoting the needs of consumers.	TERMS OF REFERENCE: To advise the Director-General of OFTEL on any matter they consider relevant; to report to the Director-General on their activities during the year and to be an independent voice representing and promoting the needs of consumers.
a —	a —	a —	a —
b —	b —	b —	b —
c Body*	c Body*	c Body*	c Body*
d —	d —	d —	d —
e —	e —	e —	e —
f —	f —	f —	f —
g £0.054m[†]	g £0.050m[†]	g £0.053m[†]	g £0.044m[†]
h —	h —	h —	h —
i 1F, £65pd	i 1M, £65pd	i £65pd**	i 1M, £65pd
j —	j —	j —	j —
k 5M, 2F	k 7M, 3F	k 8M, 2F	k 3M, 3F*
l —	l —	l —	l —
m —	m —	m —	m —

* Statutory Reports included in the Annual Report of the Director General of Telecommunications. Summary reports are available from the Secretariat.

† Includes an allocation of the costs of common secretarial support provided directly by OFTEL & on a repayment basis by DTI (local staff are shared with Post Office Users' Councils in Scotland, Wales & Northern Ireland).

§ Is the English Advisory Committee on Telecommunications.

\# Local support staff in Scotland, Wales and Northern Ireland also handle consumer representations & complaints on behalf of OFTEL.

** New chairman yet to be appointed.

DEPARTMENT OF TRADE AND INDUSTRY

Nationalised Industries

Department of Trade & Industry

1 Victoria Street, London SW1H 0ET

Enquiries	Kevin Byrne
Telephone	0171 215 5306
Facsimile	0171 215 5420
Internet	http://www.dti.gov.uk
GTN	215 5306

1 British Shipbuilders

89 Sandyford Road
Newcastle upon Tyne
NE99 1PL

TEL : 0191 232 8493
FAX : 0191 261 9490
CHAIR : Christopher Campbell CBE ; CORPORATIONS SECRETARY : John Murray
TERMS OF REFERENCE : The Corporation is involved in residual activities – litigation, insurance claim and other contractual matters.

2 British Coal Corporation

c/o Coal Directorate
DTI, Room UG EO4
1 Victoria Street
London SW1E 0ET

TEL : 0171 215 2626
FAX : 0171 215 2728
TERMS OF REFERENCE : The British Coal Corporation continues as a residual body within the Department of Trade and Industry after the vast majority of its activities, assets and liabilities have either been managed down, sold or transferred to other appropriate authorities.

3 British Nuclear Fuels plc

Risley
Warrington
WA3 6AS

TEL : 01925 832000
FAX : 01925 822711
http://www.bnfl.com
CHAIR : Mr John Guinness CB
TERMS OF REFERENCE : To manufacture and supply uranium and plutonium based fuels, and the provision of related fuel cycle services for, and the generation of electricity from, nuclear power stations; the reprocessing of nuclear fuels after use associated waste treatment and storage.

	1 British Shipbuilders	2 British Coal Corporation	3 British Nuclear Fuels plc
a. Number if a multiple body/system (1.4.98)	–	–	–
b. Number of staff employed by the body (1.4.98)	–	–	–
c. Annual Report	Body	Body	Body
d. Audit arrangements	–	–	–
e. Total gross expenditure of body (1997/98)	–	–	–
f. Amount funded by government (1997/98)	–	–	–
g. Other expenditure by sponsoring dept (1997/98)	–	–	–
h. Chief Executive's Remuneration (1997/98)	–	–	£232,000*
Appointments and Remuneration (1.9.98)			
i. Chairman/President	1M, £17,368	1M, £99,000*	1M, £95,000*†
j. Deputy	–	–	1M, £161,000*
k. Members	2M, up to £5,000	1M, up to £10,000*	1M, £195,000* 2M, £144,000* 4M, 1F, £10,001–£12,000
l. Tribunal cases received	–	–	–
m. Tribunal cases disposed of	–	–	–

* Annual salary. Chairman and member have been appointed for six months on a pro-rata basis. Their terms of office end on 31 December 1998.

* A performance related bonus of up to 40% of salary is available.
† Part-time (4 days per week).

DEPARTMENT OF TRADE AND INDUSTRY

Nationalised Industries

Executive Bodies

	4	5	6	7	8
	Magnox Electric plc	Post Office	Advisory, Conciliation and Arbitration Service (ACAS)	British Hallmarking Council	Coal Authority
	Berkeley Centre Berkeley Gloucestershire GL13 9PB	148 Old Street London EC1V 9HQ	Brandon House 180 Borough High Street London SE1 1RW	St Philips House St Philips Place Birmingham B3 2PP	200 Lichfield Lane Mansfield Nottinghamshire NG18 4RG
	TEL : 01453 810451 FAX : 01453 812529 MANAGING DIRECTOR : Mr Dennis Joynson TERMS OF REFERENCE : Magnox Electric plc is a major nuclear electricity generator, with power stations and non-operational sites throughout the UK.	TEL : 0171 250 2888 FAX : 0171 250 2960 CHAIR : Dr Neville Bain SECRETARY : Mr Richard Adams TERMS OF REFERENCE : The Post Office comprises of the Royal Mail, Parcelforce, Post Office Counters and Subscription Services (a provider of telebusinesses and customer management services).	TEL : 0171 210 3000 FAX : 0171 210 3708 http://www.acas.org.uk CHAIR : Mr John Hougham CBE SECRETARY : Miss Karen Hambly TERMS OF REFERENCE : The Advisory Conciliation and Arbitration Service aims to improve the performance and effectiveness of organisations by providing an independent and impartial service to prevent and resolve disputes and to build harmonious relationships at work.	TEL : 0121 200 3300 FAX : 0121 200 3330 CHAIR : Sir Adam Butler SECRETARY : Mr Michael Winwood TERMS OF REFERENCE : The British Hallmarking Council oversees the operations of the Assay Offices and advises the Government on the operation of the Hallmarking Act 1973.	TEL : 01623 427162 FAX : 01623 622072 john.delaney.webmaster@coal.gov.uk http://www.coal.gov.uk CHAIR : Sir David White ; CHIEF EXECUTIVE : Mr Kenneth J Fergusson TERMS OF REFERENCE : To license all coal mining operations, provide information on past and present mining to landowners and purchasers, and settles claims arising from past mining, and aims to solve the environmental legacy created by the coal mining industry.
a	–	–	–	–	–
b	–	–	641*	–	110
c	Body	Body	Body	Body	Body
d	–	–	X	Y	X
e	–	–	£24.41m	£0.038m	£48.027m
f	–	–	£23.88m	–	£44.926m
g	–	–	–	–	£0.088m
h	*	£181,980*	†	–	£70,000
i	1M, £130,000–£135,000†	1M, £88,000*	1M, £82,666†	{1M, £7,000}	1M, £20,000
j	1M, £125,000–£130,000*†	–	–	–	1M, £6,750
k	3M, £95,000–£100,000† 3M, 1F, £10,000–£15,000‡	2M, £259,161* 2M, £36,409	8M, 3F, £1,273 + £130pd	8M, 2F, {8M}*	4M, £6,250
l	–	–	–	–	–
m	–	–	–	–	–

* Deputy Chairman also acts as Chief Executive.
† A performance related bonus of up to 40% of basic salary is available.
‡ Circa 20 days per annum.

* A performance related bonus of up to 40% of salary is available.

* Although directly employed, staff of this body are civil servants.
† Chairman is also Chief Executive.

* Eight members are appointed by the four Assay Offices.

147

DEPARTMENT OF TRADE AND INDUSTRY

Executive NDPBs

9 Commissioner for Protection Against Unlawful Industrial Action

2nd Floor, Bank Chambers
2a Rylands Street
Warrington
Cheshire WA1 1EN
TEL : 01925 415771
FAX : 01925 415772
CHAIR : Mr Gerry Corless CBE
SECRETARY : Mr Terry Wafer
TERMS OF REFERENCE : To provide assistance to individuals taking proceedings against a trade union whose unlawful organisation of industrial action deprives the individual of goods or services.

10 Commissioner for the Rights of Trade Union Members

2nd Floor, Bank Chambers
2a Rylands Street
Warrington
Cheshire WA1 1EN
TEL : 01925 415771
FAX : 01925 415772
CHAIR : Mr Gerry Corless CBE
SECRETARY : Mr Terry Wafer
TERMS OF REFERENCE : To provide material assistance to union members taking certain legal proceedings against their union; including the infringement of industrial action or union leadership election balloting procedures and the unlawful use of union rights.

11 Design Council

34 Bow Street
London
WC2E 7DL
TEL : 0171 420 5200
FAX : 0171 420 5300
http://www.design-council.org.uk
CHAIR : Mr John Sorrell CBE
TERMS OF REFERENCE : To inspire best use of design by the UK, in the world context, to improve prosperity and well-being.

12 Gas Consumers' Council

Abford House
15 Wilton Road
London
SW1A 7AA
TEL : 0171 931 0977
FAX : 0171 630 9934
gcc@gcchead1.sonnet.co.uk
CHAIR : Ms Jenny Kirkpatrick
DIRECTOR : Ms Sue Slipman OBE
TERMS OF REFERENCE : The Gas Consumers' Council is an independent body established to look after the interests of the 19 million gas users in the United Kingdom. It exists to help everyone who use gas and gas appliances to obtain satisfactory service.

13 Monopolies and Mergers Commission

New Court
48 Carey Street
London
WC2A 2JT
TEL : 0171 324 1467
FAX : 0171 324 1400
mmc@gtnet.gov.uk
http://www.open.uk/mmc/mmchome.htm
CHAIR : Dr Derek Morris
SECRETARY : Miss Penny Boys
TERMS OF REFERENCE : To investigate and report on matters referred to it relating to mergers, monopolies and anti-competitive practices, the regulation of utilities and the performance of public sector bodies.

	9	10	11	12	13
a	–	–	–	–	–
b	5*	5*	39	105*	84
c	Body	Body	Body	Body	Body
d	X	X	X	Y	X
e	£0.074m	£0.247m	£7.359m	£3.480m	£6.600m
f	£0.074m	£0.247m	£7.258m	£3.480m	£6.600m
g	–	–	–	£0.023m	£0.109m
h	–	–	£89,000	£59,675	£73,143*
i	1M, £12,602	1M, £25,204	1M	1F, £15,352	1M, £120,000
j	–	–	–	1M, £5,771; 2 vacancies	1M, £52,530; 1F, £70,040
k	–	–	12M, 3F	2M, 3F, £5,771; 3M, 1F	28M, £15,173[†]; 6F, £15,173[‡]; 16M, £10,114[§]; 4F, £10,114[§]
l	–	–	–	–	–
m	–	–	–	–	–

* Staff are shared between the two Commissioner posts.

* Staff are shared between the two Commissioner posts.

* Includes 24 temporary staff recruited to deal with the additional demands on the GCC's services as a result of the opening up of the domestic gas market.

* Secretary to the Commission. Remuneration as at 31.3.98.
[†] Includes 14 additional members paid only when serving on references.
[‡] Includes 1 additional member paid only when serving on references.
[§] Reserve members paid only when serving on references.

DEPARTMENT OF TRADE AND INDUSTRY

Executive NDPBs

14
National Consumer Council*

20 Grosvenor Gardens
London
SW1W 0DH

TEL : 0171 730 3469
FAX : 0171 730 0191
info@ncc.org.uk
CHAIR : Mr David Hatch CBE JP
DIRECTOR : Ms Ruth Evans
TERMS OF REFERENCE : To act as the independent voice of consumers throughout the United Kingdom and to promote and safeguard the interests of the consumers of goods and services of all kinds.

15
National Research Development Corporation (NRDC)*

c/o British Technology Corporation International plc
101 Newington Causeway
London SE1 6BU

TEL : 0171 403 6666
FAX : 0171 575 0010
TERMS OF REFERENCE : A shadow body which exists only to retain ownership of certain patents following privatisation of the British Technology Group.

16
Post Office Users' Councils for Scotland, Wales and Northern Ireland

Various
Addresses

TERMS OF REFERENCE : To represent customer interests in respect of services provided by the Post Office.

17
Post Office Users' National Council

16 Hercules Road
London
SE1 7DN

TEL : 0171 928 9458
FAX : 0171 928 9076
CHAIR (POUNC) : Mr John Hackney ; SECRETARY : Mr James Dodds
TERMS OF REFERENCE : To represent customer interests in respect of services provided by the Post Office. There are separate Post Office Users' Councils for England, Scotland, Wales and Northern Ireland.

Research Councils

18
Biotechnology and Biological Sciences Research Council (BBSRC)

Central Office
Polaris House
North Star Avenue
Swindon SN2 1UH

TEL : 01793 413200
FAX : 01793 413201
bbsrc-office.wordmaster@bbsrc.ac.uk
http://www.bbsrc.ac.uk
CHAIR : Dr Peter Doyle CBE FRSE
CHIEF EXECUTIVE : Professor Raymond Baker FRS
TERMS OF REFERENCE : To promote and support high quality basic strategic and applied research and related post-graduate training relating to the understanding and exploitation of biotechnology and biological systems.

	14	15	16	17	18
a	4*	–	3	–	–
b	55†	–	18*	18*	3,607
c	Body	–	Body	Body	Body
d	Y	X	X†	X†	X
e	£2.976m	–	£0.458m*‡	£0.458m*‡	£198.676m
f	£2.404m	–	£0.458m*‡	£0.458m*‡	£189.022m
g	£0.030m	–	£0.030m*	£0.030m*	£1.877m‡
h	£56,471	–	–	–	*
i	1M, £21,775; 1F, £10,298‡; 1F, £5,149‡	1M	3M, £65pd	1M, £11,551	1M, £13,300
j	1F, £13,847‡	–	–	–	1M, £77,063*†
k	10M, 3F, £5,149; 17M, 8F, £40–£80pm	4M	17M, 14F	8M, 1F, 7 vacancies§	9M, 4F, £5,390
l	–	–	–	–	–
m	–	–	–	–	–

* Multiple body comprising National, Scottish and Welsh Consumer Councils and Consumers in Europe Group.
† Equivalent of 49.98 full-time posts.
‡ £10,298 relates to chairman of Welsh Consumer Council who receives £5,149 for chairman post and £5,149 as ex-officio member of NCC. £5,149 relates to chairman of Scottish Consumer Council currently vice-chair of NCC for which she receives £13,847 as shown in row 'j'.

* Although individual NDPBs, POUNC and the POUCS are funded collectively. This information has been merged to provide more accurate financial information.
† Expenditure forms part of DTI expenditure. Accounts for DTI are audited by the Comptroller and Auditor General.
‡ Excludes expenditure on the Post Office Advisory Committees (around 200 nationwide) which are funded via POUNC and the POUCs, but are not themselves NDPBs.
§ Excludes the chairmen of the Post Office Users Councils for Scotland, Wales and Northern Ireland who are all ex-officio members of POUNC.

* Deputy Chairman is also Chief Executive.
† Eligible for performance bonus of up to 20%.
‡ Total expenditure by departments on all Research Councils.

149

DEPARTMENT OF TRADE AND INDUSTRY

Executive NDPBs

Research Councils

19	**20**	**21**	**22**	**23**
Council for the Central Laboratory of the Research Councils*	Economic and Social Research Council	Engineering and Physical Sciences Research Council	Medical Research Council	Natural Environment Research Council
Rutherford Appleton Laboratory Didcot Oxfordshire OX11 0QX	Polaris House North Star Avenue Swindon SN2 1UJ	Polaris House North Star Avenue Swindon SN2 1UJ	20 Park Crescent London W1N 4AL	Polaris House North Star Avenue Swindon SN2 1EU
TEL : 01235 821900 FAX : 01235 446665 a.g.buckley@dl.ac.uk http://www.cclrc.ac.uk	TEL : 01793 413000 FAX : 01793 413001 exrel@esrc.ac.uk http://www.esrc.ac.uk	TEL : 01793 444000 FAX : 01793 444001 infoline@epsrc.ac.uk http://www.epsrc.ac.uk	TEL : 0171 636 5422 FAX : 0171 436 6179 corporate@headoffice. mrc.ac.uk http://www.mrc.ac.uk	TEL : 01793 411500 FAX : 01793 411501 nerccomm@nerc.ac.uk http://www.nerc.ac.uk
CHAIRMAN AND CHIEF EXECUTIVE : Dr Albert Westwood FEng NAE	CHAIR : Dr Bruce Smith OBE CHIEF EXECUTIVE : Professor Ronald Amann	CHAIR : Dr Alan Rudge CBE FEng CHIEF EXECUTIVE : Professor Richard Brook OBE	CHAIR : Sir Anthony Cleaver FBCS ; CHIEF EXECUTIVE : Professor George Radda CBE FRS	CHAIR : Mr James Smith CBE FEng FRSE ; CHIEF EXECUTIVE : Professor John Krebs FRS
TERMS OF REFERENCE : Provides advanced facilities, including large-scale radiation sources, to support basic, strategic and applied research programmes being undertaken by the UK and international scientific community and by industry.	TERMS OF REFERENCE : Supports high quality research and postgraduate training that will contribute to economic competitiveness, the quality of life and the effectiveness of public services and policy.	TERMS OF REFERENCE : Promotes and supports high-quality basic, strategic and applied research and related post-graduate training of engineering and the physical sciences.	TERMS OF REFERENCE : The Council's principle objectives are to promote the balanced development of medical and related biological research, with the aim of maintaining and improving human health.	TERMS OF REFERENCE : The leading body in the UK for basic, strategic and applied research across the spectrum of the environmental sciences, it has a dual role as a provider and customer of scientific research through its own centres, universities and other institutions.
a —	a —	a —	a —	a —
b 1,669	b 94	b 283	b 3,018	b 2,650
c Body	c Body	c Body	c Body	c Body
d X	d X	d X	d X	d X
e £106.068m	e £66.326m	e £392.973m	e £322.400m	e £211.850m
f £1.206m	f £65.227m	f £386.276m	f £292.721m	f £166.150
g £1.877m§	g £1.877m‡	g £1.877m‡	g £1.877m†	g £1.877m‡
h †	h *	h *	h *	h *
i 1M, 78,000†‡	i 1M, £9,900	i 1M, £13,300	i 1M, £13,300	i 1M, £13,300
j —	j 1M, £64,546*†	j 1M, £83,340*†	j 1M, £76,035*	j 1M, £82,500*†
k 6M, 3F, £5,390	k 7M, 5F, £5,390–£7,180	k 10M, 2F, £5,390	k 10M, 3F, £5,390–£7,180	k 11M, 2F, £5,390–£7,180
l —	l —	l —	l —	l —
m	m	m	m	m

* CCLRC came into being on 1 April 1995, taking responsibility from the EPSRC for the Daresbury and Rutherford Appleton laboratories and their staff.
† Chairman is also Chief Executive.
‡ Eligible for performance bonus of up to 20%.
§ Total expenditure by departments on all Research Councils.

* Deputy Chairman is also Chief Executive.
† Eligible for performance bonus of up to 20%.
‡ Total expenditure by departments on all Research Councils.

* Deputy Chairman is also Chief Executive.
† Eligible for performance bonus of up to 20%.
‡ Total expenditure by departments on all Research Councils.

* Deputy Chairman is also Chief Executive.
† Total expenditure by departments on all Research Councils.

* Deputy Chairman is also Chief Executive.
† Eligible for performance bonus of up to 20%.
‡ Total expenditure by departments on all Research Councils.

DEPARTMENT OF TRADE AND INDUSTRY

Executive NDPBs

Research Councils

24 Particle Physics and Astronomy Research Council

Polaris House
North Star Avenue
Swindon
SN2 1EU
TEL : 01793 442000
FAX : 01793 442106
pparcweb@coinet.demon.co.uk
http://www.pparc.ac.uk
CHAIR : Sir Peter Williams CBE PhD Eng ; DEPUTY CHAIRMAN AND CHIEF EXECUTIVE : Professor Ian Halliday PhD
TERMS OF REFERENCE : Pursues a programme of high quality basic research in astronomy, planetary science and particle physics which furthers understanding of fundamental questions, and trains high quality scientists and engineers.

25 The Simpler Trade Procedures Board

4th Floor
151 Buckingham Palace Road
London
SW1W 9SS
TEL : 0171 215 0825
FAX : 0171 215 0824
CHAIR : Amir Bhatia OBE
CHIEF EXECUTIVE : Michael Doran
TERMS OF REFERENCE : The Simpler Trade Procedures Board deals with trade facilitation which works to simplify international trade procedures.

26 United Kingdom Atomic Energy Authority

Marshall Building
Harwell
Didcot
Oxfordshire OX11 0RA
TEL : 01235 436900
CHAIR : Sir Kenneth Eaton GBE KCB
TERMS OF REFERENCE : The UKAEA's key responsibility is the safe management of its nuclear liabilities, and it is also responsible for thermonuclear fusion research and civil nuclear safety.

Advisory Bodies

27 Advisory Committee on Coal Research

1 Victoria Street
London
SW1H 0ET
TEL : 0171 215 2669
FAX : 0171 282 7969
charles.pearce@herd.dti.gov.uk
CHAIR : Mr Godfrey Bevan
SECRETARY : Mr Charles Pearce
TERMS OF REFERENCE : The specific objectives of the ACCR are to advise the DTI within the strategic framework set by the DTI, of the merits/content of programme plans and to provide a forum for continued developments of the strategic, technical and commercial aspects of the DTI's cleaner coal technology programme.

28 Aviation Committee

151 Buckingham Palace Road
London
SW1W 9SS
TEL : 0171 215 1128
FAX : 0171 215 2974
CHAIR : Mr Roy McNulty
SECRETARY : Ms Leonie Austin
TERMS OF REFERENCE : To advise Ministers and senior officials in the Department of Trade and Industry on the needs and priorities of the United Kingdom aerospace industry.

	24	25	26	27	28
a	–	–	–	–	–
b	371	12	2,120.5	–	–
c	Body	Body	Body	*	NP
d	X	X	X	–	–
e	£199.369m	£0.844m	£292.600m	–	–
f	£197.869m	£0.604m	£200.000m	–	–
g	£1.877m‡	–	£0.599m	£0.015m	£0.005m
h	*	£59,700	£135,179*	–	–
i	1M, £7,700	1M	1M, £30,000	1M	1M
j	1M, £72,000*†	1M	–	–	–
k	10M, 1F, £5,390–£7,180	8M*	4M, £75,000–£80,145 / 4M, £10,000 / 1M	12M, 2F	16M, 1F
l	–	–	–	–	–
m	–	–	–	–	–

* Deputy Chairman is also Chief Executive.
† Eligible for performance bonus of up to 20%.
‡ Total expenditure by departments on all Research Councils.

* Includes two ex-officio members from DTI and HMCE.

* Includes remuneration of two Chief Executives during 1997–98.

* Annual report published by the Energy Technology Support Unit on behalf of ACCR.

151

DEPARTMENT OF TRADE AND INDUSTRY

Advisory NDPBs

29
British Overseas Trade Board

Room 1010, Kingsgate House
66–74 Victoria Street
London
SW1E 6SW

TEL : 0171 215 4945
CHAIR : Mr Martin Laing
TERMS OF REFERENCE : To advise the Department of Trade and Industry and the Foreign Office on overseas trade and export promotion policy.

30
Council for Science and Technology

Office of Science and Technology, Albany House
94–98 Petty France
London SW1H 9ST

TEL : 0171 271 2097
FAX : 0171 271 2028
daniela.clare@osct.dti.gov.uk
http://www-cst.gov.uk
CHAIR : Rt Hon Peter Mandelson MP ; SECRETARY : Mr Steve Elton
TERMS OF REFERENCE : To advise the Prime Minister on strategic policies and framework for Science and Technology (S&T) in the UK with the overarching aim of sustaining and developing UK S&T and maximising their contribution to the nation's wealth creation and quality of life.

31
Energy Advisory Panel

136 Upper Street
Islington
London
N1 1QP

TEL : 0171 477 2121
FAX : 0171 277 2332
CHAIR : Sir Geoffrey Chipperfield
SECRETARY : Rob Potter
TERMS OF REFERENCE : The Energy Advisory panel provides advice on the structure and content of the Government's annual Energy Report, and may also offer other such advice to the Government as it considers appropriate.

32
Foresight Steering Group

Office of Science and Technology, Albany House
94–98 Petty France
London SW1H 9ST

TEL : 0171 271 2047
FAX : 0171 271 2015
martin.ridge@osct.dti.gov.uk
http://www.foresight.gov.uk
CHAIR : Sir Robert May
SECRETARY : Dr Martin Ridge
TERMS OF REFERENCE : To advise the Office of Science and Technology (OST) on the strategic direction, implementation and evaluation of the Foresight Programme.

33
Fuel Cell Advisory Panel

c/o James Marsh
DTI, Room 1.d.53
1 Victoria Street
London SW1H 0ET

TEL : 0171 215 2652
FAX : 0171 828 7969
CHAIR : Mr Adrian Hyde
SECRETARY : Ms Margaret Coombes
TERMS OF REFERENCE : To advise the Department of Trade and Industry and its agent – the Energy Technology Unit, in developing and formulating, against specific programme aims and objectives, programme plans for the Department's Advanced Fuel Cells programme

	29	30	31	32	33
a	–	–	–	–	–
b	–	–	–	–	–
c	Body	Body	NP*	NP	NP
d	–	–	–	–	–
e	–	–	–	–	–
f	–	–	–	–	–
g	£0.400m	£0.082m	£0.011m	£0.001m	£0.008m
h	–	–	–	–	–
i	1M, £23,118	–	1M, £450pd	*	1M
j	1M	1M	–	–	–
k	9M*	11M, 3F	9M, 4F	{14M, 3F}	7M
l	–	–	–	–	–
m	–	–	–	–	–

* Excluding chairman and vice chairman

* The role of the EAP is to advise Government on the information in its annual Energy report which is available from The Stationery Office.

* Chief Scientific Adviser (ex-officio appointment).

DEPARTMENT OF TRADE AND INDUSTRY

Advisory NDPBs

	34	35	36	37	38
	Human Genetics Advisory Commission	**Industrial Development Advisory Board**	**LINK Board**	**Measurement Advisory Committee**	**OSO Industry Board**
	Office of Science and Technology, Albany House 94–98 Petty France London SW1H 9ST	REG A, 3.b.41 DTI, 1 Victoria Street London SW1H 0ET	c/o LINK Directorate, Office of Science and Technology, DTI 1 Victoria Street London SW1H 0ET	TS Directorate 151 Buckingham Road London SW1W 9SS	Tay House 300 Bath Street Glasgow G2 4DX
TEL	0171 271 2131	0171 215 5580	0171 215 0053	0171 215 1406	0141 228 3664
FAX	0171 271 2028	0171 215 0009	0171 215 0054	0171 215 1978	0141 228 3627
	chris.hepworth@osct.dti.gov.uk http://www.dti.gov.uk/hgac	CONTACT: Mr Robin Lavery	link.ost@gtnet.gov.uk CHAIR: Dr David Smith CBE	alastair.hooley@tidv.dti.gov.uk http://www.dtiinfo1.dti.gov.uk/nmd	http://www.dti.gov.uk/ots/iep
CHAIR	Professor Sir Colin Campbell				Sir Ian Wood
SECRETARY	Dr Amanda Goldin			Mr Alastair Hooley	Mrs Beryl Reid
TERMS OF REFERENCE	The Human Genetics Advisory Commission takes a broad view of developments in human genetics and advises on ways to build public understanding of the new genetics, reporting to UK Health and Industry Ministers.	To advise the Secretary of State on the exercise of functions under sections 7 and 8 of the Industrial Development Act 1982; which involves advising on applications for regional assistance over £2m.	The LINK Board provides an independent, strategic overview of the LINK collaborative research scheme and advises Government on its development.	Advises the DTI on the effectiveness of its programmes of expenditure in support of the National Measurement System (NMS).	The OSO board brings together senior industrialists from the UK oil, gas and petrochemical supplies industry. Its function is to give advice on policy and direction regarding activities of the Infrastructure and Energy Projects Directorate (formerly OSO).
a	–	–	–	–	–
b	–	–	–	–	–
c	Body	HC	NP*	NP	NP
d	–	–	–	–	–
e	–	–	–	–	–
f	–	–	–	–	–
g	£0.203m	£0.013m	£0.046m	£0.041m*	£0.005m
h	–	–	–	–	–
i	1M	1M	1M	1M	1M
j	–	–	–	–	–
k	5M, 4F	12M, 1F	5M, 1F, 4 vacancies	9M, 1F†	11M
l	–	–	–	–	–
m	–	–	–	–	–

* Not published but copies available from LINK Directorate, UGA 35, 1 Victoria Street, London, SW1H 0ET.

* Includes expenditure to support 16 MAC Working Groups.
† Members are appointed by the Permanent Secretary.

DEPARTMENT OF TRADE AND INDUSTRY

Advisory NDPBs

39
Overseas Project Board*

Kingsgate House
66–74 Victoria Street
London
SW1E 6SW
TEL : 0171 215 4673
FAX : 0171 215 4222
CHAIR : Mr Andrew Buxton
SECRETARY : Mr Jeff Nuttall
FORMER TERMS OF REFERENCE : To provide expert advice to Ministers and officials on issues affecting United Kingdom industry's ability to compete effectively for major project business overseas.

40
Regional Industrial Development Boards

REG A, 3.6.41
DTI, 1 Victoria Street
London
SW1H 0ET
TEL : 0171 215 5580
FAX : 0171 215 0009
CONTACT : Mr Robin Lavery
TERMS OF REFERENCE : Regional Industrial Development Boards are established in those English regions with substantial assisted areas, and advise on applications for Regional Assistance between £250 and £2m.

41
Renewable Energy Advisory Committee

1 Victoria Street
London
SW1W 0ET
TEL : 0171 215 2651
FAX : 01946 728888
CHAIR : Mr Godfrey Bevan
SECRETARY : Mrs Grace Gordon
TERMS OF REFERENCE : The Committee advises the Chairman on the Department of Trade and Industry's new and renewable energy programme.

42
Spectrum Management Advisory Group

SMAG, Radiocommunications Agency, 10N/20.3 New King's Beam House, 22 Upper Ground, London SE1 9SA
TEL : 0171 211 0073
CHAIR : Dr John Forrest
SECRETARY : Ms Louise Odell
TERMS OF REFERENCE : Provides independent strategic advice to DTI Ministers and the Radiocommunications Agency on the management of the radio spectrum.

43
Standing Advisory Committee on Industrial Property

The Patent Office, Room 3B40
Concept House, Cardiff Road
Newport, South Wales
NP9 1RM
TEL : 01633 814553
FAX : 01633 814922
edward.smith@patent.gov.uk
CHAIR : Mr David Lewis
SECRETARY : Mr Edward Smith
TERMS OF REFERENCE : To advise the Government on industrial property matters.

	39	40	41	42	43
a	–	7	–	–	–
b	–	–	–	–	–
c	NP	HC	NP*	Body	NP
d					
e	–	–	–	–	–
f	–	–	–	–	–
g	£0.004m	£0.045m	£0.015m	£0.236m	£0.010m
h	–	–	–	–	–
i	–	7M	1M	1M	1M
j	–	–	–	–	–
k	–	73M, 14F	1M, 150pd 12M, 1F	–	{18}*
l	–	–	–	–	–
m	–	–	–	–	–

* The Overseas Board was disbanded in July 1998.

* Annual Report of the Renewable Energy Programme is published by the Energy Technology Support Unit.

* Numbers of male and female appointments not available as the Committee is made up of organisations, not individuals.

154

DEPARTMENT OF TRADE AND INDUSTRY

Advisory NDPBs

Tribunal NDPBs

44
Teaching Company Scheme Board

c/o Management Best Practice Directorate, DTI
1 Victoria Street
London SW1H 0ET
TEL : 0171 215 3866
FAX : 0171 215 3933
TERMS OF REFERENCE : To advise Ministers and officials in sponsoring Departments and Research Councils on strategic issues relating to Teaching Company Scheme development.

45
Central Arbitration Committee

Brandon House
180 Borough High Street
London
SE1 1LW
TEL : 0171 210 3738
FAX : 0171 210 3919
CHAIR : Professor Sir John Wood CBE ; OFFICE MANAGER : Mr Simon Gouldstone
TERMS OF REFERENCE : Its main role is concerned with industrial relations arbitration. It also determines disclosure of information complaints under the Trade Union and Labour Relations (Consolidation) Act 1992 (Section 183).

46
Copyright Tribunal

25 Southampton Buildings
London
WC2A 1AY

TEL : 0171 438 4776
FAX : 0171 438 4780
copyright.tribunal@patent.gov.uk
http://www.patent.gov.uk
CHAIR : Mr Christopher Tootal
SECRETARY : Miss Jill Durdin
TERMS OF REFERENCE : The main function of the Tribunal is to provide impartial settlement of disputes over copyright licenses, usually those offered by collecting societies.

47
Employment Appeal Tribunal

58 Victoria Embankment
London
EC4Y 0DS

TEL : 0171 273 1041
FAX : 0171 273 1045
CHAIR : Hon Mr Justice Morison
CHIEF EXECUTIVE : Mr Ian Jones
TERMS OF REFERENCE : To deal with appeals from the proceedings before, or the decisions of, the Certification Officer.

48
Industrial Tribunals (IT)

Field Support Unit
100 Southgate
Bury St Edmunds
Suffolk IP33 2AQ
TEL : 01345 959775
FAX : 01284 766334
TERMS OF REFERENCE : Industrial Tribunals are independent judicial bodies which determine disputes relating mainly to individual employment rights established in British and European Union Law.

	44 Teaching Company Scheme Board	45 Central Arbitration Committee	46 Copyright Tribunal	47 Employment Appeal Tribunal	48 Industrial Tribunals (IT)
a	–	–	–	2	14
b	–	–	–	–	–
c	NP	Body	NP	Body	Body
d	–	–	–	–	–
e	–	–	–	–	–
f	–	–	–	–	–
g	£0.021m	£0.094	£0.123m	£1.980m	£36.407m*
h	–	–	–	–	–
i	1M	1M, £30,351	1M, £316pd	–	1M, 1F, £91,478
					11M, 2F, £79,667
					63M, 12F, £64,889†
					196M, 28F, £285pd
j	–	2M, 1F, £286pd	2M, £316pd	–	–
k	5M, 1F, 2 vacancies	£5M, 3F, £183pd	2M, 3F, £186pd 3 vacancies	43M, 19F, £206pd	1619M, 661F, £119pd
l	–	22	16	1,451	80,435
m	–	19	7	1,503*	79,390‡

* 1,503 cases heard.

* Includes all agency head office costs.
† 14M and 5F chairmen also receive a £4,000 London Allowance.
‡ 25,877 cases heard.

155

DEPARTMENT OF TRADE AND INDUSTRY

Tribunal NDPBs

49
Insolvency Practitioners' Tribunal

The Insolvency Service
PO Box 203, Area 5.4
21 Bloomsbury Street
London WC1B 3QW
TEL : 0171 637 6357
FAX : 0171 291 6713
SECRETARY : Mr Dave Bradbury
TERMS OF REFERENCE : To hear referrals from individuals, and insolvency practitioners authorised to act by the Secretary of State, in respect of the refusal to grant, or the intention to withdraw, a license to act.

50
Persons Hearing Consumer Credit Licensing Appeals

Department of Trade and Industry, LEGAL Directorate
Room 211, 10 Victoria Street
London SW1H 0NN
TEL : 0171 215 3089
FAX : 0171 215 3242
brian.swift@sols.dti.gov.uk
TERMS OF REFERENCE : To provide secretariat services for appeals to the Secretary of State under the Consumer Credit Act 1974 from licensing decisions of the Director General of Fair Trading, the appeals being heard by a panel of independent persons.

51
Persons Hearing Estate Agents Appeals

Department of Trade and Industry, LEGAL Directorate
Room 211, 10 Victoria Street
London SW1H 0NN
TEL : 0171 215 3089
FAX : 0171 215 3240
brian.swift@sols.dti.gov.uk
TERMS OF REFERENCE : To provide secretariat services for appeals to the Secretary of State under the Estate Agent Act 1979 from warning or prohibition orders of the Director General of Fair Trading, the appeals being heard by a panel of independent persons.

	49	50	51
a	–	–	–
b	–	–	–
c	NP	NP	NP
d	*	–	–
e	£0.023m	–	–
f	£0.023m	–	–
g	£0.023m	£0.028m	£0.009m
h	–	–	–
i	1, £316pd†	1, £250pd*	1, £250pd*
j	–	–	–
k	2, £233pd†	2, £218pd*	2, £128pd*
l	2	3	1
m	2	5	1

49
* As per Insolvency Service.
† Appointed from a panel consisting of 5M chairmen and 16M, 3F members.

50
* Appointed from a panel of 16M, 1F, chairmen and 6M, 4F members.

51
* Appointed from a panel of 11M, 1F chairmen and 14M, 2F members.

Her Majesty's Treasury

Allington Towers, 19 Allington Street,
London SW1E 5EB

Enquiries	Sue Warrington
Telephone	0171 270 1539
Facsimile	0171 270 1353
E-mail	sue.warrington@hm-treasury.gov.uk
Internet	http:www.hm-treasury.gov.uk
GTN	270 1539

	Public Corporations	Executive NDPBs	Tribunal NDPBs
	1 **Bank of England**	2 **Policyholders Protection Board***	3 **Financial Services Tribunal**
Address	Threadneedle Street London EC2R 8AH	51 Gresham Street London EC2Y 7HQ	c/o HM Treasury Treasury Chambers Parliament Street London SW1P 3AG
TEL	0171 601 4444	0171 600 3333	0171 270 5273
FAX	0171 601 5771	0171 696 8999	0171 270 4694
	enquiries@bankofengland.Co.UK http://www.bankofengland.Co.UK		
CHAIR		Mr John Robins	
SECRETARY	Mr Peter Rodgers	Mr Derek Wright	Mrs Lesley Freeman MBE
GOVERNOR	Mr Eddie George		
TERMS OF REFERENCE	Its purpose is to maintain the integrity and value of the nation's currency, to ensure the stability of the financial system and promote the efficiency and competitiveness of the financial system.	To ensure that insurance liabilities to policyholders are met in full where insurance is compulsory.	To consider applications by firms or individuals to whom the Financial Services Authority either issued notice that it intends to refuse, withdraw or suspend authorisation; issued a notice of disqualification or a public statement about misconduct; or where the Authority has prohibited an authorised person from carrying an investment business.
a. Number if a multiple body/system (1.4.98)	–	–	–
b. Number of staff employed by the body (1.4.98)	–	–	–
c. Annual Report	*	Body	NP
d. Audit arrangements	–	Y	–
e. Total gross expenditure of body (1997/98)	–	£27.325m	–
f. Amount funded by government (1997/98)	–	–	–
g. Other expenditure by sponsoring dept (1997/98)	–	–	£0.462m
h. Chief Executive's Remuneration (1997/98)	–	–	–
Appointments and Remuneration (1.9.98)			
i. Chairman/President	1M, £227,000	–	1M, £380pd*
j. Deputy	1M, £191,500	–	–
k. Members	1M, £153,000; 1M, £142,167; 1M, £125,500; 1M, £125,500; 10M, 2F, £500	3M, 2F, £200pd	2M, £275pd†
l. Tribunal cases received	–	–	1
m. Tribunal cases disposed of	–	–	0

* Available from the Court of Directors.

* Responsibility for the body transferred from DTI to HMT.

* Appointed from a panel of 6M chairmen.
† Appointed from a panel of 17M and 4F members.

OFFICE OF WATER SERVICES (OFWAT)

Office of Water Services (OFWAT)

Centre City Tower, 7 Hill Street,
Birmingham B5 4UA

Enquiries   Caroline Duffy
Telephone   0121 625 1434
Facsimile   0121 625 1444
E-mail   cduffy@ofwat.gtnet.gov.uk
Internet   http://www.open.gov.uk/ofwat

GTN   6176 1434

Executive NDPBs

1 Customer Services Committees

TEL : 0121 625 1300
FAX : 0121 625 1400
enquiries@ofwat.gtnet.gov.uk
TERMS OF REFERENCE : To represent the interests of customers of the water and sewerage companies in their areas; and to investigate complaints, where the companies have not dealt adequately with problems.

Advisory NDPBs

2 OFWAT National Customer Council

Centre City Tower
7 Hill Street
Birmingham
B5 4UA
TEL : 0121 625 1301
FAX : 0121 625 1444
oncc@ofwat.gtnet.gov.uk
CHAIR : Sheila Reiter
SECRETARY : Roy Wardle
TERMS OF REFERENCE : To represent the interests of customers of the water and sewerage companies at national level.

	1	2
a. Number if a multiple body (1.4.98)	10	–
b. Number of staff employed by the body (1.4.98)	48*	–
c. Annual Report	Body§	Body*
d. Audit arrangements	X†	–
e. Total gross expenditure of body (1997/98)	£1.9m†	–
f. Amount funded by government (1997/98)	£1.9m‡	–
g. Other expenditure by sponsoring dept (1997/98)	£0.4m	–
h. Chief Executive's Remuneration (1997/98)	–	–
Appointments and Remuneration (1.9.98)		
i. Chairman/President	{1F, £26,577} {2M, 1F, £17,718} {3M, £15,486} {2M, £13,256} {1M, £11,065}	{1F}
j. Deputy	–	{2M}
k. Members	{79M, 41F}	{6M, 1F}
l. Tribunal cases received	–	–
m. Tribunal cases disposed of	–	–

*   Staffed by Sponsor Department.
†   Expenditure forms part of total Office of Water Services (OFWAT) expenditure. Accounts for OFWAT are audited by Comptroller and Auditor General.
‡   All expenditure funded by OFWAT through Parliamentary Vote.
§   Annual Reports are published by the Director General.

*   Annual Reports are published by the Councill.

Welsh Office

Cathays Park, Cardiff CF1 3NQ

Enquiries	Mrs Jill Thomas
Telephone	01222 823068
Facsimile	01222 823356
Internet	http://www.wales.gov.uk
GTN	1208 3068

Executive NDPBs

	1 Agricultural Wages Committees	2 Arts Council of Wales	3 Cardiff Bay Development Corporation
	WOAD, Crown Buildings Welsh Office, Cathays Park Cardiff CF1 3NQ	9 Museum Place Cardiff CF1 3NX	Baltic House Mount Stuart Square Cardiff CF1 6DH
	TEL : 01222 825315	TEL : 01222 376500	TEL : 01222 585858
	CONTACT :Mr Peter J McAllen	FAX : 01222 221447	FAX : 01222 255651
		CHAIR : Sir Richard Lloyd Jones	CHAIR : Sir Geoffrey Inkin OBE
		SECRETARY : Ms Joanna Weston	CHIEF EXECUTIVE : Mr Michael Boyce
	TERMS OF REFERENCE : The Committees have powers which allow them to grant permits which exempt employers from paying the maximum rate to disabled workers; issue certificates approving premium arrangements between employers and learners; and re-value farm workers' houses for the purpose of counting the provision of accomodation against the minimum wage.	TERMS OF REFERENCE : To develop and improve the knowledge, understanding and practice of the arts; and to increase the accessibility of the arts to the public. The Council also distributes National Lottery funds for the arts in Wales.	TERMS OF REFERENCE : To put Cardiff on the international map as a superlative maritime city, which will stand comparison with any such city in the world, thereby enhancing the image and economic well-being of Cardiff and Wales as a whole.
a. Number if a multiple body/system (1.4.98)	6	–	–
b. Number of staff employed by the body (1.4.98)	–	69	101
c. Annual Report	NP	Body	Body
d. Audit arrangements	X*	X	Y
e. Total gross expenditure of body (1997/98)	£0.002m*	£15.501m*	£59.575m
f. Amount funded by government (1997/98)	£0.002m	£14.549m	£47.918m
g. Other expenditure by sponsoring dept (1997/98)	£0.002m	£0.046m	£0.116m
h. Chief Executive's Remuneration (1997/98)	–	£50,000	£71,475
Appointments and Remuneration (1.9.98)			
i. Chairman/President	{4M, 1F, £86pm}† 1 vacancy	1M	1M, £36,389
j. Deputy	–	1M	1M, £20,522
k. Members	{66M, 1F}‡ 4M, 6F, £68pm, 2 vacancies	10M, 6F	10M, 1F, £5,889
l. Tribunal cases received	–	–	–
m. Tribunal cases disposed of	–	–	–

* Expenditure forms part of total Welsh Office (WO expenditure. Accounts for WO are audited by the Comptroller and Auditor General.
† Appointed by various trade and farmers' unions.
‡ Representing employers and workers in agriculture.

* Figure does not include expenditure on Lottery awards but does include expenditure on Lottery administration.

WELSH OFFICE

Executive NDPBs

	4 Countryside Council for Wales	5 Qualifications, Curriculum and Assessment Authority for Wales (ACCAC)	6 Development Board for Rural Wales	7 Further Education Funding Council for Wales	8 Higher Education Funding Council for Wales
Address	Plas Penrhos, Ffordd Penrhos, Bangor, North Wales LL57 2LQ	Castle Buildings, Womanby Street, Cardiff CF1 9SX	Ladywell House, Newtown, Powys SY16 1JB	Linden Court, The Orchards, Ty Glas Avenue, Llanishen, Cardiff CF4 5DZ	Linden Court, The Orchards, Ty Glas Avenue, Llanishen, Cardiff CF4 5DZ
TEL	01248 385500	01222 375400	01686 626965	01222 761861	01222 761861
FAX	01248 355782	01222 343612	01686 627 889	01222 763163	01222 763163
Web/Email	http://www.ccw.gov.uk	info@accac.org.uk http://www.accac.org.uk	enquiries@ruralwales.com.uk http://www.ruralwales.com.uk	http://www.wfc.ac.uk	http://www.wfc.ac.uk
CHAIR	Mr Michael Griffith	Mr Brian Connolly	Mr David Rowe-Beddoe	Mr Richard Webster	Sir Phillip Jones
SECRETARY / CHIEF EXECUTIVE	SECRETARY: Mr Paul Loveluck	SECRETARY: Mr John Valentine Williams	CHIEF EXECUTIVE: Sian Lloyd-Jones	CHIEF EXECUTIVE: Professor John Andrews	CHIEF EXECUTIVE: Professor John Andrews
TERMS OF REFERENCE	The Council is the statutory adviser to government on sustaining natural beauty, wildlife and the opportunity for enjoyment in rural Wales and its inshore waters. It is the national conservation authority in Wales.	To promote the raising of the overall level of educational achievement of pupils and schools in Wales.	The Board aims to promote the economic and social well being of the people in the areas of Wales for which it is responsible which are, Ceredigion, Powys, Merionydd and Gwynedd.	To ensure the provision of further education in Wales. It administers funds made available by the Secretary of Wales and others, and is required to secure a high quality and cost-effective further education system, which plays its part in meeting the social, economic and cultural needs of Wales.	To administer funds made available by the Secretary for Wales in support of the provision of education and the undertaking research by higher education institutions of Wales.
a	–	–	–	–	–
b	342.5	54	88	49	28
c	Body	Body	Body	Body	Body
d	X	X	X	X	X
e	£24.535m	£8.673m	£17.870m	£182.938m	£236.787m
f	£23.200m	£8.524m	£9.480m	£182.983m	£236.787m
g	£0.080m	£0.085m	£0.179m	£0.050m	£0.040m
h	£58,207	£55,670	£73,541	£89,000	£89,000
i	1M, £33,306	1M, £23,186	1M, 39,522	1M, £11,256	1M, £12,168
j	1M, £14,358	1M, £5,574	–	–	–
k	7M, 2F, £7,179 1F, £10,049*	7M, 6F	9M, £7,179 2F, £7,179	8M, 4F, £2,437 1M*	7M, 1F, £2,437 3 vacancies 1M*
l	–	–	–	–	–
m	–	–	–	–	–

* One member works 3.5 days a month.

* Member draws salary as Chief Executive of the Further and Higher Education Funding Councils.

* Member draws salary as Chief Executive of the Further and Higher Education Funding Councils.

WELSH OFFICE

Executive NDPBs

	9 Land Authority for Wales	10 National Library of Wales	11 National Museums and Galleries of Wales	12 Residuary Body for Wales	13 Royal Commission on Ancient and Historical Monuments of Wales
	Custom House Custom House Street Cardiff CF1 5AP	Aberystwyth Ceredigion SY23 3BU	National Museum and Galleries of Wales, Cardiff Cathays Park Cardiff CF1 3NP	Fynnon-Las Ty Glas Avenue Llanishen Cardiff CF4 5DZ	Crown Building Plas Crug Aberystwyth Cardiganshire SY23 1NJ
	TEL: 01222 223444 FAX: 01222 223330	TEL: 01970 623816 FAX: 01970 615709	TEL: 01222 397951 FAX: 01222 373219	TEL: 01222 681244 FAX: 01222 681308	TEL: 01970 621233 FAX: 01970 627701
	CHAIR: Sir Geoffrey Inkin CHIEF EXECUTIVE: Mr Bernard Ryan TERMS OF REFERENCE: To assemble land suitable for all types of development and make it available to both private and public sectors for development. The Land Authority for Wales will be amalgamated with the Development Board for Rural Wales and the Welsh Development Agency to form a single economic development agency for Wales.	PRESIDENT: Dr Brinley Jones SECRETARY: Mr Andrew Green TERMS OF REFERENCE: The collection, preservation and maintenance of manuscripts, printed matter, maps, photograhs, visual and audio-visual material relating to Wales and the Celtic peoples; and of similar material which furthers the aims of higher education and of literary and scientific research.	PRESIDENT: Mr Matthew Prichard CBE; DIRECTOR: Mr Colin Ford CBE (Anna Southall from 1 November 1998) TERMS OF REFERENCE: The National Museums and Galleries of Wales, exist to promote the wider knowledge and better understanding of Wales, its history, culture and place in the world, through their knowledge and multi-disciplinary collections, which are international in scope, importance and quality.	CHAIR: Mr D Hugh Thomas CBE ACTING CHIEF EXECUTIVE: Mr Walton Griffiths TERMS OF REFERENCE: To advise the Secretary of State for Wales on the transfer and/or disposal of properties surplus to requirements as a consequence of local government re-organisation; and the management of such properties whilst in the ownership of the Residuary Body.	CHAIR: Professor Beverley Smith; SECRETARY: Mr Peter White TERMS OF REFERENCE: The Commission records the historic buildings of Wales.
a	–	–	–	–	–
b	50	209.5	465	3.5	31
c	Body	Body	Body	Body	Body
d	X	X	X	*	X*
e	£16.514m	£5.895m	£15.361m	£0.576m†	£1.425*
f	–	£5.155m	£12.327m	–	£1.418m
g	£0.089m	£0.065m	£0.065m	–	£0.009m
h	£75,887	£56,914	£65,548	£50,018	£55,140
i	1M, £35,953	{1M}*	{1M}*	1M	1M†
j	1M, £10,213	{1M}*	{1M}*	–	–
k	6M, £7,179	{14M, 3F}† 2M, 1F‡	{9M, 4F, 1 vacancy}† 1M, 3F‡	2M, 1F, £3,410	6M, 1F, 3 vacancies†
l	–	–	–	–	–
m	–	–	–	–	–

* The President and Vice-President are elected by the Court of Governors of the body.
† 10 members of the Council, including the Treasure, are elected by the Court of Governors of the National Library. The Council itself may co-opt up to 6 members.
‡ These appointments are to the Council; members of the Council also sit on the Court of Governors.

* The President and Vice-President are elected by the Court of Governors of the body.
† 6 members of the Council, including the Treasurer and Immediate Past Presidents, are elected by the Court of Governors of the NMGW. The Council itself co-opts 4 members.
‡ These appointments are to the Council; members of the Council also sit on the Court of Governors.

* District Audit
† The costs of this body are met by levies from all Welsh Local Authorities.

* Expenditure forms part of total Welsh Office (WO) expenditure. Accounts for WO are audited by the Comptroller and Auditor General.
† Appointments are made by the Queen on the advice of the Secretary of State for Wales and the Prime Minister.

WELSH OFFICE

Executive NDPBs

14 Sports Council for Wales

Sophia Gardens
Cardiff
CF1 9SW

TEL : 01222 300500
FAX : 01222 300600
CHAIR : Mr Ossie Wheatley CBE
SECRETARY : Dr Huw Jones
TERMS OF REFERENCE : To encourage and help more people take part in sport; to help sportsmen and women improve their performances and reach high standards; and to promote the best use of Wales's man-made and natural sports facilities.

15 Tai Cymru

25–30 Lambourne Crescent
Llanishen
Cardiff
CF4 5ZJ

TEL : 01222 741500
FAX : 01222 741501
CHAIR : Mr Gerry Corless CBE
CHIEF EXECUTIVE : Mr Adam Peat
TERMS OF REFERENCE : To fund, regulate and promote the development of affordable homes by registered social landlords in Wales.

16 Wales Tourist Board

Brunel House
2 Fitzalan Road
Cardiff
CF2 1UY

TEL : 01222 499909
FAX : 01222 485031
press.office@tourism.wales.gov.uk
http://www.tourism.wales.gov.uk
CHAIR : Mr Tony Lewis ; CHIEF EXECUTIVE : Mr John French
TERMS OF REFERENCE : To encourage people to visit Wales and people living in Wales to take their holidays in Wales; and to encourage the provision and improvement of tourist amenities and facilities in Wales.

17 Welsh Development Agency (WDA)

Principality House
The Friary
Cardiff
CF1 4AE

TEL : 0345 775566 (Welsh)
TEL : 0345 775577 (English)
enquiries@wda.co.uk
http://www.wda.co.uk
CHAIR : Mr David Rowe-Beddoe
CHIEF EXECUTIVE : Mr Brian Willot
TERMS OF REFERENCE : To further the economic and social development of Wales or any part of Wales; and in that connection to provide, maintain or safeguard employment.

18 Welsh Language Board (WLB)

Market Chambers
5–7 St Mary Street
Cardiff
CF1 2AT

TEL : 01222 224744
FAX : 01222 224577
ymholiadau@bwrdd-yr-iaith.org.uk
http://www.netwales.co.uk/byig
CHAIR : Lord Elis-Thomas
CHIEF EXECUTIVE : Mr John Walter Jones
TERMS OF REFERENCE : To promote and facilitate the use of the Welsh language.

	14	15	16	17	18
a	–	–	–	–	–
b	155	67	111.5	337*	29.5
c	Body	Body	Body	Body	Body
d	X	Y	X	X	X
e	£9.339m	£84.223m	£16.702m	£164.621m	£5.671m
f	£6.596m	£82.110m	£15.135m	£88.057m	£5.756m
g	£0.041m	£0.100m	£0.126m	£0.294m	–
h	£50,002	£76,964	£59,457	£100,117†	£64,604
i	1M, £19,431	1M, £26,521*	1M, £35,328	1M, £39,522	1M, £23,365
j	1M, £9,862	–	–	1M, £25,531	1M, £5,685
k	6M, 5F	3M, 3F†, £6,754‡	4M, 1F, £6,987 1 vacancy	5M, 2F, £7,242 1M, £10,863 1M‡	10M, 2F, £5,685
l	–	–	–	–	–
m	–	–	–	–	–

* Remuneration until 1.11.98. After 1.11.98, £255 per day, one day a week until 31.3.99.
† After 1.11.98, 1M, 1F until 31.3.99.
‡ Remuneration until 1.11.98. After 1.11.98, £2,251pa, one day a month until 31.3.99.

* This figure does not include 26 European and Welsh Office funded posts.
† The WDA's Acting Chief Executive emoluments from 1.4.97 to 17.8.97 were £37,021. A substantive Chief Executive was appointed with effect from 18.8.97 whose emoluments from this date to 31.3.98 were £63,096.
‡ One member draws salary as Chief Executive of the WDA.

WELSH OFFICE

Executive NDPBs

Advisory NDPBs

19
Welsh National Board for Nursing, Midwifery and Health Visiting

Pearl Assurance House
Cardiff
CF1 3XX

TEL : 01222 395535
FAX : 01222 229366
CHAIR : Mr Stanley Wyn Jones OBE ; CHIEF EXECUTIVE : Mr David Ravey
TERMS OF REFERENCE : The Board is responsible for approving and monitoring the education of nurses, midwives and health visitors in Wales.

20
Advisory Committee for Wales (in relation to the Environment Agency)*

c/o Environment Division
Welsh Office
Cathays Park
Cardiff CF1 3NQ

TEL : 01222 825204
FAX : 01222 825008
philip.bishop@wales.gov.uk
CHAIR : Professor Eric Sunderland ; SECRETARY : Mr Philip Bishop
TERMS OF REFERENCE : To advise the Secretary of State for Wales on matters affecting or otherwise connected with the Environment Agency's functions in Wales.

21
Agricultural Dwelling House Advisory Committees

WOAD, Crown Buildings
Welsh Office
Cathays Park
Cardiff CF1 3NQ

TEL : 01222 825315
CONTACT : Peter J McAllen
TERMS OF REFERENCE : To advise housing authorities on the agricultural case when farmers or woodland owners ask those authorities to find alternative housing for their tenants as protected occupiers, so that the owner may re-allocate the house to another farm or forest worker.

22
Ancient Monuments Board for Wales

Crown Buildings
Cathays Park
Cardiff
CF1 3NQ

TEL : 01222 826376
FAX : 01222 826375
CHAIR : Professor Robert Rees Davies ; SECRETARY : Mrs Jean Booker
TERMS OF REFERENCE : To advise the Secretary of State for Wales on his functions under the terms of the Ancient Monuments and Archaeological Areas Act 1979.

23
Hill Farming Advisory Sub-Committee for Wales

WOAD 1A
Welsh Office
Cathays Park
CF1 3NQ

TEL : 01222 825735
FAX : 01222 825121
CHAIR : Mr John Vaughan ; SECRETARY : Miss Priscilla Thomas
TERMS OF REFERENCE : To advise Ministers on any matters relating to farming in the less favoured areas of Wales, including the operation of hill farming support measures, animal health, and general conditions and prospects for hill farming.

	19	20	21	22	23
a	–	–	6	–	–
b	24.27	–	–	–	–
c	Body	Body	NP	Body	NP
d	X	–	–	–	–
e	£1.029m	–	–	–	–
f	£0.903m	–	–	–	–
g	£0.144m	£0.002m	–	£0.017m	£0.006m
h	£50,644	–	–	–	–
i	1M, £9,000	1M	4M, 6F, £86pm, 2 vacancies	1M	1M*
j	–	–	–	–	–
k	2M, 4F, 1 vacancy	7M, 1F	4M, 6F, £86pm, 2 vacancies	5M, 2F	7M, 2F*
l	–	–	–	–	–
m	–	–	–	–	–

* Established under Section 11 of the Environment Act 1995.

* Appointments made jointly by MAFF Minister and Secretary of State for Wales.

163

WELSH OFFICE

Advisory NDPBs

24
Historic Buildings Council for Wales

Crown Building
Cathays Park
Cardiff
CF1 3NQ
TEL : 01222 500200
FAX : 01222 826375
CHAIR : Mr Thomas Lloyd
SECRETARY : Mr Richard Hughes
TERMS OF REFERENCE : To advise the Secretary of State for Wales on grant assistance for, and planning matters relating to, historic buildings and within conservation areas.

25
Library and Information Services Council (Wales)

CRD
Welsh Office Education Dept
Cathays Park
Cardiff CF1 3NQ
TEL : 01222 826040
FAX : 01222 826112
CHAIR : Dr Lionel Madden
SECRETARY : Miss Penny Hall
TERMS OF REFERENCE : To advise the Secretary of State for Wales on library and information matters; and to provide guidance, advice and comment on library and information services for providers and users.

26
Local Government Boundary Commission for Wales

1st Floor
Caradog House
1–6 Saint Andrew's Place
Cardiff CF1 3BE
TEL : 01222 395031
FAX : 01222 395250
lgbcfw@ndirect.co.uk
CHAIR : Professor Eric Sunderland ; SECRETARY : Mr Roger Knight
TERMS OF REFERENCE : Responsible for the administration of boundaries in Wales and it has a duty to conduct the electoral reviews of the unitary authorities.

27
Place Names Advisory Committee

4 Clos
Llywelyn
Creigau
Cardiff CF4 8JR
TEL : 01222 890534
CHAIR : Professor Gwynedd Pierce
TERMS OF REFERENCE : To advise the Secretary of State for Wales on correct place names.

28
Social Services Inspectorate for Wales Advisory Group

Welsh Office
Cathays Park
Welsh Office
CF1 3NQ
TEL : 01222 823197
SECRETARY : Mr Richard Tebboth
TERMS OF REFERENCE : To make the national inspection programme the mutual concern of central and local government and lay interests. To consider the proposals of the Social Services Inspectorate for inspection of local authority and allied personal social services; to review inspections which have taken place and the response to those inspections; and to consider from time to time the scope for future work.

	24	25	26	27	28
a	–	–	–	–	–
b	–	–	11*	–	–
c	Body	Body	Body	NP	–
d	–	–	–	–	–
e	–	–	£0.447m	–	–
f	–	–	£0.447m	–	–
g	£0.029m	£0.038m	–	£0.001m	–
h	–	–	£44,794	–	–
i	1M, £4,670	1M	1M, £232pd, £116hd	1M, £350*	*
j	–	–	1M, £202pd, £101hd	–	*
k	4M, 2F	5M, 3F	1F, £171pd, £85hd	1M, £250*	*
l	–	–	–	–	–
m	–	–	–	–	–

* Includes two Direct and nine Secondees, including Secretary.

* Honoraria.

* Currently recruiting new membership.

Advisory NDPBs

29
Welsh Advisory Committee on Drug and Alcohol Misuse*

c/o Welsh Drug & Alcohol Unit
4th Floor, St David's House
Wood Street
Cardiff CF1 1EY
TEL : 01222 667766
FAX : 01222 665940
welshdav@welshdav.demon.co.uk
CHAIR : Dr William Clee
SECRETARY : Ms Sue Morgan
TERMS OF REFERENCE : To advise the Secretary of State for Wales on all matters relating to drug and alcohol misuse in Wales.

30
Welsh Committee for Professional Development of Pharmacy

c/o The Welsh School of Pharmacy, UWCC
Cardiff
CF3 1XF
TEL : 01222 874784
FAX : 01222 874149
CHAIR : Dr Anthony Armstrong
SECRETARY : Dr David Temple
TERMS OF REFERENCE : To organise and co-ordinate postgraduate pharmaceutical education and continuing professional development education within the National Health Service in Wales – at all levels and in all specialities, including community General Practice Pharmacy.

31
Welsh Dental Committee

HPSU, Welsh Office
Cathays Park
Cardiff
CF1 3NQ
TEL : 01222 823777
FAX : 01222 823430
CHAIR : Dr Anthony Glenn
SECRETARY : Mrs Angela Parry
TERMS OF REFERENCE : To advise the Secretary of State for Wales on the provision of dental services in Wales; and to consider and comment or advise on any matter referred to it by the Secretary of State.

32
Welsh Industrial Development Advisory Board

c/o Industrial Development Division, Welsh Office
Cathays Park
Cardiff CF1 3NQ
TEL : 01222 823309
FAX : 01222 825214
CHAIR : Mr Keith Hodge OBE
SECRETARY : Mrs Helen Usher
TERMS OF REFERENCE : To advise the Secretary of State for Wales on applications for grants of over £250,000 under the Regional Selective Assistance Scheme, and on the operation of the Scheme.

33
Welsh Medical Committee

HPSU, Welsh Office
Cathays Park
Cardiff
CF1 3NQ
TEL : 01222 823777
FAX : 01222 823430
CHAIR : Mr D J Thomas
SECRETARY : Mrs Angela Parry
TERMS OF REFERENCE : To advise the Secretary of State for Wales on the provision of Medical Services in Wales; and to consider and comment or advise on any matter referred to it by the Secretary of State.

	29	30	31	32	33
a	–	–	–	–	–
b	–	–	–	–	–
c	NP	Body	Body	HC	Body
d	–	–	–	–	–
e	–	–	–	–	–
f	–	–	–	–	–
g	£0.006m	£0.007m	£0.013m	£0.061m	£0.042m
h	–	–	–	–	–
i	1M	1M	{1M}*	1M	{1M}*
j	–	–	{1M}*	–	{1F}*
k	17M, 6F, 3 vacancies	7M, 3F	{11M, 3F}*	5M, 2F	{19M, 1F}*
l	–	–	*	–	–
m	–	–	–	–	–

* Inaugral meeting held on 28 November 1996.

* Various specialities within the profession represented on the Committee.

* Various specialities within the profession represented on the Committee.

WELSH OFFICE

Advisory NDPBs

Tribunal NDPBs

34 Welsh Nursing and Midwifery Committee

HPSU, Welsh Office
Cathays Park
Cardiff
CF1 3NQ
TEL : 01222 823121
FAX : 01222 823430
CHAIR : Mrs B Rees
SECRETARY : Mrs J E Tester
TERMS OF REFERENCE : To advise the Secretary of State for Wales on the provision of nursing, midwifery and health visiting services in Wales; and to consider and comment or advise on any matter referred to it by the Secretary of State.

35 Welsh Optometric Committee

HPSU, Welsh Office
Cathays Park
Cardiff
CF1 3NQ
TEL : 01222 823121
FAX : 01222 823430
CHAIR : Mr R Roberts
SECRETARY : Mr Gareth Brydon
TERMS OF REFERENCE : To advise the Secretary of State for Wales on the provision of optical services in Wales; and to consider and comment or advise on any matter referred to it by the Secretary of State.

36 Welsh Pharmaceutical Committee

HPSU, Welsh Office
Cathays Park
Cardiff
CF1 3NQ
TEL : 01222 823121
FAX : 01222 823430
CHAIR : Mr Frank Mansell
SECRETARY : Mr Gareth Brydon
TERMS OF REFERENCE : To advise the Secretary of State for Wales on the provision of pharmaceutical services in Wales; and to consider and comment or advise on any matter referred to it by the Secretary of State.

37 Welsh Scientific Advisory Committee

HPSU, Welsh Office
Cathays Park
Cardiff
CF1 3NQ
TEL : 01222 823121
FAX : 01222 823430
CHAIR : Mr Keith Davies
SECRETARY : Mr Gareth Brydon
TERMS OF REFERENCE : To advise the Secretary of State for Wales on the provision of scientific services in Wales; and to consider and comment or advise on any matter referred to it by the Secretary of State.

38 Agricultural Land Tribunal (Wales)

New Crown Buildings
Cathays Park
Cardiff
CF1 3NQ
TEL : 01222 823165
FAX : 01222 825121
CHAIR : Mr W John Owen
SECRETARY : Mr Michael Jones
TERMS OF REFERENCE : To settle disputes and other issues between agricultural landlords and tenants; and also to settle drainage disputes between neighbours.

	34	35	36	37	38
a	–	–	–	–	–
b	–	–	–	–	–
c	Body	Body	Body	Body	NP
d	–	–	–	–	–
e	–	–	–	–	–
f	–	–	–	–	–
g	£0.020m	£0.007m	£0.022m	£0.032m	£0.007m
h	–	–	–	–	–
i	{1F}*	{1M}*	{1M}*	{1M}*	1M, £239pd†
j	{1F}*	–	–	–	1M, £239pd†
k	{4M, 17F}*	{11M}*	{11M, 2F}*	{14M, 4F}*	35M, 1F, 2 vacancies†
l	–	–	–	–	34
m	–	–	–	–	41

* Various specialities within the profession represented on the Committee.

* Various specialities within the profession represented on the Committee.

* Various specialities within the profession represented on the Committee.

* Various specialities within the profession represented on the Committee.

* Data reflects relocation and reorganisation of ALT Secretariat.
† Appointments made by the Lord Chancellor.

WELSH OFFICE

Tribunal NDPBs

39
Mental Health Review Tribunal for Wales

4th Floor
Crown Buildings
Cathays Park
Cardiff CF1 3NQ
TEL : 01222 825328
FAX : 01222 825671
CHAIR : His Honour Geoffrey Jones ; CLERK : Mrs Caroline Thomas
TERMS OF REFERENCE : To review, in individual cases, the need for the continuing detention of patients who are subject to the Mental Health Act.

40
Registered Inspectors of Schools Appeals Tribunal (Wales)

Welsh Office
Schools Performance Division
Cathays Park
Cardiff CF1 3NQ
TEL : 01222 826013
FAX : 01222 826016
TERMS OF REFERENCE : To hear registered Inspectors' of Schools appeals against any decision by the Chief Inspector of Schools in Wales to remove their name from the Register of Inspectors, either during, or at the end of a period of registrations. or to vary their conditions of registration.

41
Rent Assessment Panel for Wales (RAP)*

1st Floor, West Wing
Southgate House
Wood Street
Cardiff CF1 1EW
TEL : 01222 231687
FAX : 01222 236146
PRESIDENT : Mr Gareth Morgan
VICE PRESIDENT : Mr Rhys Davies
TERMS OF REFERENCE : The Rent Assessment Panel deals with appeals over rent levels from landlords and tenants in the private rented sector and fixes the maximum rent. It also settles disputes between freeholders and leaseholders over a range of leasehold issues.

42
Valuation Tribunals (Wales)

East Wales VT
23 Gold Tops
Newport NP9 4PG
TEL : 01633 266367
FAX : 01633 253270
NATIONAL PRESIDENT : Councillor Peter J Law JP ; SECRETARY : Mrs A H Smith
TERMS OF REFERENCE : To hear and determine appeals against council tax valuations and liability, and against non-domestic rating assessments (including land drainage rates).

NHS Bodies

43
Health Authorities (HA)

85M1B
Welsh Office
Cathays Park
Cardiff CF1 3NQ
CONTACT : Mr Paul Hopkins
TERMS OF REFERENCE : Responsible for implementing national policy on public health care within the area served by the Authority.

	39	40	41	42	43
a	–	–	–	4	5
b	–	–	–	19*	841*
c	Body	NP	Body	Body	Body
d	–	–	–	–	–
e	–	–	–	–	£2,225.595m[†‡]
f	–	–	–	–	£2,243.900m[†‡§]
g	£0.531m	–	£0.226m[†]	£0.819m	–
h	–	–	–	–	£84,200[¶]
i	1M, £3,000*+£340pd	*	1M, £37,630[‡]	{4M}[†]	1M, 4F, £19,285
j	1M, £239pd*	–	1M, £11,860[‡]	{34M, 6F}[†]	–
k	1M, £340pd* 8M, 4F, £239pd* 19M, 3F, £226pd* 6M, 9F, £97pd* 2M	1M, 1F, £228pd	11M, 3F, £258pd 18M, 1F, £206pd 7M, 5F, £132pd	{141M, 49F}[†]	20M, 13F, £5,000, 2 vacancies
l	754	–	378	15,798	–
m	683	–	295	21,248	–

* Appointments made by the Lord Chancellor.

* Appointments are made only when required and on an ad-hoc basis, by the Lord Chancellor's Department. The Tribunal was not convened during 1996/97.

* Rent Assessment Committees, Rent Tribunals and Leasehold Valuation Tribunals are drawn from the RAP.
† Includes salaries and fees for members not previously included.
‡ Appointments made by the Lord Chancellor.

* Staff are directly employed by the Tribunals.
† Appointments made by Welsh County Borough Councils.

* Number of staff at 31.3.98.
† Includes capital charges.
‡ Includes Dental Service expenditure £56.17m by the Dental Practice Board (see page 73).
§ The net national cash limit for HAs is entirely funded by Government.
¶ Average figure relating to HA Chief Executives. Total remuneration was £421,600.

167

WELSH OFFICE

National Health Service Bodies

44
Health Promotion Authority for Wales

Ffynnon-Ias
Tŷ Glas Avenue
Llanishen
Cardiff CF4 5DZ
TEL : 01222 752222
FAX : 01222 765000
CHAIR : Mr John Davies
SECRETARY : Mr Michael Ponton
TERMS OF REFERENCE : To exercise functions in relation to health promotion in Wales.

45
National Health Service Trusts

85M1B
Welsh Office
Cathays Park
Cardiff CF1 3NQ
CONTACT : Mr Paul Hopkins
TERMS OF REFERENCE : Responsible for implementing national policy on public health care within the area served by the Authority.

46
Welsh Health Common Services Authority (WHCSA)

Crickhowell House
Pierhead Street
Capital Waterside
Cardiff CF1 5XT
TEL : 01222 500500
FAX : 01222 502502
CHAIR : Mr Tim Rees OBE
SECRETARY : Mr Nigel Kirk
TERMS OF REFERENCE : To provide a range of support services to the National Health Service in Wales; and to advise the Welsh Office on National Health Service related matters.

	44	45	46
a	–	29	–
b	63*	51,637*	858*
c	Body	Body	Body
d	–	–	–
e	£3.745m	£1,589.738m†	£148.397m†
f	–	‡	£146.651m†
g	–	–	–
h	£82,000	£75,000§	£71,000
i	1M, £15,125	26M, 3F 7 x £19,235 15 x £17,145 6 x £15,125 1 x £11,020	1M, £15,125
j	–	–	–
k	3M, £5,000, 2 vacancies	91M, 42F, £5,000, 6 vacancies	1M, 1F, £5,000, 1 vacancy
l	–	–	–
m	–	–	–

* Number of staff as at 31.3.98.

* Number of staff as at 31.3.98.
† Expenditure relates to 29 Trusts during 1997–98.
‡ Not directly funded. Funding via purchasers.
§ Average figure relating to Trust Chief Executives. Total remuneration for all Chief Executives was £2,175,000.

* Number of staff as at 31.3.98
† Includes capital charges.

Annex A

Local Public Spending Bodies

Introduction

The term 'local public spending body' is a relatively new term within Government, having first been used by the Committee on Standards in Public Life in 1996. The Committee, in their Second Report on Local Public Spending Bodies, formally defined such bodies as:

> ... not for profit bodies which are rarely elected and whose members are not appointed by Ministers. They provide public services, often delivered at a local level, and are largely or wholly publicly funded.

There are a number of different bodies falling within the Committee's definition which have come to be recognised by Government as local public spending bodies. These are:

- Higher Education Institutions;
- Further Education Institution;
- Grant-Maintained Schools;
- Training and Enterprise Councils;
- Local Enterprise Companies;
- Registered Housing Associations; and
- Registered Social Landlords.

Details on the number and membership of the different local public spending bodies are given in Figure 1.

Further and Higher Education Institutions

This includes all old and new universities, higher education colleges and further education colleges. Detailed information is available from the following sources:

* information on each higher and further education institution can be found in the institution's Annual Report. Copies are available direct from the body concerned, although many institutions now make such information available over the Internet;

* summary information on all further education institutions in England and in Wales is available from the Further Education Funding Council for England[1] and the Further Education Funding Council for Wales[2]; and

- summary information on all higher education institutions in England is available from the Higher Education Funding Council for England[3]. Similar information on higher education institutions in Scotland and Wales is available from the Scottish Higher Education Funding Council[4] and the Higher Education Funding Council for Wales[5] respectively.

Grant-Maintained Schools

Grant-maintained schools (known as self governing schools in Scotland) are schools in which responsibility for budgets, staff appointments, pay and the ability to shape the overall aims and policy of the school — previously vested in representatives of local authorities — have been transferred to voluntary governors of individual schools. Information on each school can be found in the school's Annual Report. Copies of Reports are available from the schools concerned. Financial responsibility for grant-maintained schools in England rests with the Funding Agency for Schools[6]. Financial responsibility for grant-maintained schools in Scotland and Wales remains directly with the Government.

Training and Enterprise Councils and Local Enterprise Companies

Training and Enterprise Councils (TECs) are locally based companies with employer-led Boards which operate throughout England and Wales. Their role is to work in partnership to foster economic growth and contribute to the regeneration of their local areas, focusing in particular on the human resource aspects of regeneration. They have specific responsibility for developing the quality, effectiveness and relevance to the local labour market of the Government-funded training and business assistance programmes.

In Scotland, the Government established Scottish Enterprise and Highlands and Islands Enterprise with responsibility for training, economic development and environmental programmes. These activities are however contracted out to a network of Local Enterprise Companies (LECs) which have responsibility for delivery in their areas.

Detailed information on both TECs and LECs is available from the following sources:

- each TEC and LEC publishes its Business Plan, an Annual Report and an audited statement of accounts. Copies of TEC and LEC Annual Reports are available from individual bodies; and

- inter-TEC comparison tables for England and Wales are published annually by the Department for Education and Employment and the Welsh Office respectively. The Government Offices for the Regions and the Welsh Office produce and publish annual reports on the performance of Training and Enterprise Councils.

Registered Housing Associations and Registered Social Landlords

Registered Housing Associations (in Scotland and Northern Ireland) and Registered Social Landlords (in England and Wales) are voluntary bodies which are the major suppliers of new social rented housing in the UK. Detailed information is available from the following sources:

- information on individual associations and landlords can be found in bodies' Annual Reports. Copies of Reports are available direct from the associations or landlords concerned; and

- summary information on all registered housing associations in Scotland is available from Scottish Homes[7]. Similar information on registered social landlords in England and Wales is available from the Housing Corporation[8] and Tai Cymru[9] respectively. Information on registered housing associations in Northern Ireland is available from Northern Ireland Department of the Environment.[10]

1. Further Education Funding Council for England, Cheylesmore House, Quinton Road, Coventry CV1 2WT. Tel: 01203 863000.
2. Further Education Funding Council for Wales, Linden Court, The Orchards, Ty Glas Avenue, Llanishen, Cardiff CF4 5DZ. Tel: 01222 761861
3. Higher Education Funding Council for England, Northavon House, Coldharbour Lane, Bristol BS16 1QD. Tel: 0117 931 7317
4. Scottish Higher Education Funding Council, Donaldson House, 97 Haymarket Terrace, Edinburgh EH12 5HD. Tel: 0131 313 6500
5. Higher Education Funding Council for Wales, Linden Court, The Orchards, Ty Glas Avenue, Llanishen, Cardiff CF4 5DZ. Tel: 01222 761861
6. Funding Agency for Schools, Albion Wharf, 25 Skelderdale, York YO1 2XL. Tel: 01904 661661
7. Scottish Homes, Thistle House, 91 Haymarket Terrace, Edinburgh EH12 5HE. Tel: 0131 313 0044.
8. The Housing Corporation, Maple House, 149 Tottenham Court Road, London W1P 0BN. Tel: 0171 393 2000
9. Tai Cymru, 25–30 Lambourne Crescent, Llanishen, Cardiff CF4 5ZJ. Tel: 01222 741500
10. Department of the Environment (NI), Room 301, Clarence Court, Adelaide Street, Belfast BT2 8GB. Tel: 01232 540580

Figure 1 : Numbers and Non-executive Board Membership*

HIGHER EDUCATION INSTITUTIONS	NO	BOARD MEMBERS
England	135	3,375
Northern Ireland	4	100
Scotland	20	500
Wales	14	350

FURTHER EDUCATION INSTITUTIONS	NO	BOARD MEMBERS
England	435	8,700
Northern Ireland	17	340
Scotland	43	860
Wales	29	580

GRANT MAINTAINED SCHOOLS	NO	BOARD MEMBERS
England	1,199	21,582
Scotland	2	36
Wales	17	306

TRAINING AND ENTERPRISE COUNCILS	NO	BOARD MEMBERS
England	72	1,080
Wales	6	90

LOCAL ENTERPRISE COMPANIES	NO	BOARD MEMBERS
Scotland	22	264

REGISTERED HOUSING ASSOCIATIONS	NO	BOARD MEMBERS
Northern Ireland	41	402[†]
Scotland	259	3,108

REGISTERED SOCIAL LANDLORDS	NO	BOARD MEMBERS
England	2,237	26,844
Wales	98	1,176

| TOTAL | 4,650 | 69,693 |

* Membership figures have been estimated on the following basis:
Higher Education Institutions — 25 members per body;
Further Education Institutions — 20 members per body;
Grant-maintained Schools — 18 members per body;
Training and Enterprise Councils — 15 members per body;
Local Enterprise Companies — 12 members per body;
Registered Housing Associations — 12 members per body; and
Registered Social Landlords — 12 members per body.
Actual numbers will vary. In particular, figures for Higher Education may be underestimated as some institutions have much larger governing bodies.

† Actual figure.

Public Bodies 1998
Index of Bodies

INDEX OF BODIES

A

Administration of Radioactive Substances Advisory Committee	60
Advisory Board on Family Law	85
Advisory Board on Restricted Patients	76
Advisory Board on the Registration of Homeopathic Products	61
Advisory Body on Fair Trading in Telecommunication	144
Advisory Committee for the Public Lending Right	25
Advisory Committee for Wales (in relation to the Environment Agency)	163
Advisory Committee on Advertising	14
Advisory Committee on Borderline Substances	61
Advisory Committee on Business and the Environment	49
Advisory Committee on Business Appointments	10
Advisory Committee on Coal Research	151
Advisory Committee on Conscientious Objectors	29
Advisory Committee on Dangerous Pathogens	61
Advisory Committee on Dental Establishments (Scotland)	131
Advisory Committee on Design Quality in the NHS	61
Advisory Committee on Distinction Awards	61
Advisory Committee on Genetic Testing	62
Advisory Committee on Hazardous Substances	49
Advisory Committee on Historic Wreck Sites	25
Advisory Committee on Juvenile Court Lay Panel (Northern Ireland)	86
Advisory Committee on Legal Education and Conduct	87
Advisory Committee on NHS Drugs	62
Advisory Committee on Novel Foods and Processes	5
Advisory Committee on Overseas Economic and Social Research	84
Advisory Committee on Packaging	49
Advisory Committee on Pesticides	5
Advisory Committee on Plant and Machinery	49
Advisory Committee on Releases to the Environment	49
Advisory Committee on Sites of Special Scientific Interest (Scotland)	132
Advisory Committee on Telecommunications for Disabled and Elderly People	144
Advisory Committee on the Government Art Collection	25
Advisory Committee on the Micro-biological Safety of Food	62
Advisory Committees on General Commissioners of Income Tax	86
Advisory Committees on General Commissioners of Income Tax (NI)	86
Advisory Committees on Justices of the Peace (Northern Ireland)	86
Advisory Committees on Justices of the Peace in England and Wales	86
Advisory Committees on Justices of the Peace in Lancashire, Greater Manchester and Merseyside	15
Advisory, Conciliation and Arbitration Service (ACAS)	147
Advisory Council on Libraries	25
Advisory Council on Public Records	87
Advisory Council on the Misuse of Drugs	77
Advisory Group on Hepatitis	62
Advisory Panel on Standards for the Planning Inspectorate	50
Agricultural Dwelling House Advisory Committees (ADHAC)	6
Agricultural Dwelling House Advisory Committees (Wales)	163
Agricultural Land Tribunal (Wales)	166
Agricultural Land Tribunals (England)	8
Agricultural Research Institute of Northern Ireland	93
Agricultural Wages Board for England and Wales	2
Agricultural Wages Board for Northern Ireland	93
Agricultural Wages Committees for England	2
Agricultural Wages Committees (Wales)	159
Alcohol Education and Research Council	74
Ancient Monuments Board for Scotland	132
Ancient Monuments Board for Wales	163
Animal Procedures Committee	77
Animal Welfare Advisory Committee	30
Appeal Board (DVTA)	73
Apple and Pear Research Council (APRC)	3
Armed Forces Pay Review Body	30
Arts Council of England	17
Arts Council of Northern Ireland	100
Arts Council of Wales	159
Ashworth Hospital Authority	70
Audit Commission for Local Authorities and the National Health Service in England and Wales	42
Authorised Conveyancing Practitioners Board	85
Aviation Committee	151

B

Bank of England	157
Belfast Education and Library Board	102
Better Regulation Task Force	10
Biotechnology and Biological Sciences Research Council (BBSRC)	149
Birmingham Heartlands UDC	47
Black Country UDC	47
Boards of Visitors and Visiting Committees	92
Boards of Visitors to Penal Establishments	81
Boundary Commission for Northern Ireland	92
Britain-Russia Centre	56
British Association for Central and Eastern Europe	56
British Board of Agrément	42
British Broadcasting Corporation	16
British Coal Corporation	146
British Council	56
British Educational Communications and Technology Agency (BECTA)	32
British Film Institute	17
British Government Panel on Sustainable Development	10
British Hallmarking Council	147
British Library	17
British Museum	20
British Nuclear Fuels plc	146
British Overseas Trade Board	152
British Pharmacopoeia Commission	62
British Potato Council	3
British Railways Board	41
British Shipbuilders	146
British Tourist Authority	18
British Waterways Board	42
Broadcasting Standards Commission	18
Broadmoor Hospital Authority	71
Building Regulations Advisory Committee	50
Building Standards Advisory Committee (Scotland)	132

C

Caledonian MacBrayne Ltd	124
Cardiff Bay Development Corporation	159
Castle Vale Housing Action Trust	44
Central Adjudication Services	141
Central Advisory Committee on Justices of the Peace (Scotland)	132
Central Advisory Committee on War Pensions	140
Central Arbitration Committee	155
Central Council for Education and Training in Social Work (UK)	59
Central Rail Users' Consultative Committee (CRUCC)	118
Centre for Information on Language Teaching and Research (CILT)	32
Charities Advisory Committee (Northern Ireland)	110
Channel Four Television Corporation	16
Child Support Appeal Tribunals	142
Child Support Appeal Tribunals (CSATs) (Northern Ireland)	111
Children's Panel (Scotland)	137
Civil Aviation Authority	41
Civil Justice Council	87
Civil Procedure Rule Committee	87
Civil Service Appeal Board	11
Clinical Standards Advisory Group	63
Coal Authority	147
Commission for New Towns	42
Commission for Racial Equality	74
Commission for Racial Equality for Northern Ireland	95
Commissioner for the Rights of Trade Union Members	148
Commissioner for Protection Against Unlawful Industrial Action	148
Committee for Monitoring Agreements on Tobacco Advertising and Sponsorship	63
Committee of Investigation for Great Britain	6
Committee on Agricultural Valuation	6
Committee on Carcinogenicity of Chemicals in Food, Consumer Products and the Environment	63
Committee on Chemicals & Materials of Construction For Use in Public Water Supply and Swimming Pools	50
Committee on Medical Aspects of Food and Nutrition Policy	63
Committee on Medical Aspects of Radiation in the Environment	64
Committee on Mutagenicity of Chemicals in Food, Consumer Products and the Environment	64
Committee on Standards in Public Life	11
Committee on the Medical Effects of Air Pollutants	63
Committee on the Safety of Medicines	64
Committee on Toxicity of Chemicals in Food, Consumer Products and the Environment	64
Common Services Agency for the NHS in Scotland	138
Commons Commissioners	53
Commonwealth Development Corporation	83
Commonwealth Institute	57
Commonwealth Scholarship Commission in the United Kingdom	83
Communications for Business	144
Community Development Foundation	74
Construction Industry Training Board (Northern Ireland)	95
Construction Industry Training Board	33
Consultative Panel on Badgers and Bovine Tuberculosis	6
Consumer Communications for England	145
Consumer Panel	7
Consumers' Committee for Great Britain under the Agricultural Act 1958	6
Copyright Tribunal	155
Council for Catholic Maintained Schools (Northern Ireland)	100
Council for Nature Conservation and the Countryside (Northern Ireland)	104
Council for Science and Technology	152
Council for the Central Laboratory of the Research Councils	150
Council on Tribunals	87
Countryside Commission	42
Countryside Council for Wales	160
County Court Rule Committee	88
Covent Garden Market Authority	2
Crafts Council	18
Crime Prevention Agency Board	77
Criminal Cases Review Commission	75
Criminal Injuries Compensation Appeals Panel (CICA)	78
Criminal Injuries Compensation Authority (CICA)	75
Criminal Injuries Compensation Board (CICB)	79
Crofters' Commission	125
Crown Agents Holding and Realisation Board	83
Crown Court Rule Committee	88
Customer Services Committees	158

D

Dairy Produce Quota Tribunal	8
Dartmoor Steering Group and Working Party	30
Darwin Initiative Advisory Committee	50
Data Protection Tribunal	79
Deer Commission for Scotland	126
Defence Scientific Advisory Council	30
Dental Practice Board	73
Dental Rates Study Group	64
Dental Vocational Training Authority	71
Design Council	148
Development Awareness Working Group	84
Development Board for Rural Wales	160
Diplomatic Service Appeal Board	57
Disability Appeal Tribunals	142
Disability Appeal Tribunals (DATs) (Northern Ireland)	111
Disability Living Allowance Advisory Board	141
Disability Living Allowance Advisory Board for Northern Ireland	110
Disability Rights Task Force	35
Disabled Persons Transport Advisory Committee	50
Distinction and Meritorious Service Awards Committee	110
Doctors' and Dentists' Review Body	65
Drainage Council for Northern Ireland	94

INDEX OF BODIES

E

East Midlands Region Electricity Consumers' Committee	37
East of Scotland Water Authority	123
Eastern Health and Social Services Board (Northern Ireland)	112
Eastern Health and Social Services Council (Northern Ireland)	113
Eastern Region Electricity Consumers' Committee	37
Economic and Social Research Council	150
Education Assets Board (EAB)	32
Employment Appeal Tribunal	155
Energy Advisory Panel	152
Engineering and Physical Sciences Research Council	150
Engineering Construction Industry Training Board (ECITB)	34
English Heritage (The Historic Buildings and Monuments Commission for England)	19
English National Board for Nursing, Midwifery and Health Visiting	59
English Nature	46
English Partnerships	43
English Sports Council	18
English Tourist Board	18
Enterprise Ulster	95
Environment Agency	43
Equal Opportunities Commission (EOC)	33
Equal Opportunities Commission for Northern Ireland	96
Expert Action Group for Building Materials	51
Expert Advisory Group on AIDS	65
Expert Group on Airborne Particles	51
Expert Group on Cryptosporidium In Water Supplies	51
Expert Panel on Air Quality Standards	51
Expert Panel on Sustainable Development Education	51
Export Guarantees Advisory Council	55
Extra Parliamentary Panel (Scotland)	132

F

Fair Employment Commission for Northern Ireland	96
Fair Employment Tribunal	98
Family Health Services Appeal Authority	71
Family Proceedings Rule Committee	88
Farm Animal Welfare Council	7
Financial Services Tribunal	157
Fire Authority for Northern Ireland	107
Firearms Consultative Committee	77
Fisheries Conservancy Board for Northern Ireland	93
Fleet Air Arm Museum	28
Food Advisory Committee	7
Food from Britain	3
Football Licensing Authority	19
Football Task Force	26
Foreign Compensation Commission	58
Foresight Steering Group	152
Foyle Fisheries Commission	94
Fuel Cell Advisory Panel	152
Funding Agency for Schools	33
Further Education Funding Council for England (FEFC)	33
Further Education Funding Council for Wales	160

G

Gaming Board for Great Britain	75
Gas Consumers' Council	148
Geffrye Museum	20
Gene Therapy Advisory Committee	65
General Commissioners of Income Tax (GCIT)	90
General Consumer Council for Northern Ireland	96
General Teaching Council for Scotland	133
Government Hospitality Fund Advisory Committee for the Purchase of Wine	58
Great Britain Sports Council	19

H

Hannah Research Institute	124
Health and Safety Agency for Northern Ireland	97
Health and Safety Commission	43
Health and Safety Executive	44
Health and Social Services Trusts (Northern Ireland)	114
Health Appointments Advisory Committee (Scotland)	133
Health Authorities (HA) (Wales)	167
Health Authorities (HAs)	70
Health Boards (Scotland)	138
Health Education Authority	71
Health Education Board for Scotland	138
Health Promotion Authority for Wales	168
Higher Education Funding Council for England (HEFC)	33
Higher Education Funding Council for Wales	160
Highlands and Islands Airports Ltd	124
Highlands and Islands Enterprise	126
Hill Farming Advisory Committee for England, Wales and Northern Ireland (HAFC)	7
Hill Farming Advisory Committee for Scotland	133
Hill Farming Advisory Sub-Committee for Wales	163
Historic Buildings Council for Scotland	133
Historic Buildings Council for Wales	164
Historic Buildings Council (Northern Ireland)	105
Historic Monuments Council (Northern Ireland)	105
Historic Royal Palaces	19
Home-Grown Cereals Authority	3
Honorary Investment Advisory Committee	88
Horniman Museum and Gardens	20
Horserace Betting Levy Appeal Tribunal for Scotland	138
Horserace Betting Levy Appeal Tribunal for England and Wales	79
Horserace Betting Levy Board	75
Horserace Totalisator Board (The Tote)	75
Horticultural Development Council (HDC)	3
Horticulture Research International	4
Housing Benefit Review Boards (Northern Ireland)	106
Housing Corporation	45
Human Fertilisation and Embryology Authority	59
Human Genetics Advisory Commission	153

I

Imperial War Museum	20
Independent Board of Visitors for Military Corrective Training Centres (MCTC)	30
Independent Television Commission	16
Independent Tribunal Service	142
Indian Family Pensions Funds Body of Commissioners	84
Industrial Development Advisory Board	153
Industrial Development Board for Northern Ireland	98
Industrial Injuries Advisory Board	141
Industrial Research and Technology Unit (Advisory Board)(Northern Ireland)	98
Industrial Tribunals (IT)	155
Inland Waterways Amenity Advisory Council	52
Insolvency Practitioners' Tribunal	156
Insolvency Rules Committee	88
Intelligence Services Tribunal	58
Interception of Communications Tribunal	79
Investors in People UK(IiP UK)	34

J

Joint Committee on Vaccination and Immunisation	65
Joint Nature Conservation Committee (JNCC)	45
Judicial Studies Board	89
Justices of the Peace Advisory Committees (Scotland)	133
Juvenile Justice Board	91

K

Know-How Fund Advisory Board	84

L

Labour Relations Agency	96
Laganside Corporation	104
Land Authority for Wales	161
Land Registration Rule Committee	89
Lands Tribunal for Scotland (LTS)	122
Law Commission	89
Law Reform Advisory Committee for Northern Ireland	108
Legal Aid Advisory Committee (Northern Ireland)	89
Legal Aid Board	85
Library and Information Commission	26
Library and Information Services Council (Wales)	164
LINK Board	153
Liverpool Housing Action Trust	44
Livestock and Meat Commission for Northern Ireland	94
Local Enterprise Development Unit	96
Local Government Boundary Commission for Scotland	134
Local Government Boundary Commission for Wales	164
Local Government Commission for England	52
Local Government Property Commission (Scotland)	134
Local Government Residuary Body	45
Local Government Staff Commission (England)	52
Local Government Staff Commission (Northern Ireland)	107
London Docklands Development Corporation	47
London Pensions Fund Authority	46
London Region Electricity Consumers' Committee	38
London Regional Passengers' Committee	46
London Regional Transport	41

M

Macauley Land Use Research Institute	125
Magnox Electric plc	147
Marshall Aid Commemoration Commission	57
Measurement Advisory Committee	153
Meat and Livestock Commission (MLC)	4
Meat Hygiene Appeals Tribunals (England and Wales)	8
Medical Appeal Tribunals	142
Medical Appeal Tribunals (MATs) (Northern Ireland)	111
Medical Practices Committee	60
Medical Research Council	150
Medical Workforce Standing Advisory Committee	65
Medicines Commission	66
Mental Health Act Commission	71
Mental Health Commission for Northern Ireland	109
Mental Health Review Tribunal	69
Mental Health Review Tribunal for Northern Ireland	111
Mental Health Review Tribunal for Wales	167
Mental Welfare Commission for Scotland	139
Merseyside and North Wales Region Electricity Consumers' Committee	38
Merseyside UDC	48
Metropolitan Police Committee	77
Microbiological Research Authority	72
Microbiology Advisory Committee	66
Midlands Region Electricity Consumers' Committee	38
Milk Development Council (MDC)	4
Millennium Commission	19
Misuse of Drugs Advisory Board	79
Misuse of Drugs Professional Panel	80
Misuse of Drugs Tribunal	80
Monopolies and Mergers Commission	148
Moredun Research Institute	125
Museum of London	20
Museum of Science and Industry in Manchester	21
Museums and Galleries Commission	23

N

National Army Museum	28
National Biological Standards Board (UK)	60
National Blood Authority	72
National Board for Nursing, Midwifery and Health Visiting for Northern Ireland	109
National Board for Nursing, Midwifery and Health Visiting for Scotland	126
National Consumer Council	149
National Consumers' Consultative Committee (NCCC)	37
National Disability Council	35
National Employers' Liaison Committee	31
National Film and Television School (NFTS)	23

INDEX OF BODIES

National Forest Company	46
National Galleries of Scotland	126
National Gallery	21
National Health Service Litigation Authority	72
National Health Service Supplies Authority	72
National Health Service Tribunal	69
National Health Service Trusts	70
National Health Service Trusts (Scotland)	139
National Health Service Trusts (Wales)	168
National Heritage Memorial Fund	23
National Library of Scotland	126
National Library of Wales	161
National Lottery Charities Board	23
National Maritime Museum	21
National Museum of Science & Industry	21
National Museum of Scotland	127
National Museums and Galleries of Northern Ireland	101
National Museums and Galleries of Wales	161
National Museums and Galleries on Merseyside	21
National Portrait Gallery	22
National Radiological Protection Board	60
National Research Development Corporation (NRDC)	149
Natural Environment Research Council	150
Natural History Museum	22
New Deal Task Force	35
New Millennium Experience Company Ltd	24
North Eastern Education and Library Board (Northern Ireland)	102
North Eastern Region Electricity Consumers' Committee	38
North Hull Housing Action Trust	44
North of Scotland Region Electricity Consumers' Committee	39
North of Scotland Water Authority	123
North Western Region Electricity Consumers' Committee	38
Northern Health and Social Services Board (Northern Ireland)	112
Northern Health and Social Services Council (Northern Ireland)	113
Northern Ireland Advisory Committee on Telecommunications	145
Northern Ireland Advisory Committee on Travellers	105
Northern Ireland Blood Transfusion Service Agency	114
Northern Ireland Building Regulations Advisory Committee	105
Northern Ireland Central Services Agency (NICSA)	114
Northern Ireland Commissioner for Protection Against Unlawful Industrial Action	97
Northern Ireland Commissioner for the Rights of Trade Union Members	97
Northern Ireland Construction Industry Advisory Council	105
Northern Ireland Consumer Committee for Electricity	116
Northern Ireland Council for Postgraduate Medical and Dental Education	109
Northern Ireland Council for the Curriculum, Examinations and Assessment (NICCEA)	100
Northern Ireland Disability Council (NIDC)	110
Northern Ireland Economic Council	108
Northern Ireland Fishery Harbour Authority	94
Northern Ireland Guardian Ad Litem Agency (NIGALA)	114
Northern Ireland Health Promotion Agency	114
Northern Ireland Higher Education Council	101
Northern Ireland Housing Executive (NIHE)	107
Northern Ireland Industrial Court	99
Northern Ireland Industrial Tribunals	99
Northern Ireland Local Government Officers' Superannuation Committee	104
Northern Ireland Museums Council	101
Northern Ireland Regional Medical Physics Agency (NIRMPA)	115
Northern Ireland Review Body (Operator and Vehicle Licensing)	106
Northern Ireland Tourist Board	97
Northern Ireland Transport Holding Company	107
Northern Ireland Water Council	106
Northern Lighthouse Board	43
Nuclear Powered Warships Safety Committee	31
Nuclear Weapons Safety Committee	31
Nurses', Midwives' and other NHS Professions' Review Body	66

O

Occupational Pensions Regulatory Authority (OPRA)	140
Office of the Data Protection Registrar	76
OFWAT National Customer Council	158
Oil and Pipelines Agency	28
OSO Industry Board	153
Overseas Project Board	154
Overseas Service Pensions Scheme Advisory Board	84

P

Parliamentary Boundary Commission for England	78
Parliamentary Boundary Commission for Scotland	134
Parliamentary Boundary Commission for Wales	78
Parole Board	76
Parole Board for Scotland	127
Particle Physics and Astronomy Research Council	151
Pensions Appeal Tribunal for Scotland (PATS)	122
Pensions Compensation Board	140
Pensions Ombudsman	143
Persons Hearing Consumer Credit Licensing Appeals	156
Persons Hearing Estate Agents Appeals	156
Pharmacists' Review Panel	66
Pig Production Development Committee	94
Place Names Advisory Committee (Wales)	164
Planning Appeals Commission (Northern Ireland)	106
Plant Varieties and Seeds Tribunals	9
Plymouth UDC	48
Poisons Board	78
Poisons Board (Northern Ireland)	110
Police Arbitration Tribunal	80
Police Authority for Northern Ireland	91
Police Complaints Authority	76
Police Discipline Appeals Tribunal	80
Police Information Technology Organisation (PITO)	76
Police Negotiating Board	78
Policyholders Protection Board	157
Political Honours Scrutiny Committee	13

INDEX OF BODIES

Post Office	147
Post Office Users' Councils for Scotland, Wales and Northern Ireland	149
Post Office Users' National Council	149
Post Qualification Education Board for Health Service Pharmacists in Scotland	134
Prescription Pricing Authority	72
Probation Board for Northern Ireland	91
Property Advisory Group	52
Public Health Laboratory Service Board	60

Q

Qualifications, Curriculum and Assessment Authority for Wales (ACCAC)	160
Qualifications Curriculum Authority (QCA)	34

R

Radio Auithority	17
Radioactive Waste Management Advisory Committee	52
Rail Users' Consultative Committee for Eastern England	118
Rail Users' Consultative Committee for North Eastern England	119
Rail Users' Consultative Committee for North Western England	119
Rail Users' Consultative Committee for Scotland	119
Rail Users' Consultative Committee for Southern England	119
Rail Users' Consultative Committee for the Midlands	118
Rail Users' Consultative Committee for Wales	119
Rail Users' Consultative Committee for Western England	120
Rampton Hospital Authority	73
Regional Flood Defence Committees	4
Regional Industrial Development Boards	154
Registered Homes Tribunal, Northern Ireland	111
Registered Homes Tribunals	69
Registered Inspectors (RgI) Appeals Tribunal	36
Registered Inspectors of Schools Appeals Tribunal (Wales)	167
Registrar of Public Lending Right (PLR)	24
Remploy Limited	34
Renewable Energy Advisory Committee	154
Rent Assessment Panel (RAP) (Northern Ireland)	106
Rent Assessment Panel for Scotland	138
Rent Assessment Panel for Wales (RAP)	167
Rent Assessment Panels (RAPS)	54
Residuary Body for Wales	161
Review Board for Government Contracts	31
Reviewing Committee on the Export of Works of Art	26
Rowett Research Institute	125
Royal Air Force Museum	29
Royal Armouries Museum	24
Royal Botanic Garden, Edinburgh	127
Royal Botanic Gardens, Kew	4
Royal Commission on Ancient and Historical Monuments of Wales	161
Royal Commission on Environmental Pollution	53
Royal Commission on Historical Manuscripts	24
Royal Commission on Long Term Care for the Elderly	66
Royal Commission on the Ancient and Historical Monuments of Scotland	127
Royal Commission on the Historical Monuments of England	24
Royal Fine Art Commission	26
Royal Fine Art Commission for Scotland	134
Royal Marines Museum	29
Royal Military College of Science Advisory Council (RMCS)	31
Royal Mint Advisory Committee on the Design of Coins, Medals, Seals and Decorations	121
Royal Naval Museum	29
Royal Navy Submarine Museum	29
Rural Development Commission	46

S

Scheme of Compensation for Loss of Employment through Civil Unrest	99
School Teachers' Review Body	35
Scientific Committee on Tobacco and Health	67
Scottish Advisory Committee on Drug Misuse	135
Scottish Advisory Committee on Telecommunications	145
Scottish Advisory Committee on the Medical Workforce	135
Scottish Agricultural Consultative Panel	135
Scottish Agricultural Wages Board	127
Scottish Arts Council	128
Scottish Children's Reporter Administration	128
Scottish Community Education Council	128
Scottish Consultative Council on the Curriculum	135
Scottish Conveyancing and Executry Services Board	128
Scottish Council for Educational Technology	128
Scottish Council for Postgraduate Medical and Dental Education	139
Scottish Crime Prevention Council	135
Scottish Crop Research Institute	125
Scottish Enterprise	129
Scottish Environment Protection Agency	129
Scottish Further Education Unit	129
Scottish Higher Education Funding Council	129
Scottish Homes	129
Scottish Hospital Endowments Research Trust	130
Scottish Hospital Trust	139
Scottish Industrial Development Advisory Board	136
Scottish Law Commission	122
Scottish Legal Aid Board	130
Scottish Medical Practices Committee	130
Scottish Natural Heritage	130
Scottish Qualifications Authority	131
Scottish Records Advisory Council	136
Scottish Screen	130
Scottish Sports Council	131
Scottish Standing Committee for the Calculation of Residual Values of Fertilizers and Feeding Stuffs	136
Scottish Studentship Selection Committee	136
Scottish Tourist Board	131
Scottish Transport Group	124
Scottish Valuation and Rating Council	136
Scottish Water and Sewerage Customers Council	131
Sea Fish Industry Authority	5

177

INDEX OF BODIES

Secretary of State (Electricity) for Scotland's Fisheries Committee	137
Secretary of State for Scotland's Advisory Committee on Scotland's Travelling People	137
Secretary of State for Scotland's Advisory Group on Sustainable Development	137
Secretary of State for Scotland's Advisory Panel of Economic Consultants	137
Section 706 Tribunal	82
Security Commission	11
Security Service Tribunal	80
Security Vetting Appeals Panel	11
Senior Salaries Review Board	11
Sinal Pedwar Cymru (Welsh Channel Authority)	17
Sir John Soane's Museum	22
Skills Task Force	36
Social Security Advisory Committee	141
Social Security Appeal Tribunals	142
Social Security Appeal Tribunals (SSATs) (Northern Ireland)	112
Social Services Inspectorate for Wales Advisory Group	164
South Eastern Education and Library Board (Northern Ireland)	102
South Eastern Region Electricity Consumers' Committee	39
South of Scotland Region Electricity Consumers' Committee	39
South Wales Region Electricity Consumers' Committee	39
South Western Region Electricity Consumers' Committee	39
Southern Health and Social Services Board (Northern Ireland)	112
Southern Health and Social Services Council (Northern Ireland)	113
Southern Education and Library Board (Northern Ireland)	102
Southern Region Electricity Consumers' Committee	40
Special Educational Needs Tribunal (SENT)	36
Spectrum Management Advisory Group	154
Spongiform Encephalopathy Advisory Committee	7
Sports Council for Northern Ireland	101
Sports Council for Wales	162
Staff Commission for Education and Library Boards (Northern Ireland)	103
Standing Advisory Commission on Human Rights	92
Standing Advisory Committee on Industrial Property	154
Standing Advisory Committee on Trunk Road Assessment	53
Standing Committee on Postgraduate Medical and Dental Education	67
Standing Dental Advisory Committee	67
Standing Medical Advisory Committee	67
Standing Nursing and Midwifery Advisory Committee	67
Standing Pharmaceutical Advisory Committee	68
State Hospitals Board for Scotland	139
Statistics Advisory Committee (Northern Ireland)	98
Statistics Advisory Committee	117
Statute Law Committee for Northern Ireland	108
Steering Committee on Pharmacy Postgraduate Education	68
Stonebridge Housing Action Trust	44
Student Loans Company Ltd (SLC)	34
Sugar Beet Research and Education Committee	8
Supported Employment Consultative Group	36
Supreme Court Rule Committee	89

T

Tai Cymru	162
Tate Gallery	22
Teacher Training Agency (TTA)	35
Teaching Company Scheme Board	155
Teesside	48
The Accounts Commission for Scotland	124
The Great Britain-China Centre	57
The Independent Commission for Police Complaints for Northern Ireland	92
The Simpler Trade Procedures Board	151
Theatres Trust	26
Tower Hamlets Housing Action Trust	45
Traffic Commissioners	54
Traffic Director for London	47
Trafford Park UDC	48
Training and Employment Agency (Advisory Board)	98
Treasure Valuation Committee	27
Tribunal Under Schedule 11 to the Health and Personal Social Services (NI) Order 1972	112
Trinity House Lighthouse Service	43
Tyne and Wear UDC	48

U

UK Advisory Panel for Health Care Workers Infected with Blood Borne Viruses	68
UK Round Table on Sustainable Development	53
Ulster Supported Employment Ltd	97
United Kingdom Atomic Energy Authority	151
United Kingdom Eco-labelling Board (UKEB)	47
United Kingdom Register of Organic Food Standards	5
United Kingdom Sports Council	25
United Kingdom Transplant Support Service Authority	73
United Kingdom Xenotransplantation Interim Regulatory Authority	68
Unrelated Live Transplant Regulatory Authority	68

V

Vaccine Damage Appeal Tribunals	143
Valuation Tribunals	54
Valuation Tribunals (Wales)	167
Veterinary Products Committee	8
Victoria and Albert Museum	22

W

Wales Tourist Board	162
Wallace Collection	23
Waltham Forest Housing Action Trust	45
War Pensions Committees	141
Water Appeals Commission (Northern Ireland)	107
Water Regulations Advisory Committee	53
Welsh Advisory Committee on Drug and Alcohol Misuse	165
Welsh Advisory Committee on Telecommunications	145

Welsh Committee for Professional Development of Pharmacy	165
Welsh Dental Committee	165
Welsh Development Agency (WDA)	162
Welsh Health Common Services Authority (WHCSA)	168
Welsh Industrial Development Advisory Board	165
Welsh Language Board (WLB)	162
Welsh Medical Committee	165
Welsh National Board for Nursing, Midwifery and Health Visiting	163
Welsh Nursing and Midwifery Committee	166
Welsh Optometric Committee	166
Welsh Pharmaceutical Committee	166
Welsh Scientific Advisory Committee	166
West of Scotland Water Authority	123
Western Health and Social Services Board (Northern Ireland)	113
Western Health and Social Services Council (Northern Ireland)	113
Western Education and Library Board (Northern Ireland)	102
Westminster Foundation for Democracy	57
Wider Health Working Group	69
Wilton Park Academic Council	58
Wine Standards Board of the Vintners' Company	5
Women's National Commission	12

Y

Yorkshire Region Electricity Consumers' Committee	40
Youth Council for Northern Ireland	101

Printed in the United Kingdom for The Stationery Office
J67808 C11 12/98 5673